FORD
MUSTANG

Forty Years
of Fun

BY THE AUTO EDITORS OF
CONSUMER GUIDE®

Publications International, Ltd.

Louis Weber, CEO
Publications International, Ltd.
7373 North Cicero Avenue
Lincolnwood, Illinois 60712

Manufactured in China.

8 7 6 5 4 3 2 1

ISBN: 0-7853-9872-4

Library of Congress Control Number: 2004100670

The editors gratefully acknowledge those who supplied photography for this book:

Ford Motor Company; Mitch Frumkin; Chuck Giametta; Bud Juneau; Dave Kutz; Dan Lyons; Vince Manocchi; Doug Mitchel; Mike Mueller; David Newhardt; Rick Popely; Saleen Corporation; Steve Statham; W.C. Waymack; Nicky Wright.

Special thanks to the owners of the cars featured in this book:

Quentin Bacon; Gary Blackman; Eugene & Sharon Blanc; June & Rudy Bleakely; Bill Bolle; David & Linda Burpeau; Tim Carle; Luis A. Chanes; Dr. Randy & Freda Cooper; Corey D. Cross; Hank D'Amico; Detroit Public Library; Ron Edgerly; Andrew Esposito; Clarence E. Ferguson; Bill Fioretti; Louise Gibino; George & Tony Gloriosa; Alive Greunke; Siegfried Grunze; Keith Hazley; Teresa & Doug Hvidston; Jeff Kapla; David Klemenz; Darrell Kombrink; Leroy Lasiter; Mitch Lindahl; Rob Long; Arnold Marks; Doug Mitchel; Mike Moore; Michael Mulcahy; James Nair; John C. Nelson; Erin O'Neill; Darryl Peck; Charles Plylar; Ted Pope; Steve Potseck; Phil Quinn; Mike Rice; Steve Riley; Allan St. Jacques; Merritt G. Sargent; Albert Schildknecht; Southwest Gallery of Cars; Mike Vanarde; Edward J. Whey; Karl & Betty Zrnich.

The editors also express their thanks for the generous assistance of:

Leslie G. Armbruster; Dan Bedore; John Clinard; Addam Ebel; Larry Erickson; Kevin George; Scott Jensen; Bob Johnston; Keith C. Knudsen; Phil Martens; J Mays; Sonia Mishra; Mark Rushbrook; Wes Sherwood; Sean Tant; Hau Thai-Tang; Holly Clark Walker; Ford Motor Company.

Mustang

Table of Contents

Mustang's galloping stallion is among motoring's landmark logos. A key
moment in the emblem's design was this sketch by Phillip Thomas Clark,
a Ford designer in the 1960s and one of the stylists on the two-seat
Mustang I. Ford lore has it that the pony runs to the left because it
was easiest for the right-handed Clark to draw it that way.

Foreword

What can I say about the Mustang? I can give you the facts. Mustang created its own market segment—the ponycar. Mustang is celebrating its 40th birthday in 2004 and is one of the longest-surviving single models manufactured by Ford Motor Company. Maybe most importantly, Mustang has remained true to its value-oriented, sports-car vision.

But none of that would do the Mustang justice. For most of us, Mustang wasn't just a car—it was a piece of our lives, a part of who we really are.

The Mustang and I ventured out onto the road together. With a brand new driver's license on my 16th birthday, my father, Henry Ford II, gave me a 1964½ Mustang fastback. It was pearl white and as clean as my driving record (at the time). During the summer of 1968, I worked for Carroll Shelby in California and delighted in his Mustang GT-350s and Shelby Cobras.

Yet it didn't stop there. At 21, I took a year off from college and went to work at Ford Motor Company. That year, I bought a candy-apple-red Mustang Boss 351. In the summer of that year, my best friend Bill Chapin and I drove across America following the SCCA Trans Am series where the Mustangs took on the AMC Javelins and the Chevrolet Camaros. This was a summer where Mustang distinguished itself repeatedly.

Mustang has played a special role in my life, as I suspect it has in yours. Your personal affair with the Mustang probably wasn't too much different than mine. But whether your first Mustang was brand-new or well-worn, whether it was a classic or a new 2005—we all have stories, wonderful stories.

What the Model T did for working families, the Mustang did for the youth culture of the '60s, and for every generation of young, and young-at-heart, since. This book captures that energy, the youthful enthusiasm that was, and is, Mustang. I sincerely hope it will bring back as many fond memories and evoke as many personal stories for you as it has for me.

Edsel B. Ford II

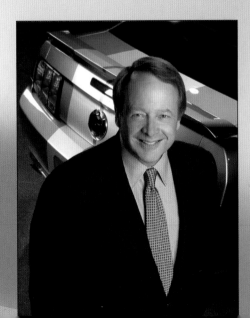

Chapter One:
1961-1964

It was the right car at the right time, but it had to await the early 1960s, when a savvy, up-and-coming Ford executive realized that America's youth was looking for a car to call its own. Lee Iacocca pushed hard for his "better idea," and a high-style, low-cost sporty compact galloped from drawing board to showroom—though not without plenty of hard work.

The biggest automotive success of the 1960s was actually some 20 years in the making. Since World War II, Americans had shown growing enthusiasm for British and European sports cars with their rakish looks, handy size, tight handling, and intriguing "foreign" features like tachometer, floorshift, and individual "bucket" seats. Sports cars attracted few sales but tons of attention. That's why Detroit paraded yearly fleets of sporty two-seat "dream cars" in the Fifties and offered sporty versions of some existing models. Struggling independent manufacturers Nash and Kaiser-Frazer actually built credible sports cars as "a difference to sell." But among the Big Three, only General Motors offered anything like a genuine sports car. Even then, the Chevrolet Corvette met a poor reception on its 1953 debut and was almost killed after two years for lack of sales.

Ford achieved far more success with the 1955–57 Thunderbird, a "personal" two-seat convertible with the V-8 power, boulevard ride, and convenience features Americans craved. But Ford Division chief Robert S. McNamara figured a four-seat model would sell even better. The replacement 1958 T-Bird proved him right.

At the same time, however, Americans were fast turning from Detroit's gaudy, gas-guzzling giants to small European cars and thrifty new domestic compacts like the Studebaker Lark. The Big Three responded for 1960 with the compact Ford Falcon, Chevy Corvair, and Chrysler Valiant. Though the affordable, orthodox Falcon was soon way outselling its rivals, the unconventional Corvair scored a surprise hit in mid-1960 with the snazzy Monza coupe featuring vinyl bucket seats, floorshift, and snazzy trim. Ford fired back the next year with a similar Falcon Futura.

It was in 1961 that an astute new Ford Division chief broached the idea of a more distinctive sporty Ford. A self-professed car-crazy and nobody's fool, Lee Iacocca had worked in the rental-car business as a high-schooler, attended Lehigh University, and earned a master's in mechanical engineering at Princeton on a scholarship. After joining the Ford sales force in Pennsylvania, he devised a novel and successful sales scheme that McNamara used nationwide. By age 35, Iacocca was a Ford vice-president. A year later, in 1960, he was promoted to head Ford Division.

The new chief moved quickly to rejuvenate Ford's profitable but stodgy lineup. He rushed out the Futura, added more "Lively Ones" for mid-1962 and again for "1963 ½," and put fastback rooflines on several models. He also launched an all-out racing program under the same "Total Performance" banner. By mid-decade, Ford was a consistent winner on racetracks and road courses the world over, which boosted sales and the division's bottom line.

But Iacocca wanted something more, suspecting there was a market looking for a new kind of car. He took his hunch to a 1961 meeting of the Fairlane Group, an informal planning committee composed of top company execs and Ford advertising people. Iacocca pointed out that America's huge "baby boom" generation was coming of age, would have money to spend, and would probably go big for a smaller car with high style, a low price, sporty features, and enough space for two adults and two children. The committee agreed, and Iacocca tapped engineer and product-planning manager Donald N. Frey to head up a new project dubbed T-5. The Mustang was on its way.

Mustang I: Experimental Bell-Ringer

As the effort got rolling, other Ford hands were finishing up a very different think-young car, the Mustang I. Petite and curvy, this open two-seater borrowed a front-wheel-drive powertrain from Ford Germany's mainstream Cardinal/Taunus sedan but put it behind the cockpit. Lead designer John Najjar suggested this mechanical format, then becoming *de rigueur* for racing cars. He also came up with the horsey name. Though simply a what-if exercise at first, the Mustang I impressed design vice-president Eugene Bordinat. As it happened, Bordinat wanted a newsworthy "bell-ringer" for Ford's autumn-1961 new-model press preview and ordered that Mustang I be transformed from clay-model dream to drivable reality. Engineers Herb Misch and Roy Lunn were called in and rushed to meet a tight 60-day deadline, working closely with Najjar's staff and interior designers

ABOVE: Small, light, and innovative, the midengine Mustang I began as an early-1961 paper exercise. Impressed Ford execs soon ordered up a realistic full-size mockup. RIGHT AND OPPOSITE PAGE: A fully operable model was built later in the year for publicity and to test public reaction. Sports-car purists raved, but Ford deemed the car too costly and impractical to produce.

led by Damon Woods. Construction was assigned to Southern California race-car fabricator Troutman-Barnes.

Riding a trim 90-inch wheelbase, the Mustang I measured 154.3 inches long and barely three feet tall at its highest point, a racy built-in rollover bar. Curb weight was a feathery 1500 pounds, so although the small, 1.5-liter German V-4 engine was tuned for only 90 horsepower, the car could do 0–60 mph in a brisk 10 seconds while squeezing out up to 30 mpg. Predictably, Mustang I was polo-pony agile, thanks to the low weight, a ground-hugging stance, and sophisticated European-style all-independent suspension.

The Mustang I was not only Dearborn's first true sports car, it was very innovative and thus quite unexpected from tradition-bound Detroit. Jaded reporters pleaded for a ride at the new-model preview, then went home to write glowing stories. The public didn't get to see Mustang I in person until October 1962, when race driver Dan Gurney drove it around the Watkins Glen circuit in New York before the start of the U.S. Grand Prix.

For a time, there was talk that Ford would build Mustang I for sale, and Najjar's studio devised a larger windshield, door windows, and a lightweight removable hardtop with that possibility in mind. But as Iacocca later told the press, Mustang I never had a chance. Where sports-car purists saw a dream come true, Ford's market-savvy chief saw a car that would be costly to produce. He

also knew that a tight two-seater with hardly any luggage space would be tough to sell in sufficient numbers to return a sizable profit. "That's sure not the car we want to build, because it can't be a volume car," he declared. "It's too far out." Exit Mustang I.

Decisions, Decisions

Ford briefly considered another two-seat idea, the "XT-Bird," a revival of the 1957 Thunderbird proposed by the Budd Company, which had built the original bodies and still had tooling. Budd pitched a prototype using a Falcon chassis and a '57 T-Bird body with updated styling and a tiny rear seat added. But though claimed production costs were temptingly low, Ford couldn't see a two-seater of any kind drawing the sales and profits Iacocca was after.

Even so, two-seaters persisted for a while in T-5 work, which produced scores of sketches, renderings, and clay models. Major themes were refined through several groups of designs labeled Avventura, Allegro, Mina, Median, and Stilletto, to name a few. The Allegro series alone comprised some 13 workouts differing in appearance, size, projected cost, and other key factors. One Allegro, a fastback coupe, was publicly shown as a "styling experimental car" in August 1963, but it was already a dead duck. Of the many sporty-car concepts churned out in 1961 and into '62, none satisfied Iacocca and other Ford execs.

John Najjar: In his own words

Of the many cars and trucks shaped by John Najjar over his 43 years with Ford Motor Company, none is more famous than the experimental mid-engine Mustang I of 1961. He's also long been credited with the horsey name and logo that survived to the production Mustang, but his work on the production-car interior is less widely known. Recruited by Ford out of high school in 1936, Najjar was a machinist trainee when Henry Ford himself happened by and asked if he was happy with the job. When Najjar said he'd rather be drawing cars, he was assigned to the fledgling design department to work with pioneer Ford stylist E.T. "Bob" Gregorie and scion Edsel Ford. Najjar rose to become Lincoln chief stylist in the mid-Fifties and held a number of other high-level design jobs for "Mother Ford" until he retired in 1979.

By early '62, Gene Bordinat had replaced George Walker as Ford's design vice-president, and I was in Advanced Vehicles under Bob Maguire. Bordinat had given out a directive that each studio was to take a crack at a small, sporty car.

We had one clay model that somehow looked globby and bulky. A modeler who worked for me, Joe Siebold, was interested in midget cars, and I had been reading about engines in race cars being placed ahead of the rear axle. Then it hit me! A small midship-engine passenger car. I started talking to Joe, and he started to draw. I remembered the power package from the little German Ford Cardinal from when I worked on that. "Why not take the front-engine drive and move it aft to drive the rear wheels?" So we did. Finally we showed our drawing to Maguire. He said, "That's pretty good, but keep it on the side 'til we see how it goes"—meaning the executives' reactions to the other designs.

Bordinat brought Iacocca around to all the studios, but Iacocca didn't like any of the cars. Then came news that race driver Dan Gurney was coming in to see if we had anything. So in comes Gurney, and Maguire said, "Turn the blackboard around, John." This is after he'd looked at all the other models. And Gurney said, "Now there's a nice little car." So that's how the Mustang I started.

As it happened, the company needed a "bell ringer" for the fall press introduction of the 1962 products, and Bordinat thought of our little car. He was out of money in that year's budget, but he got hold of Herb Misch, the vice-president for engineering. Misch comes in with Bordinat and some

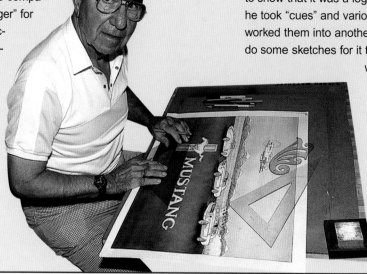

other people. "Can it be made?" they asked. "Yeah, we can do a fiberglass model." They said, "We'll need more than that." They wanted an operable vehicle to show the press. Misch put Roy Lunn in charge of building it. Roy had been a racing-car designer, and he worked with us on engineering. He really brought our concept to life. Jim Sipple, from Damon Woods' studio, did the interior, and I did the exterior.

We finished a clay model and took fiberglass casts of it. Roy only had something like 60 days, and his staff worked feverishly designing the tube work for the frame, the front suspension, steering mechanism, all the operating parts. He elected to have the drawings and fiberglass panels shipped to Troutman-Barnes, a racing-car fabricator in California, which would build the car in metal. It was an exciting time. The finished vehicle came back to the Design Center by late August or early September. It was driven on the Ford test track by a race driver named Dan Jones, who applauded its handling, but there was no other testing before it was shown to the press. Certain press people were allowed to ride in it, and it became the topic for the day, giving our 1962 program a much-needed lift.

Later on, a movie was made of the Mustang I, along with a ⅒ scale model. These were taken to different college campuses by company people who gave talks about Ford being the wave of the future, having youth in mind. Wherever possible, the drivable Mustang I was shown too. The Mustang I was a viable, marketable car, but Mr. Iacocca had a higher volume goal and wanted a 2+2 design. But it did kick off his dream of a sporty, youthful car that could be produced in huge volume.

After the Mustang I, I helped develop the interior for the production Mustang. One of my ideas was to save money by eliminating the door trim panel. At first we were going to use a cloth insert on steel, but I found a vendor that could supply textured metal that resembled vinyl. I had some samples made, and everyone said let's do it. I also got approval for making the rear seat curve up from the cushion into the backrest for an integrated look. It was that kind of thinking and attitude that made the whole car a pleasure to work on.

When the production Mustang was finalized, Bordinat wanted to show that it was a logical development from the Mustang I, so he took "cues" and various parts from the production car and worked them into another show car, the Mustang II. He had me do some sketches for it that went to Don DeLaRossa's team, which did the full-size design.

I would say it's absolutely true that Lee Iacocca is the "father" of the Mustang. He was the one who assigned the people and assigned money to build the early clay vehicles and get the project through. I understand that Mr. Ford was not all for it, but Iacocca was able to convince him to go ahead. I'm sure he had even had the car researched with the dealers.

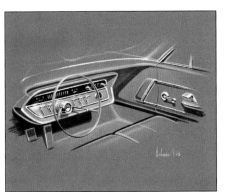

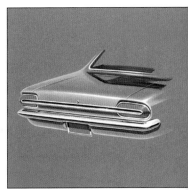

ABOVE AND LEFT: The Mustang began in 1961 as Project T-5, which produced scores of styling ideas in sketches and clay models into mid-1962. None, however, satisfied Lee Iacocca and other Ford brass. TOP: Ford PR staged this photo to show how engineers use a series of templates to transfer body surfaces from a full-size clay model to production tooling. The design here is another early T-5 reject.

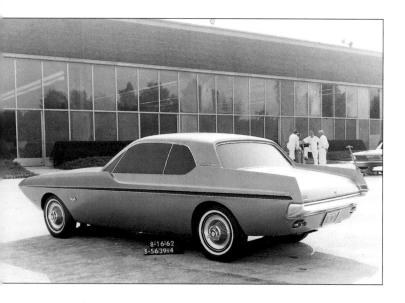

To get things moving, an impatient Iacocca had the program restarted in August 1962. A new package was laid down, and the company's three design studios were assigned to come up with fitting proposals. Iacocca felt the in-house competition was bound to produce the car everyone was searching for. The requirements were daunting: a $2500 target price, 2500-pound curb weight, 180-inch overall length, seating for four, standard floorshift, and maximum use of Falcon components. Styling was to be "sporty, personal, and tight." Marketers threw in the notion of an arm-long option list so buyers could equip the car for economy, luxury, performance, or any combination.

The contest pitted the Ford and Lincoln-Mercury divisional studios against a team from the Advanced Design section under Don DeLaRossa, all guided by Bordinat. Each studio had just two weeks to come up with one or more full-size clay models. Ultimately, seven candidates were wheeled into the Ford Design Center courtyard for an August 16 executive review. Each had its own character, some more formal than others, but most featured a long hood and a relatively short rear deck surmounted by a close-coupled "greenhouse." This look was at least partly inspired by the sporty yet elegant 1956-57 Continental Mark II, a design benchmark among recent Dearborn cars, but it was also the basic look of many genuine sports cars. Other shared traits included full rear-wheel openings and crisp body lines.

At Last, a Winner

Among the gathered seven, one design leaped out, a white notchback coupe. "It was the only one that seemed to be moving," Iacocca said.

Fittingly perhaps, it came from the Ford Studio headed by veteran designer Joe Oros, studio manager Gale Halderman and executive designer L. David Ash. Oros had his team paint their clay white so as to catch management eyes, which it obviously did. It looked much like the eventual showroom Mustang except for different side treatments left and right—the former would be

OPPOSITE PAGE: After an August 1962 restart, the Mustang styling effort came down to an executive review of seven proposals in the Ford Design Center courtyard. Lincoln-Mercury sent a crisp notchback (top) and a busy fastback (center). A candidate convertible (bottom) represented Advanced Design's "Allegro" series. ABOVE: A bit later, the chosen Ford Studio design was posed with a Corvair Monza, a prime marketing target. Note Cougar insignia and right-side body styling.

chosen for production—plus rectangular headlamps, different trim, and nameplates (more of which shortly). Ironically, this mockup was a second-thought rush job, completed in only three days after the group spent its first week on a design that Oros immediately vetoed upon returning from an outside seminar.

Gallop to the Starting Gate

Iacocca's baby now moved ahead with unusual speed. The Ford Studio model was "validated" for production on September 10, 1962, less than a month after the courtyard showdown. Except for changes typically made for mass production—suitable bumpers, round headlights, less windshield rake—the design was essentially untouched. And most Ford people didn't want it touched anyway. That included engineers, who bent a good many in-house rules to keep the styling intact.

The task of "productionizing" the Mustang fell to executive engineer Jack Predergast and development engineer C. N.

Reuter. It was mainly a body engineering job, because the basic chassis, suspension, and driveline were, by design, shared with the Falcon and the related "intermediate" Fairlane, new for '62. Overall length ended up at 181.6 inches, a bit over the specified limit but identical to that of the reskinned 1964 Falcon. Wheelbase was set at 108 inches, 1.5 inches shorter than Falcon's, but enough to accommodate four passengers. Though Falcon relied mainly on six-cylinder engines, the Oros team had left plenty of underhood space for Ford's light and lively new "Challenger" V-8, which arrived with the Fairlane and became a new option for top-line '63 Falcons.

Though Mustang development focused mainly on a hardtop coupe, the effort more or less assumed that a convertible would also be offered despite its inevitably higher price and lower sales. But with racy fastbacks starting to make a comeback in the market, designers felt a sloped-roof coupe was essential to give Mustang a credible performance image with American youth.

TOP AND ABOVE LEFT: Publicly shown as a "styling experimental" in August 1963, the Allegro X-car was one of many ideas to come from the T-5 program. It hinted that Ford was working on a new sporty compact but proved a literal red herring, as this fastback design had been rejected a year earlier. RIGHT: The Mustang had many "fathers," not just Lee Iacocca. Chief among them was engineer and product-planning manager Donald N. Frey, who spearheaded initial development under Iacocca's guidance.

Joe Oros: In his own words

You can thank motivational management techiques for the original Mustang design, abetted by a shrewd chief designer, Joe Oros. Oros first worked for GM in the Thirties and early 1940s, then joined the independent George Walker group that shaped the vital all-new 1949 Ford and the cars and trucks that built on its timely success. When Walker became Ford's in-house design vice president in 1955, he made Oros an assistant, then named him to head the Ford Studio in 1956. Though Oros would supervise the design of most every U.S. Ford-brand vehicle over the next dozen years, the Mustang was undoubtedly his biggest success as studio chief. Ironic, then, that his team's winning design was something of a rush job, just like that '49 Ford.

Lee Iacocca wanted a car that was more of a personalized, sporty four-seater rather than a tight, European 2+2 package. Gene Bordinat requested proposals for it from our Ford studio, Lincoln-Mercury [and Corporate Advanced].

The request came through on a Monday, and I had gone off to a one-week seminar: training sessions on problem analysis and problem-solving methods. Dave Ash was my executive. On Tuesday I called him to find out how things are going, and he told me about the new assignment. Ash had already made some sketches, and my understanding was that the studio was rapidly putting together a clay model for me to see the following Monday. I could hardly wait. I had difficulty concentrating on the seminar.

The following Monday, I went to the Design building very early and hot-trotted down to the Ford studio. And there was this car with a low mouth-type front end, a bumper integral with the grille opening, and a greenhouse with a reverse backlight like those on recent Lincolns, Mercurys, and the British Ford Anglia. I thought, "we can't use a reverse backlight if this car is supposed to be new. And the front end is going to be expensive and add weight." The bodysides were not new and exciting either. So I didn't think we would win all the marbles against the other studios. Then the designers started trickling in, and I asked Gale Halderman and John Foster, two managers working under Ash, "What happened here?" They said, "It's what Dave wanted to start with." Then Dave walks in and I said, "Please cover this model."

I then called a meeting with all the Ford studio designers, including the truck designers. We talked about the sporty car for most of that afternoon, setting parameters for what it should look like—and what it should not look like—by making lists on a large pad, a technique I adapted from the management seminar. We taped the lists up all around the studio to keep ourselves on track. We also had photographs of all the previous sporty cars that had been done in the Corporate Advanced studio as a guide to themes or ideas that were tired or not acceptable to management.

Within a week we had hammered out a new design. We cut templates and fitted them to the clay model that had been started. We cut right into it, adding or deleting clay to accommodate our new theme, so it wasn't like starting all over. But we knew Lincoln-Mercury would have two models. And Advanced would have five, some they had previously shown and modified, plus a couple extras. But we would only have one model because Ford studio had a production schedule for a good many facelifts and other projects. We couldn't afford the manpower, but we made up for lost time by working around the clock so our model would be ready for the management review.

It took us another two weeks or so to finish it. Lee Iacocca first saw it when it was about five-eighths to three-quarters complete. I met him at the studio door and talked with him about what we were trying to accomplish. I could tell he was really pleased with the concept we were on, but he was noncommittal. Still, our car won hands-down. And we did it in under three weeks' time.

I guided the overall appearance, especially the front end, but Dave Ash, Gale Halderman, and John Foster did an outstanding job in guiding the Mustang's development with the various committees that came through the studio-manufacturing, engineering, product planning. Charlie Phaneuf, another manager with a lot of ideas, also helped tremendously, as did the interior studio headed by Damon Woods. It was a tremendous all-around effort that shows what teamwork can do when properly coordinated. Interestingly enough, the car fell together naturally as a design theme. It wasn't forced. Engineering development came together very well. We were always conscious of the packaging requirements, the manufacturing requirements as far as feasibility. From approval to the showroom floor, we only had to make minor adjustments.

When Lee Iacocca saw our finished car, he just rolled his cigar in his mouth. I could see the gleam in his eye, and he was pleased as punch. Of course, that made me feel very good too.

Oros (2nd from right) and the original Mustang team.

Planners okayed the fastback, and it was all but wrapped up by mid-October 1963. However, it wouldn't start sale until some six months after its stablemates.

Why the delay? One reason was that the Mustang was a new idea and thus not a guaranteed success, however promising it seemed. While many Ford people thought it would be quite popular, there were a few—including chairman Henry Ford II—who feared a replay of the recent Edsel fiasco. They needn't have worried. Indeed, market research conducted during the program's final months strongly indicated that Ford had a winner on its hands. But the Edsel's outlook had been just as rosy, hence a certain amount of hand-wringing in late 1963.

Names and Icons

By that point, Ford had settled on the Mustang name after months of search and debate. Cougar had emerged as the early favorite, one reason the Oros team model wore Cougar name-plates and a big stylized cat within its grille. But countless other names were considered along the way, including Torino, Turino, and even T-5. Chairman Ford liked "Thunderbird II" and "T-Bird II." Iacocca, Frey, and others argued for Mustang, though other horses were in the running for a time, including Colt, Bronco, Maverick—and Pinto.

In any case, the name wasn't finally decided until late in the game. Indeed, some early Mustang press photos showed production prototypes with another big cat in the grille. But a galloping horse soon took its place. This icon was cast from a mahogany carving by sculptor Waino Kangas working from sketches by John Najjar and Phil Clark for the Mustang I. Equine name aside, the only other legacy from the little midships roadster was a small tri-color logo designed by Najjar, which appeared on the production model's dashboard and lower front fenders.

In many ways, Mustang was a perfect name for the sporty new Ford, evoking romantic images of free-spirited cowboys astride powerful steeds. Just as important, it was easy to spell and easy to remember. As one Ford ad man said, Mustang "had the excitement of the wide-open spaces, and it was American as all hell."

continued on page 22

OPPOSITE PAGE: Save a few details, Mustang styling was locked up by October, 1963, when this hardtop was photographed in the Design Center courtyard. Stylists always focused on a notchback, which was projected to be the most popular body style. ABOVE AND RIGHT: But designer Joe Oros felt a fastback coupe would give Mustang a truly sporty image and got it approved. This model, also made of fiberglass and shot at the same time as the hardtop, is very close to the showroom version released in autumn 1964.

Gale Halderman: In his own words

Recruited to Dearborn in 1954, designer Gale Halderman had helped shape the 1957 standard Ford before moving to the Corporate Advanced Studio, where he worked on ideas for a new low-cost sporty car favored by Ford division boss Lee Iacocca. As fate would have it, Halderman was transferred to the Ford Studio just in time to help Joe Oros' team create the design chosen for the production Mustang over proposals from Corporate Advanced and the Lincoln-Mercury Studio. Oros credits Halderman not only for contributing to the design but also for skillfully guiding the Mustang from clay-model dream to realistic, fully producible car.

I worked on a little electric-car proposal with Colin Neale and Alex Tremulis, who each did one side of a clay model. Elwood Engel said he liked both sides and wanted to do two full clays, which were then built in fiberglass. Lee Iacocca and Hal Sperlich came through and saw them. They said, "You know, they have flair and lots of excitement. Why don't we give the sporty-car package one more shot?" Those proposals encouraged them to reopen the design process for the car that became the Mustang. They had Ray Smith prepare a 2+2 package on the blackboard, and that's where the Mustang program started.

We did a design series called Median based on that package—what the car would look like proportioned in different ways and with different engine options. We did maybe six. We were still searching for the right-sized car and package arrangement. They were good-looking cars, except I think none of them were exciting enough.

About that time, I was transferred to the Ford studio again. They were just starting work on the '65 full-size Ford and I was assigned to work on it with Joe Oros. But one day Joe said, "We've just been told by Bordinat to do a proposal for a small car that Lee wants to build." I told Joe, "I won't have time. I'm doing the '65 Ford." He told me I had to give him some designs. So I went home and sketched. I took about five or six sketches with me the next morning and put them up on the board. Joe picked one of those to be clay-modeled.

Dave Ash had already done a clay—very boxy, very stiff-looking. Joe came back from a management conference and said, "No, no, no, we're not going to do that!" That's when he said he wanted me to submit some designs. So we actually started over on the clay model using the theme from one of my designs, which had scoops on the sides and the hop-up quarter lines. The front end was primarily designed afterward. We built the clay model in our Corporate Advanced Studio. George Schumaker was assigned to follow my sketch into the full-sized clay model. I was still working on the big '65 Ford across the hall, but during the day I kept going over to where the Mustang clay was to help interpret my sketch. Then Joe got me in there working on the taillamps and rear end while he and Charlie Phaneuf did the front end.

After the Mustang clay was approved, Joe asked me to manage the feasibility process. We had to modify the hood and headlamp area, and the front bumpers a little to accommodate the parking lamps. We lifted them up a little bit, but we didn't change the theme. We had to reproportion it slightly for manufacturing.

The fastback was Joe Oros' idea and designed in Charlie Phaneuf's studio. There was a lot of discussion about whether the roofline should come back all the way, or if it should leave a little bustleback, which is what Joe strongly wanted. But we all felt that for Mustang to be seen as a really sporty car, it had to have a fastback model. We did it in secret. No one, including Sperlich or Iacocca, saw it until it was finished. We cast it in fiberglass, painted it bright red, and then showed it to Iacocca. He said, "We've got to do it!"

No one knew the Mustang was going to be as popular as it was, but it created a huge stir in the company. Everybody just loved it, even the engineers, though we must have bent 75 in-house engineering and manufacturing rules. The Mustang had the first floating bumpers. The whole front end was a die-casting with a floating hood. There were so many things the engineers said we shouldn't be doing, but they didn't want to change them either. There was so much enthusiasm right from the beginning. Even the drivers at the test track loved it. We would go there for meetings, and the crowds of people around it were huge. That was totally unusual, so we suspected the Mustang was going to be a hit.

Lee Iacocca pushed the Mustang through and is entitled to the credit for it. Mr. Ford knew that Iacocca had assigned Hal Sperlich to determine where the holes were in our car lines, markets where we didn't have cars. He came back and said we don't have an entry-level car for young people, something exciting for them to drive to work, and for newly married couples, and so forth. At first, Henry Ford II didn't want it because it was a brand-new vehicle, and we just had a failure called the Edsel. But Lee loved it.

Many newspapers and magazines previewed Ford's new sporty car with these early PR photos of a "Mustang" convertible wearing a Cougar grille emblem. The Mustang name wasn't decided until almost the 11th hour, but Cougar was too good to lose and would return for 1967 on an upscale "Mercury Mustang."

continued from page 18

But it wasn't yet a household name, and Ford publicists wanted to build on the buzz created by the Mustang I. The result was a new showpiece, a convertible logically named Mustang II. Though billed as another "experiment," this was really an exaggerated preview of the showroom models, built after tooling was ordered with mostly production-line parts. Differences included a five-inch longer hood, a more pointed front, a bulkier tail, a cut-down windshield, matching liftoff hardtop, no bumpers, and an elaborately trimmed custom interior. Ford returned to Watkins Glen in October 1963 to unveil the Mustang II. Response was

enthusiastic, which must have lessened some anxiety in Dearborn. Reporters, noting the car looked factory-ready, now knew what they'd suspected for months: Ford was up to something potentially very big.

The Mustang II kicked off a six-month publicity buildup to announcement day. The next major step came on January 21, 1964, when invited reporters went to Dearborn for a "Mustang Technical Press Conference." Iacocca played host, beaming like a proud new papa. "Frankly, we can hardly wait for you to get behind the wheel of a Mustang," he gushed. "We think you're in for a driving experience such as you've never had before."

A revolution was about to begin.

Unveiled in October 1963, the "experimental" Mustang II was actually the fully engineered production Mustang with exaggerated nose and tail styling, a cut-down windshield, custom liftoff hardtop, and jazzy "show car" interior. It kicked off a carefully orchestrated publicity buildup to the showroom Mustang's scheduled debut in April 1964.

Chapter Two:
1965-1966

Mustang thundered onto America's automotive landscape like no car in history, captivating the nation to capture a million sales in its first model year alone. This runaway success wasn't hard to understand. Sporty, yet practical and affordable, the Mustang could be almost anything to anybody, thanks to a mile-long options list—the ultimate "personal" car.

With Mustang ready to meet the public in early 1964, Dearborn marketers shifted into overdrive to get the public ready for Mustang. Though Ford previewed the showroom model at a January 1964 press conference, it put the information revealed under an "embargo," meaning reporters weren't supposed to go public with it before a date Ford had set. This tactic is still widely observed in various industries, a sort of cat-and-mouse game between manufacturers and the Fourth Estate.

But the embargo didn't prevent reporters from engaging in "informed speculation." It certainly didn't prevent Ford itself from baiting the press or leaking information—which it did. For example, on March 11, just two days after the first production Mustang was built, young Walter Buehl Ford II, nephew of chairman Henry Ford II, was allowed to drive an undisguised prototype convertible to a luncheon in downtown Detroit. Fred Olmsted, auto editor for the Detroit *Free Press,* spotted it and hurriedly called photographer Ray Glonka. *Newsweek* and other publications quickly picked up Glonka's pictures—just as Ford intended. *Time,* meanwhile, had been allowed inside the corporate walls to follow the Mustang's gestation, again with the understanding that it wouldn't publish anything until the appointed day. *Time* kept its word but got no scoop. In a coup for Ford PR, both *Time* and *Newsweek* ran cover stories on Lee Iacocca and his brainchild the same week.

The Big Day Arrives

The weeks leading up to Mustang's debut saw big stories in all sorts of places: *Business Week, Esquire, Life, Look, Sports Illustrated, U.S. News & World Report, The Wall Street Journal*— and, of course, most every "buff book" car magazine. Finally, the wraps came off. On April 16, Ford presented its new baby to some 29 million TV viewers, buying the 9 P.M. slot on all three networks. Friday, April 17, was the public rollout. That morning, 2600 newspapers ran announcement ads and articles while the Mustang was revealed to opening-day visitors at the New York World's Fair.

Ford invited some 150 journalists to the unveiling—and some sumptuous wining and dining. The next day, it set them loose in a herd of Mustangs for a 750-mile cruise to Motown. "These were virtually hand-built cars. Anything could have happened," a Ford official remembered. "Some of the reporters hot-dogged the cars the whole way, and we were just praying they wouldn't crash or fall apart. Luckily, everyone made it, but it was pure luck."

The publicity bliz didn't end there. A flood of print and TV advertising insured that most everyone in America knew the "unexpected" Mustang had arrived. Ford also stoked public interest with numerous promotions and events. A highlight was getting Mustang named official pace car for the 1964 Indy 500. Though a white convertible with blue dorsal racing stripes led the field on Memorial Day, Ford built another 35 ragtops and some 195 hardtops decked out in the same regalia. The convertibles were later sold, the hardtops given away in dealer-sponsored contests.

It all added up to a not-so-small fortune, but the money was well spent. Mustang caused more excitement than any Ford in a generation. It surely provided a welcome mood lift for a nation still coming to terms with the assassination of President John F. Kennedy the previous fall.

America Catches "Mustang Fever"

Public reaction was beyond even Ford's expectations, and "Mustang Fever" was soon a national epidemic. One trucker was so distracted by a Mustang in a San Francisco showroom that he drove right through the window. A Chicago dealer had to lock its doors to keep people from rushing in and crushing the cars—and each other. A Pittsburgh retailer hoisted his only Mustang on a lube rack, only to find crowds pressing in so thick and fast that he couldn't get the car down until suppertime. Another dealer found itself with 15 customers wanting to buy the same new Mustang, so the car was auctioned. The winning bidder insisted on sleeping in it until his check cleared.

It was the same story everywhere. And why not? Mustang looked sharp and was priced right. The hardtop started at just

$2368 f.o.b. Detroit, a fact naturally trumpeted in early advertising. Dealers couldn't get cars fast enough. Early models sold at or above retail—with very unliberal trade-in allowances.

Though first-year sales were originally pegged at 100,000 units, Iacocca upped the estimate to 240,000 as announcement day approached. But even that proved conservative. Ford needed only four months to move 100,000 Mustangs. By mid-September 1965, the total was 680,989, an all-time industry record for first-year sales, though a 17-month model "year" helped. The millionth. Mustang was built the following March.

To Dearborn's delight, most of these sales were "plus" business, with fully 53 percent of trade-ins being non-Ford products. Even better, the average 1965-66 Mustang left the showroom with a healthy $400 in options, contributing to gross profits for Ford Motor Company estimated at $1.1 billion for those two model years. Casting a glow over the entire Ford line, Mustang was largely responsible for lifting the division's market share from 20 percent to 22.5 percent by 1966, a sizable gain.

Magic for Everyone

Despite this runaway success, some automotive experts could muster only qualified enthusiasm for the Mustang. After all, wasn't it basically a humble Falcon beneath that striking exterior? Perhaps, yet somehow it didn't matter, certainly not to buyers. "That was the magic of this car," Iacocca said later. "It stood out, yet it was everyman's car." He might have added that women loved—and bought—Mustangs as much as men did.

Advertising was quick to play on the car's wide appeal by sketching stories of fictional wallflowers transformed into swingers once they owned a Mustang. Typical of the approach, a fetching lady in a toreador outfit was pictured with a hardtop coupe above these words: "If they're still waiting for Agnes down

at the Willow Lane Whist and Discussion Group, they'll wait a long time. Agnes hasn't been herself since she got her Mustang...[It's] more car than Willow Lane has seen since the last Stutz Bearcat bit the dust. (And Agnes has a whole new set of hobbies, none of which involves cards.) Why don't you find out if there's any truth in the rumor—Mustangers have more fun?" Another ad told the tale of "Wolfgang," who "used to give harpsichord recitals for a few close friends. Then he bought a Mustang.... Sudden fame! Fortune! The adulation of millions! Being a Mustanger brought out the wolf in Wolfgang. What could it do for you?"

The cars claimed to work these life-changing miracles were divided between the "1964 ½" hardtops and convertibles produced through August 1964 and the "true" '65s built from then on. Among the latter were the 2+2 fastbacks that arrived at dealers on September 9, 1964, when the formal '65 model year began. Incidentally, Ford officially regarded all these cars as '65 models but has usually used 1964 in dating Mustang anniversaries since.

More Than a Prettier Falcon

Though Ford used many Falcon components to achieve a low base price, the Mustang was rather more than just a slicker version of the workaday compact. Indeed, Iacocca and Mustang engineers liked to talk of significant advancements in "weight control" made possible by "platform construction," basically a modified unibody. As one brochure stated: "The Mustang with its galvanized structural members and torque boxes is designed for strength and rugged support of both chassis and body components. The uninterrupted tunnel which runs straight through the center of the platform from the toe-board to the rear axle kick-up gives firm support, and the whole structure is reinforced by a practical use of ribs and reinforcements." Even so, the convertible

OPPOSITE PAGE: The Mustang convert-ible struts its stuff in one of two photos used for announcement-week ads. The other shot was of a well-equipped hardtop in profile. Headlines read "Presenting the unexpected...new Ford Mustang!" THIS PAGE, TOP: Mustang fast eclipsed the all-time first-year sales record set by Ford's own 1960 Falcon. This PR photo shows the popular duo flanking division executives Donald Frey (left) and Lee Iacocca. RIGHT AND BELOW: Early Mustang ads naturally played up the hardtop's low $2368 base price. Even no-frills models were quite dressy, as vinyl bucket seats, carpeting, and wheel covers were all included.

Mustang caused more buyer excitement than any Ford in a generation. Terrific styling was one big reason. Almost everyone loved it—even hard-boiled critics. Small front-fender emblems, as on this hardtop, identified cars with one of four optional V-8 engines, which initially ranged from a 164-bhp 260 to a potent 271-bhp 289.

required quite a bit of additional bracing to keep body flex tolerable.

More obvious was how dressy even a basic Mustang seemed compared to the typical Falcon, thanks to standard front bucket seats, vinyl interior, full carpeting, and full wheel covers. As planned, the "starter" powerteam comprised the 170-cubic-inch Falcon six sending 101 horsepower through a three-speed manual floorshift transmission. It was a good combination, capable of returning up to 20 mpg. But who cared when gas cost a quarter a gallon? A car this sporty just had to have a V-8.

There were four to choose from. The base option was a 260-cid engine ($75) offering 164 bhp with two-barrel carburetor and a bore and stroke of 3.80 × 2.87 inches. Next came a 289 with a 4.00-inch bore and either 195 bhp with two-barrel carb ($108) or 210 with four-barrel ($162). The top option was a four-barrel "Hi-Performance" (HP) 289 with 271 bhp (yours for $443). For the "true" '65s, the 170 six was replaced by an improved 200-cid unit with 120 bhp, the 260 V-8 gave way to a two-barrel 200-bhp 289, and the four-barrel 289 was tuned up to 225 bhp.

Save the HP V-8, all Mustang engines could be ordered with stick-overdrive manual transmission, Borg-Warner T-10 four-speed manual ($116 for sixes, $76 for V-8s), or three-speed Cruise-O-Matic ($180/$190). The four-speed was a "mandatory option" with the HP, a profit-boosting tactic then popular in Detroit. The HP came with a 3.50:1 rear-axle ratio and was the only engine available with the "short" (high-numerical) gearing favored by drag racers (3.89:1

Lee Iacocca: In his own words

Mustang was introduced to the press at the New York World's Fair, April 13, 1964. These are excerpts from that historic unveiling.

We appreciate your coming here to share this moment with us, one of the most important occasions in Ford Division history. Incidentally, this is Ford's first international press introduction. Here in New York we have newsmen from Canada and Puerto Rico as well as the United States. And while we meet here, the Mustang is being introduced in 11 European capitals to some 2000 reporters, editors, and photographers.

From the beginning, the Mustang has been an exciting venture for all of us. We haven't been able to contain our excitement entirely, with the result, I'm happy to say, that the public has caught some of our fever. We hope it's highly contagious.

We can't think of any [Ford] product... that has generated more advance interest than the Mustang. People in every state and from as far away as England, Malta, and Australia have written to ask for more information about the car. Many were ready to order it sight unseen!...One customer we may have to disappoint. He wants a Mustang [with] a 427 high-performance engine in it. We've forwarded his name to Project Mercury at Cape Kennedy.

Let me put the Mustang into perspective. First, it is a completely new line of cars—separate from Ford, Fairlane, Falcon, and Thunderbird.... Second, Mustang will be available in two-door hardtop and convertible models with probably the longest list of options and accessories ever offered on a new car.

Third, the Mustang will have an astonishingly low price—so low we plan to introduce it with an intensive campaign of price advertising. The suggested retail price for a two-door Mustang hardtop with standard equipment, delivered at a Detroit dealership, will be just $2368. Fourth, the Mustang will be built at two assembly plants—Dearborn, Michigan, and San Jose, California.

Fifth, our introduction program will be one of the most extensive on record. We will run Mustang announcement ads in 2600 newspapers reaching 75 percent of the households in the country, and in 24 top magazines with a combined circulation of 68 million. Beyond that, we have lined up a television introduction unlike any other ever attempted. On Thursday evening we will sponsor three half-hour shows simultaneously on the three major networks from

9:30 to 10 P.M. Eastern Standard Time. We expect to show the Mustang on TV screens in more than half the homes in the country—an estimated 29 million.

Finally, we plan to fit the Mustang into our program of performance events. We'll use it in such famous road rallies as the Midnight Sun in Sweden, the Alpine in France, and the Spa-Sofia-Liege between Belgium and Yugoslavia.

We don't claim the Mustang...can be all things to all people. But we do believe it will be more things to more people than any other automobile on the road.

The secret lies in its remarkable versatility. For a modest price it can be an economical compact car with traditional Ford quality and all the flair of a high-priced, highly styled European road car. For a little less-modest price, customers can buy high performance to match the flair. The Mustang straddles price brackets in a way that will enable buyers to position it depending on their individual needs, wants, and pocketbooks.

From the outset, compact-car customers have wanted bucket seats, deluxe trim packages, high-performance engines, four-on-the-floor stick shifts, and just about every other option we could devise. [They] wanted basic economical compacts, to be sure. But they also wanted to be able to dress them up to suit their own individual tastes. The compact-car market reflected the flavor of youth—young Americans out to have a good time.

By next year, 40 percent of the U.S. population will be under 20 years of age, and the 16–24 group is growing faster than any other segment. Not only are there more young people, they are settling down at an earlier age, marrying, and having families.

We designed the Mustang with young America in mind. We like to think that in the process we have achieved a new dimension in American motoring—perhaps in world motoring. We believe we have succeeded in wrapping up—in one package—all the elements of what we call "total performance." Best of all, we offer the package at a modest price.

You know, it's easy to design a car with a spacious interior if you are willing to sacrifice exterior flair. And it's also easy to design a car with a racy, sporty exterior if you're willing to throw out a couple of seats or give up most of your trunk space. The trick is finding the right combination of roominess and high style—and that's exactly what we think we've accomplished with our new line of cars. Ladies and gentlemen—the Mustang!

and a tight 4.11:1). Sixes came with a 3.20:1 axle, two-barrel V-8s a 2.80:1 gearset, and the regular four-barrel V-8 with a 3.00:1 cog.

Light and Lively V-8s

All Mustang V-8s used the efficient "thinwall" design inaugurated for 1962 with the 221-cid Fairlane unit. The nickname referred to the advanced casting techniques employed to make these engines the lightest iron-block V-8s in the industry. Shared features included full-length, full-circle water jackets; high-tubulence, wedge-shaped combustion chambers; hydraulic valve lifters; automatic choke; and centrifigual-vacuum-advance distributor. Four-barrel engines achieved their extra power via higher-flow intake systems, more aggressive valve timing, and increased compression, all of which dictated premium fuel. The Hi-Performance 289 naturally went further. Besides tight 10.5:1 compression (vs. 8.8 or 9.0:1), it benefited from a high-lift camshaft, solid valve lifters, chrome-plated valve stems, free-flow exhaust, and low-restriction air cleaner.

For those who didn't order (or couldn't get) the HP V-8 and later wished they had, Ford dealers soon offered a slew of bolt-on performance enhancers. Many were marketed under the Cobra banner, a canny move, as the same basic engine already powered Carroll Shelby's fierce Cobra sports cars, already making their mark. As one ad urged: "Mix a Mustang with a Cobra for the performance rod of the year!" A good starting point was the big-port aluminum manifold available with single four-barrel carb ($120), triple two-barrels ($210), or dual quads ($243). A "Cobra cam kit" ($73) delivered the HP's solid lifters and camshaft, a "cylinder head kit" ($222) the HP heads, big valves, and heavy-duty valve springs. An "engine performance kit" combined those two packages with matched pistons ($343). Other over-the-counter goodies included a dual-point Cobra distributor ($50), heavy-duty clutch, dual exhausts (where not already stock), and engine dress-up kits with plenty of gleaming chrome.

Only the Start

But deciding on a powertrain was just the first step in personalizing a Mustang. Further down the long options list were power brakes ($42); power steering ($84); tinted windshield ($22); the same with tinted windows ($31); 14-inch whitewall or red-band tires (to replace 13-inch blackwalls); spinner wheel covers ($18 the set); and 14-inch wire-wheel covers ($46). Minor items like backup lights and padded dash and sunvisors are common standard equipment now, but cost extra then. The priciest single option was air conditioning at $283 (but not available with the HP V-8). Also on the menu: a "Rally-Pac" tachometer and clock in a small pod atop the steering column ($69); deluxe steering wheel ($32); sports center console ($52); pushbutton AM radio with antenna ($59); rear-seat speaker ($12); a vinyl roof covering for the hardtop ($76); and power operation for the convertible top ($54).

ABOVE: Ford kept up the promotional pace in the months after Mustang's launch. A highlight was the new pony's selection as pace car for the 1964 Indy 500, where a convertible did the honors. RIGHT: Mustang's early sales pace was too much for Ford's River Rouge plant, so production was added at two other factories.

Desmond was afraid to let the cat out...until he got his Mustang. Mustang! A car to make weak men strong, strong men invincible. Mustang! Equipped with bucket seats, floor shift, vinyl interior, padded dash, full carpeting, more. Mustang! A challenge to your imagination with options like front disc brakes, 4-on-the-floor, big 289 cu. in.V-8, you name it. Desmond traded in his Persian kitten for an heiress named Olga. He had to. She followed him home. (It's inevitable...Mustangers have more fun.)

Best year yet to go Ford
MUSTANG!
MUSTANG!
MUSTANG!

Bernard was a born loser. He couldn't win at Solitaire, even when he cheated. Enter Mustang—the car that's practical, sporty, luxurious. Your choice! Bernard chose the sporty options. Got a 289 cu. in.V-8. Four-on-the-floor. Tachometer and clock combo. Special handling package. Front disc brakes— and did Bernie's luck change! Yesterday he won San Francisco in a faro game. And now he's got his eye on New York. Mustangers always win.

Best year yet to go Ford
MUSTANG!
MUSTANG!
MUSTANG!

Then there were option *packages* to grapple with: handling suspension (V-8s only, $31); Visibility Group (remote-control driver's-door mirror, day/night inside rearview mirror, two-speed electric wipers and windshield washers, $36); Accent Group (pinstriping and rocker-panel moldings, $27); and Instrument Group (round speedometer and four smaller dials including oil-pressure gauge and ammeter, $109). Added in September were Kelsey-Hayes front-disc brakes ($57 and well worth it), "Equa-Lock" limited-slip differential ($43), "spider-web" styled-steel wheels ($120), front bench seat ($24), and a $165 GT Group comprising the disc brakes, grille-mounted driving lights, special badges, and rocker-panel racing stripes like those on Ford's GT40 endurance racer. A bit later on came the Interior Décor Group, the so-called "pony interior" now highly coveted by collectors. This $107 package bundled the GT gauge cluster with woodgrain appliqués on dash and door panels, a simulated-wood-rim steering wheel, door courtesy lights, and—the main attraction—unique duo-tone vinyl upholstery with a herd of running horses embossed on the upper seatbacks.

For the "true" '65s, Ford added a standard adjustable front passenger seat, an alternator to replace the generator—and the snazzy 2+2 coupe. Several names had been considered for the last, including GT Limited, Grand Sport, and even GTO. But 2+2 was apt, as the semi-fastback had even less rear passenger space than other

Later ads in the '65 model year sketched stories of fictional wallflowers turned into stylish, successful swingers once they started driving Mustangs. Though designed for the youth market, Mustang appealed greatly to buyers of all ages with its dashing looks, "personal" character, and exciting sports-car performance options.

Wolfgang used to give harpsichord recitals for a few close friends. Then he bought a Mustang. Things looked livelier for Wolfgang, surrounded by bucket seats, vinyl interior, padded dash, wall-to-wall carpeting (all standard Mustang)...and a big V-8 option that produces some of the most powerful notes this side of Beethoven. What happened? Sudden fame! Fortune! The adulation of millions! Being a Mustanger brought out the wolf in Wolfgang. What could it do for you?

Best year yet to go Ford
MUSTANG!
MUSTANG!
MUSTANG!

This "true" 1965 convertible carries several highly desirable options, including 289 V-8, "Rally Pac" tachometer/clock combo, styled-steel wheels, and the GT Equipment Group with grille-mounted driving lights, special emblems, racing stripes, and more.

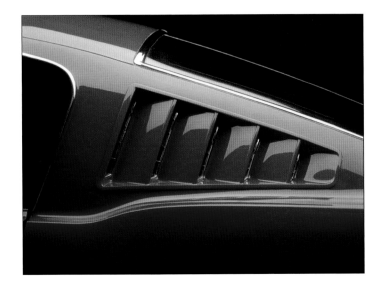

After a six-month run of "1964 ½" Mustangs, Ford adjusted standard equipment and added more options for "true" '65 models that started sale in September 1964. Among them was the planned 2+2 semi-fastback coupe with a racy roofline featuring single side windows ahead of gill-like air-extractor vents, part of an exclusive flow-through ventilation system. The 2+2 pipped the convertible as the second most popular body style for the formal '65 model year.

Mustangs. There was compensation, however, in greater utility via an optional rear seatback and trunk partition that could be dropped down to form a usefully long, flat load floor. The racy roofline incorporated gill-like air vents instead of windows in the rear quarters, part of a flow-through ventilation system. The 2+2 also stood apart by omitting the dummy-scoop rear fender trim, as did cars with pinstriping and/or the GT package.

The Critics Speak

Mustang's vast option list obviously covered all the bases. It helped give the car its wide appeal and was a big reason why sales took off so quickly. Perhaps more than any car before it, a Mustang could be equipped to reflect an individual owner's precise tastes and budget—provided he or she was willing to wait for their dream to be built. Yet your custom carriage needn't cost a king's ransom. Even easily tempted spendthrifts were hard-pressed to push delivered price above $3000. With so many ways to go, a Mustang's personality could range from mild to wild, spartan to sybaritic, anything you wanted—which explains why initial press reviews were no less varied.

To be sure, the car had some built-in flaws. Few testers faulted the styling, but many griped that the steering wheel was too close to the driver's chest and the interior too snug for the exterior size.

As *Motor Trend* noted: "Five passengers can fit, but the fifth one usually sits on the others nerves." *Road & Track* carped about the sparse, Falcon-sourced instrumentation and flat bucket seats.

Most all reviewers hurled barbs at the fade-prone drum brakes, slow steering (even with available "fast" ratio), and especially the standard suspension. *R&T* was particularly critical in its initial test of three base-chassis hardtops: "The ride is wallowy, there's a tendency [to float] at touring speeds, and the 'porpoise' factor is high on undulating surfaces....The Mustangs we tested [were] indistinguishable from any of half a dozen other Detroit compacts. There's just nothing different about it in this respect. And this, we think, is unfortunate." As for straight-line performance, *R&T*'s 210-bhp 289/four-speed car did about what the editors expected: 0–60 mph in nine seconds (vs. 11.2 for an automatic 260), a standing quarter-mile of 16.5 at 80 mph, 110 mph all out, and 14–18 mpg.

As the voice for what Iacocca termed "the sports-car crowd, the real buffs," *Road & Track* was harsher on the Mustang than most other publications. Yet even *R&T* allowed that any shortcomings had to be weighed against the low price. And the magazine did find a few things to cheer, including, perhaps surprisingly, good workmanship. "The car is...trimmed and neatly finished in a manner that many European sports/touring cars would do well to emulate."

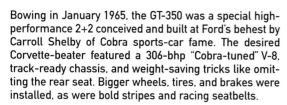

Bowing in January 1965, the GT-350 was a special high-performance 2+2 conceived and built at Ford's behest by Carroll Shelby of Cobra sports-car fame. The desired Corvette-beater featured a 306-bhp "Cobra-tuned" V-8, track-ready chassis, and weight-saving tricks like omitting the rear seat. Bigger wheels, tires, and brakes were installed, as were bold stripes and racing seatbelts.

The thing is, *R&T* became downright enthused about the Mustang once it tested a Hi-Po V-8 model equipped with the inexpensive handling package. The editors went out of their way to praise the chassis upgrades, which included stiff springs and shocks, larger-diameter front anti-sway bar, 5.90 × 15 Firestone Super Sports tires, and quicker steering ratio (3.5 turns lock-to-lock vs. nearly four). "The effect is to eliminate the wallow we experienced...and to tie the car to the road much more firmly....There is a certain harshness to the ride at low speeds over poor surfaces, but this is a small price to pay for the great improvement in handling and roadholding." Acceleration was naturally better too, *R&T* getting 8.3 seconds 0-60 mph.

Sports Car Graphic also tested an HP Mustang, but with the tight 4.11:1 axle that delivered 7.6 seconds 0-60 and a slightly faster quarter-mile than *R&T* posted. *Motor Trend,* which traditionally favors Detroit cars, loved every Mustang it tested, even an automatic-equipped six-cylinder job that needed a lengthy 14.3 seconds 0–60.

The HP Mustang got a glowing endorsement from none other than ace race driver Dan Gurney, whose mount reached 123 mph and consistently beat a similarly equipped Corvette in quarter-mile sprints. "This car will run the rubber off a Triumph or MG," he wrote in *Popular Science*. "It has the feel of a 2+2 Ferrari. So what *is* a sports car?" Clearly, the right options could make a Mustang fully worthy of that term.

An Even More Fiery Steed

An even more exciting and capable Mustang premiered at California's Riverside Raceway on January 27, 1965. Though created by Carroll Shelby, the GT-350 was instigated by Lee Iacocca, who wanted a Corvette-beater for Sports Car Club of America (SCCA) B-Production racing. The idea was to give every Mustang a "competition-proved" aura in line with Ford's "Total Performance" racing and ad campaign, then nearing high tide.

Shelby laid down the specifics in the fall of 1964. SCCA required that at least 100 cars be built to qualify as production, and Ford sent that many 2+2 fastbacks to Shelby's small facility in Venice, California, for conversion. The first dozen GT-350s were hand-built by Christmas; the remaining 88 by New Year's Day (a feat that much impressed SCCA officials).

Anatomy of a Thoroughbred

Each GT-350 started as a white fastback supplied with the Hi-Po V-8, four-speed gearbox, a stouter rear axle from the big Galaxie, and no hood, grille, side trim, or wheel covers. Shelby muscled up the engine to 306 bhp via a "hi-rise" manifold, larger carburetor, free-flow exhaust, and other changes. Additional component upgrades included Koni adjustable shocks, a bigger front sway bar, rear torque arms (added to lessen axle hop in hard takeoffs), Shelby-cast 6 × 15 alloy wheels, 7.75 × 15 Goodyear Blue Dot performance tires, larger brakes with sintered-metallic friction surfaces, and fast-ratio steering on relocated upper-suspension control arms. A hefty steel tube was added to bridge the front shock towers to lessen body flex in hard cornering. Shelby installed a fiberglass hood with functional air scoop and competition-style tiedowns and applied Ford-blue racing stripes above the rocker panels and atop the hood, roof, and deck. Inside were three-inch competition seatbelts, mahogany-rim racing steering wheel providing more arm room, and steering-column-mount tachometer and oil-pressure gauge. To meet racing rules for "sports cars" (defined as two-seaters), the stock rear seat was omitted and the spare tire lashed in its place, though Shelby offered a different bolt-in bench seat as an option.

As planned, there was also a race-ready GT-350R. This used basically the same high-tune 289 as competition Cobras, which meant 340-360 bhp. A low-restriction side-exit exhaust system helped, as did replacing the front bumper with a fiberglass airdam containing a large central air slot. Also to save weight, the gearbox got an aluminum case, plastic replaced glass for door and rear windows, and the cockpit was stripped down to a single racing seat, roll bar, and safety harness. Super-duty suspension and tires were naturally included, and a "locker" differential was installed. A few GT-350Rs were built with all-disc brakes and ultra-wide tires under flared fenders.

Mustangs went racing even before they went on sale. Many showed up at dragstrips, where they often won. Typical of that highly modified breed is this 2+2 campaigned in 1965 by Royal Oak, Michigan, dealer Stark Hickey Ford in NHRA's "factory experimental" class.

The street GT-350 was priced at $4547, about $1500 more than a standard V-8 Mustang. A real sizzler, it could storm 0-60 mph in around 6.5 seconds, hit 130–135 mph, and make genuine track-star moves. The R-model was even faster—and at a nominal $5950 an incredible bargain for a showroom car that could race straight to victory lane. Though no GT-350 was easy to drive, orders quickly overwhelmed the small Venice shop, prompting the newly formed Shelby American, Inc., to move into two huge hangars at nearby Los Angeles International Airport in the spring of 1965. Model-year production totaled 562, of which an estimated 25 were racing versions.

Mustang seemed born to race and did so even before it went on sale. In late winter of 1963-64, Ford prepped several hardtops for the European rally circuit. The effort was sincere enough, but the team's only major win came in the Tour de France, where Peter Proctor and Peter Harper finished one-two in class. Mustang was more successful in drag racing, where 2+2s stuffed full of Ford big-block 427 V-8s racked up numerous wins in the National Hot Rod Association (NHRA) A/FX class and, less often, as "funny cars." Ford itself jumped in for the '65 season, fielding wild "altereds" with two-inch-shorter wheelbases. And not unexpectedly, GT-350s tore up the tracks—and more than a few Corvettes—winning the National B-Production Championship three years running (1965–67).

More of a Good Thing for 1966

Typical for a new car in its second year, the 1966 Mustangs weren't greatly changed—not that they needed to be with sales roaring along. Thin bars replaced the grille's honeycomb background, and non-GT models discarded the grille's thick horizontal chrome bar and small vertical supports, leaving the galloping horse's "corral" to seemingly float in space. Fuel-filler cap, stock wheel covers, the simulated bodyside scoops, emblems, and nameplates were all revised. Designers had always wanted three separate taillamps per side instead of a cluster, but though some '66 press photos showed this, the idea was again rejected on cost grounds. Ford did splurge on interiors, though, adding new seat and door trim, standard padded dash and sunvisors (with a nod to Congress, then starting to grumble about auto safety), and the five-dial GT instrumentation (replacing the original cluster with dated strip speedometer). Six-cylinder cars went from 13- to 14-inch standard wheels and tires, and all models got new engine

mounts to reduce vibration. Engine offerings carried over from the "true" '65s, but options expanded again with the addition of 8-track stereo tape player ($128) and deluxe seatbelts with reminder light and inertia-reel retractors (about $8).

Ford pushed six-cylinder Mustangs more heavily for '66, in part to keep sales going during a temporary shortage of V-8s that occured during the model run. Highlighting this effort was the Sprint 200, advertised as the "Limited Edition," announced in spring 1966 to mark the first million Mustangs built and sold. The Sprint 200 was basically a package available for any body style, though most were built as hardtops. The 200-cid six (hence the name) was given a chrome air cleaner with "Sprint 200" decal. Wire-look wheel covers, center console, and bodyside pinstriping were also included. In all, it was an attractive package for any buyer, though Ford pitched it mainly to women.

Though six-cylinder Mustangs looked like V-8 models at a glance, there were some technical differences. Chief among them were four-lug wheels instead of five-bolt, nine-inch drum brakes versus 10-inch diameter, slightly narrower front track, a lighter rear axle, and lower spring rates.

There were two other reasons to push sixes for '66. As one Ford executive said later, "We felt there was a need to emphasize the economy aspect at that time. Also, the six-cylinder coupe was by then the only Mustang selling for less than Mr. Iacocca's original target figure."

Not that prices had risen much since introduction. The hardtop had gone up only $4 during '65 and started at $2416 for '66. The convertible, which had listed for $2614 through the entire first year, went to $2653. The 2+2 had arrived at $2589 and was upped to $2607.

Predictably, model-year 1966 sales were down on extra-long '65, but for comparable 12-month periods the '66s actually ran ahead by 50,000 units. Model-year sales kept galloping along at close to half a million hardtops, 72,000 convertibles, and 36,000 fastbacks.

ABOVE: Another press photo rounds up prototype '66s, also with the the separate taillamps that were axed at the last minute. FAR RIGHT AND BELOW: The '66s did get slightly tidier detailing around the nose but were otherwise hard to tell from '65s at a glance. NEAR RIGHT: Engines carried over from the "formal" '65 model year. The strong 271-bhp "Hi-Performance" 289 remained the top power option.

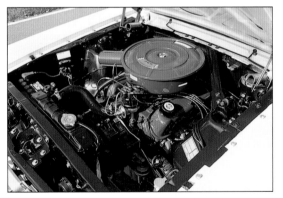

Unlike other '66 Mustangs, GT-package cars kept the original horizontal grille bar, again with outboard driving lights. This convertible carries the now highly desired "pony" interior trim with wood-effect steering wheel and dash appliques, plus available underdash air conditioner. LEFT ABOVE AND BELOW: Ads still played on the milquetoast-to-Mustanger theme, but text took a more hard-sell approach.

Mustang reminded many of certain European tourers, so it was fitting that the car started sale in Germany during 1966. But it couldn't be a Mustang in the land of Bimmers and Benzes, because a local company already owned the name and wouldn't give it up. Accordingly, Ford substituted badges reading T-5, the code name of the original development program, and removed all other "Mustang" labels, though the powerful steed still appeared on the grille and steering wheel. The cars were otherwise all-American except for minor changes needed to satisfy German regulations. Interestingly, German T-5 Mustang sales would continue until the late 1970s.

A Kinder, Gentler Shelby-Mustang

As a small manufacturer, Shelby American didn't observe strict model years, generally making changes only after parts in stock were used up. As a result, there's no "official" distinction between the 1965 and '66 GT-350s. However, the first 262 cars designated as '66s were actually leftover '65s retrofitted with the thin-bar grille (also sans "corral"), rear-brake air scoops behind the doors, and plexiglas windows replacing the roof vents. Subsequent '66s

Carroll Shelby:
"Total Performance" Man

Ford Division chief Lee Iacocca suspected Mustang would be popular but thought a true "Total Performance" aura would cinch its success. What better than a racing Mustang capable of trouncing Chevy Corvettes in big-league sports-car competition? To build it, Iacocca sought out Carroll Shelby. He couldn't have made a better choice. By the time the Mustang debuted, Shelby and his furiously fast Cobra were already performance legends. Even better for the marketing-minded Iacocca, the Cobra was festooned with "Powered by Ford" logos, and Shelby had the racing experience and mechanic talent needed to make a winner of Mustang.

Born in 1923 in Leesburg, Texas, Shelby served as an Army Air Corps flight instructor during World War II, then worked as a truck driver, ranch hand, and salesman. He was into chicken ranching when he turned to racing sports cars, starting in 1952 with a humble MG-TC.

Even now, the name Carroll Shelby conjures images of a lanky country boy with a thick Texas drawl and a wide "aw shucks" grin beneath a black cowboy hat. This down-home manner was somewhat calculated. In 1953, for example, Shelby was late getting to a race and had no time to change out of his farmer's overalls. Noticing how people reacted, he made the "Texas tuxedo" a sartorial signature. He might play to crowds, but Shelby was as smart about business as he was about racing and building cars. He was, as one writer put it, "a promoter in the most flattering sense. Like an alchemist, he had the unique ability to combine elements so that their sum becomes greater than the total of their parts."

Shelby raced successfully in the U.S., Europe and Latin America in the mid- to late-Fifties, wheeling Aston Martins, Maseratis, Ferraris, and other sports cars with stellar teammates including Masten Gregory, Dan Gurney, and Phil Hill. He also had a few Formula rides during the 1955 and '58 seasons.

A natural but fierce competitor, Shelby would often steal a quick pre-race snooze, saying "Wake me up when it's time to grid." His high point as a driver came in 1959. Shelby's friendship with John Weyer of Aston Martin led to his being paired with Ray Salvadori in an Aston DBR for that year's LeMans 24 Hours. Carroll and Ray won the always-grueling event outright.

The very next year, a heart condition forced Shelby to retire from driving, but not from working with cars. Settling in Southern California, he became a Goodyear tire distributor and opened America's first performance driving school. Meanwhile, he dreamed of building a pure "sport car"—trim, light, powerful, and fast enough to beat anything on street or track.

He got his chance in September 1961. Ford had just introduced its revvy "Fairlane 221" small-block V-8, and Shelby heard that

England's AC Cars was losing the engine supplier for its lithe two-seat Ace roadster. There are various stories about what happened next, but basically Carroll decided the engine and car were made for each other. He cajoled AC into selling him Aces and Ford into supplying engines, only he opted for the more powerful 260-cubic-inch V-8. Thus was born the Cobra in February 1962. By year's end, Shelby was offering an even faster 289-cid version, built at his small shop in Venice, California. By 1965 he had the brutal 427 Cobra and was turning out his first high-performance Mustangs, the GT-350s.

Like the Cobra, the GT-350 was all business and tough to beat, even in street tune. Racing R-models fulfilled Iaccoca's hopes by running away from Corvettes in the Sports Car Club of America's B-Production class, winning the national championship in 1965, '66, and again in '67. But then Ford and the stock Mustang began changing in ways that Shelby didn't like, and he parted company with Dearborn in 1970.

For the next 10 years, Shelby tended to various businesses, most all of which succeeded by dint of his fame. Notable among these ventures was marketing a spicy Texas chili mix and, believe it or not, a deodorant called—what else?—"Pit Stop." Meanwhile, a slew of imitation Cobras had cropped up. Not surprisingly, Shelby took the counterfeiters to court, putting many out of business even though some cases ran on for years. In the early 1980s, Shelby again teamed with Lee Iaccoca, this time at Chrysler, where the former Ford exec had become chairman. There, Shelby brokered a string of coarse but potent turbocharged Dodges, then served as the "spiritual conscience" for the Cobra-like 1990 Dodge Viper.

Despite a subsequent heart transplant, Shelby would keep going strong. Shrewd, colorful, and feisty as ever, he set up a modern new shop in Las Vegas to build the capable, though ultimately star-crossed, Series I "new Cobra" of 1999, as well as more "continuation" Cobras assembled from new-old-stock parts and even a few "new" GT-350s converted from 1960s Mustangs.

Then, in 2003, Shelby officially returned to Ford as a consultant on high-performance models. Announcing his return was the exciting 2004 Shelby Cobra concept based partly on the mid-engine Ford GT supercar.

Though a Mustang could still be equipped to be most anything a buyer wanted, most enthusiasts would probably opt for the goodies on this beautifully maintained '66 2+2. A special front-fender badge signals "Hi-Po" V-8 under the hood, and the GT-package driving lights, rocker-panel stripes, and bright exhaust tips are easily spotted. Note, too, the larger-than-stock redline tires and "spider web" styled steel wheels. Inside are Rally-Pac, air conditioning, and a sports console with T-handle selector for the optional "Select Shift" automatic transmission.

got slightly softer damping and other suspension tweaks, plus the new options of automatic transmission and the stock fastback's fold-down rear seat. Paint colors expanded to red, blue, green, and black, all with white stripes. More typical of ol' Shel was a Paxton centrifugal supercharger option, available factory-installed for $670 or as a $430 kit. Boosting horsepower by a claimed 46 percent to more than 400, it cut the 0–60 dash to around five seconds. Few were sold, however, and the option was dropped after a single season.

Shelby's Rent-A-Racer

In another interesting move for '66, Carroll concocted the GT-350H—"H" for Hertz Rent-A-Car. Exactly 936 were built, all finished in black with gold striping and equipped with Select-Shift Cruise-O-Matic. Hertz rented them for $17 a day and 17 cents a mile. Weekend racers eagerly lined up, but their unauthorized track outings made the venture a mite unprofitable, and Hertz bailed out after just one year.

In all, Shelby built 2378 GT-350s to '66 specs, including R- and

H-models, plus six prototype convertibles. But profit-minded Ford wanted far more and was starting to pressure Carroll to water down his original concept even more.

Brilliance Bound To Be Copied

Up to now, Ford's spectacularly successful ponycar (a term coined by *Car Life* magazine) had only one direct competitor: the Plymouth Barracuda, a sporty Valiant-based "glassback" that by pure coincidence bowed a month after Mustang. As a Plymouth and a less "special" sportster, Barracuda proved no sales threat. But Ford knew that archrival Chevrolet was bound to copy Mustang—probably sooner rather than later. Indeed, many journalists had predicted a whole slew of competitors inspired by Mustang's winning formula. After all, it's axiomatic in Detroit that a hot-seller doesn't go unanswered for long.

But Dearborn had more extensive changes in store for the 1967 Mustangs. The only question was, would they be enough to keep the original ponycar ahead of the expected imitators? The market would render its verdict soon enough.

IT'S WHAT'S UP FRONT THAT COUNTS!

When you take half a Mustang and half a Cobra, power it with 306 Ford horses (350 in the competition version) and call it the G.T. 350, you end up with a powerhouse from Shelby-American that's unbeatable...on the street or in competition. Take the Pomona ABC Production race on June 20...first overall. Take Elkhart Lake on the same weekend...first in B, fourth overall (the first three, all A Production, were Cobras). Let's take a look at just a small part of the record.

	Kent	Titus	1st overall
Cumberland	Johnson	1st in Bp
Lime Rock	Johnson	1st in Bp
	Donahue	2nd in Bp
	Krinner	3rd in Bp
	Owens	4th in Bp
Willow Springs	Cantwell	1st in Bp
Mid-Ohio	Johnson	1st overall
Dallas	Miles	1st in Bp

G.T. 350 STREET VERSION SPECIFICATIONS Shelby-American prepared 289 cubic inch O.H.V. Cobra V-8 engine equipped with special high riser aluminum manifold, center pivot float four barrel carburetor, hand built tubular "tuned" exhaust system featuring straight through glass-packed mufflers, finned Cobra aluminum valve covers, extra capacity finned and baffled aluminum oil pan; fully synchronized Borg Warner special Sebring close-ratio four speed transmission; computer designed competition suspension geometry; one inch diameter front anti-roll bar; fully stabilized, torque controlled rear axle; 6½" wide wheels mounted with Goodyear high-performance low-profile tires; Kelsey Hayes front disc brakes; wide drum rear brakes with metallic linings; competition adjustable shock absorbers; integrally-designed functional hood air scoop; competition instrumentation including tachometer; racing steering wheel; rear quarter panel windows; rear brake air scoop; competition seat belts; 19:1 quick ratio steering.

G.T. 350 COMPETITION VERSION Additions to the street version include: Fiberglass front lower apron panel; engine oil cooler; large capacity water radiator; front and rear brake cooling assemblies; 34 gallon fuel tank; quick fill cap; electric fuel pump; large diameter exhaust pipes; five magnesium bolt-on 7" x 15" wheels, revised wheel openings; interior safety group including roll bar; full Shelby-American competition prepared and dyno-tuned engine; every car track-tested at Willow Springs before delivery.

SHELBY G.T. 350

ABOVE: A unique black-and-gold exterior marked the 1966 Shelby GT-350H models built for Hertz Rent-A-Car. The company took 936, a big production and profit booster for Shelby, but abandoned the rent-a-racer program because many customers went on unauthorized track outings, which often damaged the cars and lost Hertz a pile of money. LEFT: Appropriate for a high-performance machine, GT-350 ads were heavy on "tech and specs," not to mention a fast-growing list of racing wins. BELOW: Privateers and Ford itself fielded wild Mustang dragsters in 1966 with altered wheelbases and huge power.

Chapter Three:
1967-1968

How do you follow a million-seller in Detroit? Make it even better. Ford did just that with the 1967 Mustang, adding a fresh "performance" look and go-power to match. A good thing, too, because the original ponycar was no longer the only ponycar and had to fight for sales. Still, Mustang galloped on in 1968 as one of America's most popular cars ever.

Lead times are a frustrating fact of life in the auto industry. In the 1960s, a new model took some three years to go from drawing board to showroom. (That's often true even now.) This means designers and engineers usually have to work without knowing how the public liked the car they just finished.

When work on the '67 Mustang began in summer 1964, the first edition was already a huge hit. But that posed the knotty problem of what to do for an encore. While Ford expected some changes would be needed after '66, it wasn't clear what those ought to be. Moreover, as program head Ross Humphries later told author Gary Witzenburg: "At the time the '67 was planned, we really didn't have any idea that the original was such a winner. Things did look awfully rosy, but we didn't know how long it was going to last." Fad or not, Mustang's instant high success got Ford cracking on a slightly larger, more luxurious ponycar by late 1964. It would emerge for '67 as the Mercury Cougar.

Meantime, Ford Division was left to ponder how archrival Chevrolet might respond—if at all. For a time, General Motors design chief Bill Mitchell insisted his company already had a Mustang-fighter in the beautiful second-generation 1965 Corvair. But that was just a smokescreen for the super-secret Camaro, a true Chevy ponycar being readied for '67. As Ford engineer Tom Feaheny recalled for Witzenburg: "It was a long ways down the road before we were aware they were coming after us."

Refinements—and Much More

Beyond that, Feaheny admitted that "[the '67 Mustang] was an opportunity to do a lot of refinement work. Frankly, the amount of engineering in [the first model] was not as great as it could have been....We really wanted to do the job right the second time around." He also noted that product planning chief Hal Sperlich wanted to "one-up the original in every respect: model availability, options, handling, performance, braking, comfort, quietness, even appearance where we could without making a major change."

Dovetailing nicely with that goal was the redesigned 1966 Falcon, which grew from cost-conscious compact to a slightly smaller sister of the midsize Fairlane. This meant Mustang would now have to share front-end components with those cars for cost and manufacturing reasons. And as the Fairlane was planned for big-block V-8s, Mustang's engine bay was bound to get wider too. Moreover, the mid-1964 arrival of Pontiac's GTO muscle car gave Ford an extra incentive to offer Mustang with a big-inch engine. After all, another "horsepower race" was on, and even a ponycar can always use more oats.

Change It...But Don't Change It

With all this, the '67s retained the original Mustang's basic chassis and inner structure but were redesigned or reengineered most everywhere else. Most obvious was fresh, "more Mustang" styling, created by the Ford Division studio under Gale Halderman. Given the tricky task of changing an instant icon without really changing it, designers explored various combinations of crisp lines and "soft," rounded forms through the usual plethora of sketches and clay models. They also toyed with Mustang's trademark mouthy grille, bodyside sculpting, and trim tail. Even so, some proposals strayed fairly far afield, ranging from bulky and square to lithe-looking, almost European. But the car that ultimately emerged was a nicely logical evolution of 1965–66. "We really took a number of cracks at it," Halderman told Witzenburg. "For '67 the theme revolved around more performance, so we made it a little stronger in appearance all over. The side scallop got deeper, for instance, and the grille and rear panel were enlarged. But we were very adamant about not changing...that rear hop-up look."

Though Don Frey took the reins at Ford Division as the '67 took shape, Lee Iacocca, promoted to corporate management, couldn't stay away. "Back in those days, Iacocca appeared [in our studio] daily," Halderman recalled. "The Mustang was his baby, and he watched it very carefully. We really didn't do anything on that car that he wasn't fully aware of and part of."

Save the 2+2, the '67 styling amounted to new outer sheet-metal from the beltline down. Wheelbase was held at 108 inches, but overall width swelled by 2.7 inches. A half-inch height increase improved headroom. Overall length tacked on two inch-

Mustang had just left the corral when work on the follow-up '67 model began in mid-1964 at the Ford Division studio under Gale Halderman. As with the original design effort, a four-door sedan (top and center) was mocked-up, then discarded as "un-Mustang." Besides stock 1964 wheel covers, these full-size clay models bear fairly rounded lines, which designers felt would impart a huskier "performance" look.

es, most of it via a tidier nose with a more aggressive grille bereft of flanking "gills." Halderman's comment notwithstanding, designers did exaggerate the rear hop-up a little. They also made the tail panel concave, as well as larger, and finally won approval for the more-expensive individual taillamps they'd long desired. For a new Exterior Decor Group option they applied thin bars to the back panel and conjured a special hood with wide, longitudinal recesses suggesting scoops. A nifty gimmick were turn-signal repeater lights nestled at the scoops' forward ends, easily visible to the driver. The 2+2 was the most radically changed '67 Mustang, gaining a sweeping full-fastback roofline inspired by that of Ford's GT40 racer, then making its mark at LeMans and other international endurance events. The new fastback retained flow-through ventilation but with air ducted through a dozen rear-quarter roof louvers instead of five vertical slots.

New Interior, New Features

Changes inside were no less numerous. Though the cabin remained a close-coupled affair with standard front bucket seats, the available console now swept up to meet a new "twin-cowl" instrument panel unique to Mustang. Drivers faced a pair of large, circular dials below three smaller gauges; ordering the optional tachometer eliminated the ammeter and oil pressure displays in the main starboard hole. Besides looking cool, the bulkier dash allowed for integrated air conditioning, though a hang-on unit was still available from dealers. Newly optional for all models was the useful Tilt-Away steering wheel recently pioneered by the posh Thunderbird, as well as AM radio with 8-track tape player and a "Convenience Control Panel" above the radio—reminder lights for door ajar, parking brake, low fuel, and seatbelts.

Interiors also added a number of "passive safety" features for '67, most per new federal decrees. Included were padded armrests, windshield pillars, sunvisors, and dashtop; double-laminate windshield; lane-change positions on the turn-signal lever; breakaway day/night mirror; standard seatbelts with pushbutton buckle releases and reminder light; built-in anchors for dealer-installed shoulder belts; four-way emergency flashers; and door locks that could not be accidentally released from the inside door handles. Serving "active safety" were a new dual-circuit brake system with trouble warning light; corrosion-resistant brake lines; safety-rim wheels; and standard backup lamps. Revised steering with a faster ratio and tighter turning circle served both active safety and driving ease.

Hardly anything was overlooked. Among other new features were Ford's handy reversible keys, manual keyless door locking, standard windshield washers (operated by foot-pedal), tighter door and window seals, and lower-effort window winders. A unique new ragtop option was a glass rear window with a middle crease that allowed more-compact top folding. It was naturally more durable than the traditional plastic affair, immune to "clouding up" with age and weathering.

A Big New Heart

For performance fans, though, the big event for '67 was availability of the planned big-block V-8, the familiar 390-cubic-inch "Thunderbird Special" with four-barrel carburetor and a rousing 320 horses. Also listed for many Fairlanes and full-size Fords (and standard in the T-Bird), it cost $264 as a Mustang option vs. $434 for the "Hi-Po" small-block. Dealers usually recommended teaming it with Ford's new "SelectShift" Cruise-O-Matic, which cost $233. SelectShift referred to a manual-override feature that allowed this automatic to be held in any of its three forward gears to engine redline for maximum acceleration, as well as manual downshifts from third to second.

The 390 raised powerteam choices to 13. The sturdy 200-cid six remained base power, while the "starter V-8" was now a two-barrel "Challenger" 289 with 200 bhp ($106). The four-barrel 225-bhp version returned as the "Challenger Special" ($158), as did the 271-bhp 289, now called "Cobra" (and priced at a stiff $434). All engines offered standard three-speed manual, a new close-ratio four-speed option, and the SelectShift automatic.

A More Nimble Pony

A 2.6-inch wider front track helped make room for the burly big-block but benefited the handling of any Mustang. So did front springs moved from below the top crossmember to above it *a la* Falcon/Fairlane. Dearborn engineers exchanged ideas with Carroll Shelby's crew, and though no GT-350 hardware showed up in regular Mustangs, the '67s did have similarly lowered upper A-arm pivots and a raised roll center. The effect was to decrease understeer by holding the outside front wheel more perpendicular to the road. As this didn't require higher spring rates, ride didn't suffer. Engineers also reduced noise, vibration, and harshness (NVH) with new rubber bushings at suspension attachment points.

"Given the more primitive hardware of the day," Tom Feaheny said later, "the '67 Mustang was really a fine-handling car…more than just cornering ability, but a feeling of real security for the driver…" Well, maybe with a small-block, but the 390 made for a front-heavy Mustang—fully 58 percent of total curb weight—and it understeered with merry abandon even though the option included F70-14 Firestone Wide-Oval tires. You were well advised to specify the Competition Handling Package, which list-

It seemed nothing was sacred in the early phases of the '67 design effort, not even established Mustang "cues." Full-fastback roofline for the 2+2 surfaced early, but so did a Plymouth Barracuda-like "glass-back" (upper center) and a "formal" Thunderbird-style wide-quarter roof (above). Also much debated were curved vs. straight-through fenderlines and plain vs. sculptured bodysides.

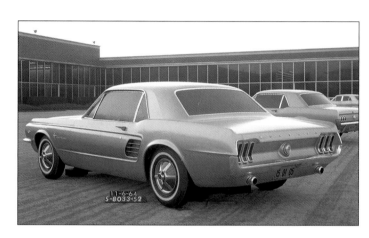

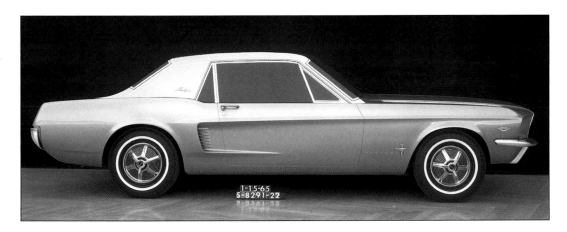

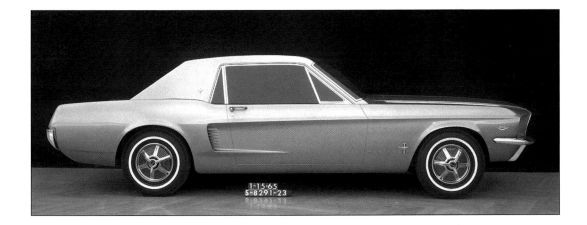

OPPOSITE PAGE, TOP LEFT AND RIGHT: The basic '67 shape and proportions began to emerge by October 1964. These two life-size clays show various ideas for bodyside and back-panel contouring. CENTER LEFT AND RIGHT AND BOTTOM: Peaked fenderlines, a more prominent nose, and a "mouthi-er" grille were mostly locked in by early November, but many other elements were still far from decided. THIS PAGE, LEFT: A trio of mockup hardtops shows how things stood in mid-January 1965. Wide-quarter roofline was still in contention, probably as a luxury option, along with '66-style "windsplits" in the simulated bodyside scoops. BELOW: Designers wanted separate taillamps and got them but still had other rear-end details to iron out as late as mid-June 1965.

ABOVE: Stock wheel covers and most other elements were settled by June 1965, but this hard-top's side scoops would be altered. TOP: Styling was mostly done by October, but GTs would not use the under-bumper driving lamps here. RIGHT: Proposed i.d. for the "HP" V-8 option.

ed for $62 but required the $205 GT Equipment Group (denoted this year only by "GT/A" fender emblems on cars with automatic). Also available with the Cobra 289, the comp package reprised stiffer springs and front stabilizer bar, 15-inch wheels and quick-ratio steering, while adding premium Koni adjustable shocks and a 3.25:1 limited-slip differential. All this improved handling at the expense of ride, which may explain why orders were relatively few.

What big-block buyers *really* cared about was blazing straight-line acceleration, and the 390 didn't disappoint. Typical figures were 0–60 mph in 7.5 seconds, the standing quarter-mile in 15.5 seconds at 95 mph, and close to 120 mph all out.

With performance like that, it was easy enough to forgive less-than-perfect handling. At least *Car and Driver* seemed to after testing a well-equipped 390 GT/A fastback. "The Mustang corners willingly, if clumsily," the editors reported. "It doesn't seek the right line instinctively...but once pointed in the proper direction, it clambers eagerly around the corner. True, initial under-steer is there, but oversteer can be induced by a flick of the wheel here, a poke at the throttle there. And it's very hard to throw it off balance or make it come unglued."

C/D praised other things beside the potent new engine. "Anyone who likes the old Mustang ought to go nuts for the '67.

It's a much better-looking car than the photographs show.... [The new interior indicates] Ford has decided the Mustang is going to be around for awhile, so why not invest some money where the occupants can enjoy it? The ride has been improved to the point that it's every bit as good as [on] most [midsize cars]." Other testers echoed many of these opinions, confirming that Ford had achieved what it set out to do.

Shelby's New "Better Idea"

If a 390 Mustang wasn't exciting enough, you could always count on Carroll Shelby, who offered two ways to go-go for '67. Typical of the man, he again one-upped Dearborn by stuffing in a bigger big-block, the 428 "Police Interceptor," for what he called the GT-500. The GT-350 returned with a Shelby-tuned 289 minus the steel-tube headers and straight-through mufflers, which reduced horsepower even though bhp was still advertised at 306. Though stock '67 Mustangs were little heavier than previous models—base curb weight rose only 140 pounds—power steer-ing and brakes were now mandatory Shelby options (you still paid extra, but couldn't get a car without them). This was prompt-ed by comments from existing owners that Shelby-Mustangs were tiring to drive.

Customer feedback led to other chassis changes. A 15/16-inch front sway bar and stiffer-than-stock springs continued, but Koni shocks gave way to cheaper Gabriel adjustables, and the rear traction bars and limited-slip differential were eliminated in the interest of ride comfort. Tires were upsized to E70×15 Goodyears on steel wheels with wheel covers or, at extra cost, 15×7-inch Kelsey-Hayes MagStars or Shelby-made cast-aluminum 10-spokes.

Styling was even more "more Mustang," announced by a shark-like fiberglass nose with larger-than-stock grille and a matching hood with a bigger scoop and racing-style tiedowns. A pair of high-intensity driving lamps mounted either dead-center of the grille or at its outboard ends, depending on local laws. Functional scoops adorned the sides (for rear brake cooling) and the roof

(for interior air extraction). A special trunklid (also fiberglass) sported a molded-in "lip" spoiler, and wide taillight clusters were borrowed from the Mercury Cougar. In all, it was a busy but arresting package. Inside was a new racing-style padded roll bar with integral inertia-reel shoulder harnesses, plus Shelby-brand wood-rimmed steering wheel, 8000-rpm tachometer, 140-mph speedometer, and Stewart-Warner oil and amp gauges. Tellingly, factory air conditioning arrived as first-time option.

Big Inches, Big Performance

Less muscle inevitably made the GT-350 a bit slower for '67, but the GT-500 more than made up for it. Shelby's big-block employed a cast-aluminum "427" medium-riser intake manifold and two high-flow Holley four-barrel carbs, plus a unique oval-

Photographed in January 1965, this full-size 2+2 was one of many mockups given the executive eye in the Ford Design Center's curtained showroom. At a glance, it's very close to the final '67, but the upper-bodyside character line would be abbreviated, and the triple rear-roof vent doors wouldn't make it. Wide, louvered taillamps (below left) were rejected too, though a ribbed, full-width back-panel appliqué would be offered. Spinner wheel covers and V-8 front-fender emblems were make-do 1965-model items that did not carry over.

finned, open-element aluminum air cleaner and cast-aluminum valve covers. Like the GT-350, the 500 was available with a "Top Loader" four-speed manual or SelectShift Cruise-O-Matic and axle ratios ranging from 3.50:1 to 4.11:1.

Carmakers were now deliberately understating power figures to avoid the ire of insurance companies, so the GT-500 doubtless packed far more bhp than its claimed 355. *Car and Driver,* which timed 6.5 seconds 0–60 mph, said that while the 428 "isn't the Le Mans winner," the GT-500 "does with ease what the old [GT-350] took brute force to accomplish." *Motor Trend*'s four-speed tester did better at 6.2 seconds and blitzed the standing quarter-mile in 15.42 seconds at 101.35 mph. But *Road & Track,* which reported 7.2 seconds 0–60, said the GT-500 "simply doesn't have anything sensational to offer...." As if to answer that, Shelby built 36 GT-500s with the 427 engine—which *was* the Le Mans winner—cautiously street-rated at 390 bhp.

Though Shelby-Mustangs were still the hairiest ponycars around, performance was now starting to take a back seat to style and luxury because that's what customers wanted and Ford wanted higher sales and profits. Indeed, Dearborn was exerting ever-more control over Shelby operations. Then, too, Carroll himself was increasingly occupied with various Ford racing programs, including development of the GT40s that won LeMans in 1966 and again in '67. Happily, Ford's heavier hand did produce

friendlier Shelby-Mustang prices. The GT-350 dropped more than $600 to $3995. The GT-500 bowed at $4195, about $150 less than 327 Corvette. All this helped boost total production to 3225 for the model year. Significantly, the big-inch version outsold its small-block sister by nearly 2 to 1 (2048 vs. 1175).

Another Trans-Am Trophy

Though Shelby-American didn't race its '67s and offered no new R-model for those who might want to, Carroll's crew did prep the Mustang hardtops that gave Ford a second consecutive championship in SCCA's Trans-Am series for ponycars. The issue wasn't decided until the season closer, where Jerry Titus and Ronnie Buckman fended off a factory-backed pack of Mercury Cougars to win the title by a mere two points.

Torrid Sales Pace Cools

Among regular '67 Mustangs, model-year sales dropped some 25 percent from the previous year's level, which was no surprise. The torrid pace of 1965-66 had to end sometime. Besides, Mustang now faced its first real competition. Not only did Chevy

RIGHT: For the '67 auto-show season, Ford recycled the Allegro coupe from the original Mustang program into the roofless Allegro II. Racing-inspired touches included a low wraparound windscreen, integral roll bar, fixed seats, and adjustable pedals. BELOW: Ford design chief Gene Bordinat shows off the '67 Mustang fastback and two other new Dearborn cars, the Mercury Cougar (left) and four-door Thunderbird.

All '67 Mustangs got new lower-body sheetmetal designed to suggest stronger performance, but the 2+2 also got a sweeping new full-fastback roofline patterned on that of Ford's LeMans-winning GT40 racer. These brochure shots also show the optional GT and Exterior Decor packages. The latter was identified by a ribbed back panel and a special hood with turn-signal repeater lights in twin "scoops."

have the Camaro, but Pontiac introduced a midyear clone called Firebird, and Plymouth trotted out a trio of handsome all-new '67 Barracudas that presented a far more serious sales threat than the previous "glassback." There was also doubtless some intramural interference from the Mercury Cougar. The top-selling hardtop took the biggest year-to-year hit, tumbling to just over 356,000. The convertible and fastback exchanged places on the popularity chart, the former dropping to only about 45,000 units, the latter moving up to over 70,000.

Still, Mustang's model-year sales tally of 472,121 units was hardly bad. In fact, the new styling and more available power allowed the original ponycar to way outpace its new imitators— more than 2 to 1 over Camaro, the closest challenger. Interestingly, '67 volume was more than *double* the most optimistic Ford estimates for Mustang's *first* year.

Slogans and Specials

Ford responded to the new competitive onslaught by advertising Mustang with an even more "hard sell" tone than in '66. Some pitches took a swipe at the ponies-come-lately with Mustang was "Bred First...To Be First!" and "still the original and lowest-priced car of its kind with bucket seats." Other ads urged buyers to "Take the Mustang Pledge!" or "Answer The Call of Mustang" and "Strike a blow for Originality!"

Marketers weren't idle, conjuring up another "package model" as a spring '67 sales boost. Called Sports Sprint, it came as a hardtop or convertible and with popular options like whitewalls, full wheel covers, and bright rocker moldings, plus chrome air cleaner and double-scoop hood. Engines were limited to the six and base V-8 in line with the slogan, "1968 Ideas at 1967 Low Prices Now!" It was a game try, but neither this tactic nor the high-pressure ads were quite enough in a suddenly crowded ponycar field.

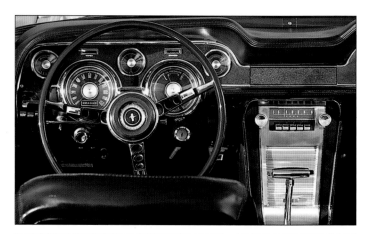

Despite greater visual bulk, Mustang's '67 styling kept the original car's lithe, ready-for-action look. This convertible wears optional "spider-web" styled-steel wheels, one of the few items continued from 1965-66. Jazzy new "twin cowl" dashboard (right) allowed for integrated air conditioning and was unique to Mustang, part of Ford's effort to give the ponycar a more upscale persona. So, too, was availability of the useful Tilt-Away steering wheel from the posh Thunderbird.

Why see a marriage counselor? Get a Select Shift.

You want a stick shift. *She* wants an automatic. And your budget says: "one car!"
No problem anymore. Get *one* car. And get it with a Ford Motor Company Select Shift.
The Select Shift is standard equipment with every automatic transmission.
Comes on the steering column or on the floor. Works like this: Shift the Select Shift
into first or second gear; it works like a *manual shift.* Real control in snow
or mud. Assists braking on hills—helps handle heavy trailer loads.
Shift the Select Shift into automatic. It's *automatic.* The Select Shift.
You get your way. *She* gets hers.
Ford has a better idea... Shift for yourself!

...has a better idea

Strike a blow for originality!
(Take the Mustang Pledge.)

Still the original and lowest-priced car of its kind with bucket seats. **MUSTANG** *Ford*

Better Than Ever for 1968

Ford hyped the '68 Mustang as "The Great Original" and "the
most exciting car on the American road." But though the cars
were improved in many ways, model-year sales plunged nearly 33
percent from '67. Still more competition was one problem, as tiny
American Motors weighed in with its shapely Javelin and clever
two-seat AMX spinoff. Also, Mustang probably lost some customers to racy new muscle midsizers like the restyled Dodge
Charger and Pontiac GTO as well as Ford's new Torino fastback.
Higher prices didn't help. The hardtop now started at $2600, the
fastback at $2700, the ragtop at $2800. Options cost more too.

Familiarity was another likely factor, as the '68s looked much
like the '67s. As before, creaselines ran from the upper front fenders to loop around simulated scoops ahead of the rear wheels
before running forward into the lower doors. GTs now accented
this shape with jazzy optional "C-stripes." All '68s wore a more
deeply inset grille, with the galloping horse (still in a bright rectangular "corral") newly flush-mounted rather than protruding.
F-O-R-D lettering was erased from the hood. So was the horizontal grille bar, leaving the pony mascot and GT foglamps to "float"
within the cavity. The rest of the GT package was happily
unchanged, so you again got dual exhausts with chrome "quad"

Humor still had a place in Mustang advertising for '67 (top left), but
most appeals took a "hard sell" tact, emphasizing features, price, and
value (right and top right) instead of telling tales of lives transformed.
The shift was needed in a year when Mustang got its first real marketplace competition, especially from archrival Chevrolet's Camaro.

take the
MUSTANG PLEDGE!

I WILL NOT...

I will not sell tickets to all the people who
want to ride in my '67 Mustang.

I will not keep the neighbors up all night by
playing my Mustang's stereo tape player.

I will not yawn when people talk about the
performance of other cars.

I will not show off my Mustang's overhead
console by turning on its map lights (at least,
not in the daytime, anyway).

I WILL...

I will tell the truth about my Mustang's low price
and not let people think I paid extra for bucket seats,
vinyl interior, plush carpeting and all those other
no-cost extras.

I will spend the money I save with Mustang on
a good cause...myself.

I will love, honor and obey the Convenience Control
Panel when its lights tell me to fasten seat belts
and release the parking brake.

I will stick to my diet even though my Mustang's
Tilt-Away steering wheel is so adjustable.

I will keep the "helpless-female" look by shifting
manually only when I'm driving alone. All other
times I will let the SelectShift work automatically.

I will catch up on my diary...one of these days.

MUSTANG *Ford*

Though down on actual power and speed for '67, the Shelby GT-350 looked faster than ever, thanks to an aggressive makeover of the new stock fastback supervised by Dearborn designer Chuck McHose. The result was a busy but eye-catching package with unique fiberglass nose, hood, and trunklid, Mercury Cougar taillamps below a purposeful spoiler, and Shelby's trademark racing stripes. The interior was less special than before, though extra gauges and Shelby-brand wood-rim wheel were included. Advertised horsepower was still 306.

outlets, pop-open fuel cap, heavy-duty suspension, and F70-14 tires on styled-steel wheels. Wide-Oval tires were again sold separately.

Satisfying the Feds

With federal safety and emissions standards now in force nationwide, some Mustang engines were detuned and "desmogged" for '68. Lower compression pushed the base 200-cid six down to 115 bhp. The two-barrel 289 V-8 withered to 195 bhp, but the 390's rating actually went up a little, to 335. And for the first time, there was an optional six: a 250 lifted from the Ford truck line, offering 155 bhp for just $26 extra. Sadly, four-speed manual was no longer available for six-cylinder Mustangs. The high-winding four-barrel 289 also departed, replaced as the middle V-8 by a considerably changed small-block stroked out to 302 cid and a rated 230 bhp. A tractable, reasonably economical compromise, it cost only about $200.

Topping the chart—at a whopping $755—was Ford's mighty 427 big-block with 10.9:1 compression and a conservative 390-bhp rating. Though restricted to Cruise-O-Matic, it was good for 0–60-mph times of around six seconds—the fastest showroom-

Carroll Shelby again one-upped Dearborn for '67 with a bigger big-block engine in a second high-performance Mustang, the GT-500. Horsepower was a claimed 355 but was probably much higher, suggested by typical 0–60-mph times of around 6.5 seconds. If nothing else, the GT-500 helped make up for the absence of R-models—and the lack of Shelby-backed cars in competition. All '67 Shelbys came with grille-mounted driving lights. Depending on local laws, they were either paired in the center or spread outboard, as shown here.

stock Mustang yet. But few were ordered because of that formidable price, as well as the added weight that tended to overwhelm the front end.

Engineers are a persistent lot, and all '68 Mustangs got more detail refinements. The front suspension was again tweaked to improve ride and handling, and Michelin radial tires, available on a limited basis for '67, were now a full factory option with any V-8. Just as laudable, the available power front-disc brakes switched from fixed to "floating" calipers, which provided extra stopping power with no extra pedal effort. The design was also claimed to promote longer brake life and, because it employed fewer parts, to be more reliable. Ford recognized the necessity of front discs for hot Mustangs by making them a mandatory option with the

TOP: Mustang's '67 styling was little altered for '68. Ford still owned the most popular ponycar, as this ad mod-ishly trumpets. ABOVE: Interior updates for '68 mostly involved new federally required add-ons.

390 and 427 engines.

Like other '68 cars, Mustang met new "fed regs" for interior safety, adding collapsible steering column, locking seatbacks with release levers, seatback and console padding, and redesigned knobs, switches, and door hardware that would be less user-unfriendly in a crash. Side marker lights appeared in the front and rear fenders. Dull-finish windshield wiper arms, steering wheel hub and horn ring, rearview mirror, and windshield pillars met government specs for glare.

Other '68 changes were strictly Ford's own doing. A standard mini-spare tire opened up a bit more trunk room, and the convertible's top boot was remade in a stretchable vinyl and given hidden fasteners for a neater appearance. A new Sports Trim Group gilded any model with woodgrain dash appliqués, two-tone hood paint (also available separately), "Comfort-Weave" vinyl seat inserts, wheel-lip moldings, and, on V-8s, styled-steel wheels and larger tires. Fingertip Speed Control (cruise control operated from the turn-signal stalk) and rear-window defogger also joined the options list. Spring ushered in another specially priced Sprint Sports hardtop and ragtop, this time wearing GT C-striping and pop-open gas cap, plus full wheel covers; cars with V-8s substituted styled wheels shod with Wide-Oval tires.

Horsing Around with Hardtops

A unique '68 confection was a special hardtop cosmetic package aimed at buyers in California and Colorado. The Golden State version was originally called GT/SC ("GT Sport Coupe") but appeared as the GT/CS—"California Special." Aping Shelby styling, it featured a plain grille with foglamps and no Mustang emblem, twist-lock hood fasteners, bespoilered trunklid, Cougar taillight clusters, dummy side scoops with large GT/CS lettering, and contrasting tape stripes around the tail and along the bodysides. Ford also threw in styled wheels and wider tires. About 5000 California Specials were built. The Colorado edition was dubbed GT/HCS—High Country Special. Except for shield-

TOP: Vinyl roof, whitewalls, and wire wheel covers remained popular 1968 dressup options for basic six-cylinder models like this hardtop. ABOVE: Sold only for '68 in the Golden State, the "California Special" hardtop offered Shelby-Mustang style for much less money. Some 5000 were built. LEFT: Exterior Decor Group was dropped for '68, but its twin-scoop hood with two-tone paint continued, as on this convertible.

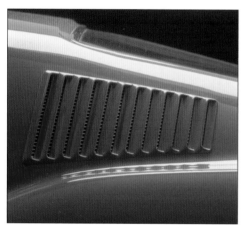

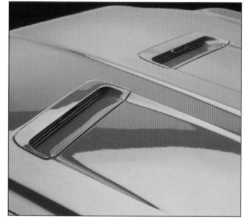

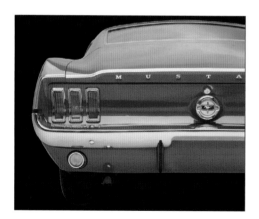

TOP: Like all '68 GTs, this 2+2 sports bodyside "C-stripes" and new multi-hole styled-steel wheels. All models exchanged a protruding grille for an inset piece without crossbars. The running-horse emblem "floated" in the cavity, as did the GT-standard outboard driving lamps. CENTER LEFT: Fastbacks retained rear-roof louvers for '68. CENTER MIDDLE: "Cheese-grater" dummy side vents gave way to a slim vertical accent. CENTER RIGHT: Useful in-hood turn-signal lights returned at extra cost. ABOVE: Fuel-filler caps were again redesigned for '68.

shaped name decals, it was virtually identical to the California package. Production is unknown but was likely less than for the CS (due to the smaller Rocky Mountain market), so an HCS would be a pretty rare find today.

Flying the Cobra Jet

Back on the engine chart, the 427 option was retired at mid-model year in favor of Ford's new 428 Cobra Jet, a huskier big-block with vacuum-actuated ram-air hood scoop. For drag racing and insurance purposes, it was advertised at 335 bhp on 10.7:1 compression, but was doubtless much stronger. A quarter-mile zip of 13.56 seconds at a trap speed of 106.64 mph caused *Hot Rod* magazine to sing its praises.

The "CJ," as it came to be known, was a better idea of Bob Tasca, then the country's number-one Ford dealer. Tasca had been backing big-block Mustang drag cars that tore up the strips in 1965-66 and had customers flocking to his Rhode Island showroom. But while Tasca welcomed the factory 390 option, he found it wasn't strong enough to be a winner in local drags, and that was costing him sales. When an employee blew up a stock 390 car, Tasca ordered his mechanics to piece together a more competitive engine using only the Ford parts catalog. Starting with the "short-block" 428 Police Interceptor, they bolted on a pair of 427 low-riser heads, a big Holley carb, and 390 cam, then turned a 13.39-second quarter-mile at 105 mph. Dearborn was impressed—even Henry Ford II took note—and used Tasca's monster mongrel as the starting point for the production Cobra Jet.

High-Velocity *Bullitt*

Bullitt. A Solar Production released by Warner Brothers/Seven Arts, October 17, 1968. 113 minutes. Director: Peter Yates. Screenplay: Alan Trustman and Harry Kleiner. Car chase designed by Carey Loftin. Starring Steve McQueen, Robert Vaughn, Jacqueline Bisset, Don Gordon.

San Francisco police Lt. Frank Bullitt has lost a government witness to professional hit men, and he's dead set on getting his hands on the killers. The opportunity for professional redemption arises when he spies the bad guys' black Charger R/T in slow-moving San Francisco traffic. For three and a half minutes, Bullitt's Highland Green GT390 Fastback Mustang tags behind the big Dodge. While paused at a light the Charger's driver fastens his lap belt with sober deliberateness. The light flips, the driver stands on the Dodge's accelerator, and two celebrated American muscle cars show what they're made of. The chase—seven glorious minutes' worth—is on.

Two identical Mustangs and two matching Chargers were used in the *Bullitt* chase sequence. So that the 4-speed Mustang could run more easily with the brawnier 4-speed 440 Magnum Charger, Hollywood engineer Max Balchowsky installed a racing cam on both Fords, milled the heads, and modified the ignition and carburetion systems. Additionally, Balchowsky bulked up the suspensions of all four cars for improved strength, handling, and control. One Mustang and one Charger were fitted with a full roll cage.

The chase was shot at normal film speed; there would be no cranked-up footage to jazz audiences. The byword was reality.

Bullitt captures legendary star Steve McQueen at the apex of his popularity and puts him in a milieu he loved in his private life: auto racing. He owned many fast cars and had particular fondness for his barely streetable XKSS Jaguar, which he liked to pilot at breakneck speeds along Sunset and serpentine Mulholland Drive high above Los Angeles. He participated in SCCA events, and was an enthusiastic motorcyclist, as well.

McQueen insisted on driving the Mustang during the carefully choreographed pursuit, but when he failed to make a turn after locking up his wheels he sealed the deal for pro driver Bud Ekins, who handled the Mustang during the jouncy maneuvers along San Francisco's famously hilly streets. Stunt driver/actor Bill Hickman piloted the Charger.

Veteran stunt coordinator Carey Loftin designed the chase, plotting a course along a variety of city avenues and landmarks: Clay & Taylor streets, York Street, Potrero Hill, Kansas Street, Russian Hill, and the bucolic Guadalupe Canyon Parkway. Longtime SF residents will see that the chase is not linear, i.e., the cars jump freely around town from cut to cut. Well, chalk that up to artistic license.

The sounds emitted by the Mustang suggest a lot of double-clutching—something that would not have been needed with a '68 Ford trans. McQueen confirmed that the sweet racket of the car's engine and transmission were overdubbed recordings of a Ford GT40 driven at full tilt.

The highest compliment one can offer to Loftin and director Peter Yates is that the chase is completely believable. No "super-hero" stunts, no impossible tricks—just adrenaline-pumping speed, heightened by razor sharp cinematography (William Fraker) and Oscar-winning editing (Frank Keller), plus multiple points of view: drivers' eye, worm's eye, bird's eye, over the shoulder, close on McQueen and Hickman, and setups that suck us along inches behind the cars' back bumpers. Pat Houstis drove the camera car, which was built atop a Corvette chassis.

Dramatically, the chase works for a multitude of reasons, not least the human silence: neither Bullitt nor the hit men speak, not one syllable—not when Bullitt's Mustang is momentarily blocked by oncoming traffic, not when the Charger nearly annihilates itself on a guardrail, not when assassin #2 (Paul Genge) loads his Winchester pump and pokes the barrel from the Charger's rear side window—not even when Bullitt's windshield absorbs a blast of buckshot. Instead, the soundtrack vibrates with the Charger's thrumming baritone and the hornet-like growl of the Mustang; the squeal of abused rubber; the deep, thudding thumps as the cars repeatedly bottom out on the city's hills; and the harsh reports of the Winchester. The mute concentration of the participants seems to underscore the chilly professionalism of Bullitt and the men he hunts. Deadly pursuit and flight, like rail-splitting or high-iron work, are masculine occupations best performed in silence.

The sequence did wonders for the Mustang mythos, of course, and didn't do Charger any harm, either. Ford offered a limited edition anniversary "Bullitt" Mustang for model-year 2001.

The chase altered the tone of cop films and upped the ante for writers and directors who felt obliged to attempt to surpass it. Some gems came later, notably in *The French Connection* and *The Seven-Ups* (both by Bill Hickman). Although the *Bullitt* chase is no longer the most kinetic in movie history, it almost certainly is still the best.

One for the Trans-Am

Announced at about the same time as the CJ was a fortified 302 with high-compression heads, larger valves, wild cam timing, and a pair of four-barrel carbs. Humorously rated at 240 bhp, it was Ford's new weapon in Trans-Am racing, but unexpected troubles delayed production after SCCA approved it, and few were actually installed this year. Not that it mattered. Mark Donohue's Camaro won 10 Trans-Am contests to Mustang's three, and Chevy collected the manufacturer's trophy.

Buyers Shift Gears

At over 300,000 units, Mustang's 1968 model-year sales were far below the heady days of 1965-66 and thus a disappointment to Ford executives hoping for an upturn. In fact, the ponycar market was nearing its peak, though no one could know that at the time, least of all Ford.

But there was a hint of a trend in optional equipment orders, which showed a shift in buyer preferences from low-priced sportiness toward convenience and luxury features. Cruise-O-Matic, for example, was fitted to 72 percent of '68 production vs. just six percent for four-speed manual. V-8s claimed fully 70 percent of sales. Power steering was specified by 52 percent of buyers, air

conditioning by 18 percent, tinted windows by 32 percent. By contrast, only 13 percent ordered power brakes, another 13 percent the power front discs, and a scant 3.7 percent a limited-slip differential. Increasingly it seemed, Mustangers were less concerned with price and pure performance than with going fast in comfort and looking good while doing it.

Kings and Convertibles

This year's Shelby-Mustangs got a heavier facelift than their parents. The hood sprouted louvers and a full-width scoop placed nearer the panel's leading edge to improve airflow to the carburetors. Below was a wider grille with square foglamps (not driving lamps) sitting outboard. Taillamps adopted Cougar's gimmicky sequential-turn-signal feature. Carroll had built a few '66 convertibles as gifts for friends, but now offered ragtops as regular models—a 350 and 500 with a built-in roll-over hoop that enhanced safety but looked a bit awkward with the top down. Though some '68 advertising used the name Shelby Cobra instead of Shelby GT, the cars again displayed GT-350 or GT-500 labels.

To meet emissions limits, the GT-350 switched to the new 302 V-8. Despite a deep-breathing four-barrel Holley carb and hydraulic lifters, rated power was down to 250. To compensate,

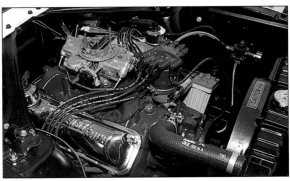

OPPOSITE PAGE: "Mustang to the max" described the production-based Mach 1 seen at major 1968 auto shows. THIS PAGE, TOP AND ABOVE, LEFT AND RIGHT: Drag racers were quick to seize on the potent 428 Cobra Jet V-8 that became a regular Mustang option for mid-1968. "CJ" fastbacks were always a threat in the National Hot Rod Association's Super Stock class. RIGHT: Bob Tasca, a Rhode Island Ford dealer and a top power in national drag racing, started running Mustang "funny cars" in 1968 with supercharged, nitro-fueled engines. BELOW LEFT AND RIGHT: Mustang scored a creditable fourth overall at the 1968 Daytona 24 Hours but failed to win a third straight Trans-Am championship, which went to Mark Donohue and his Chevy Camaro.

Shelby revived his Paxton supercharger option from '66. It added about 100 horses but again found few takers.

That's because Shelby buyers still much preferred big-block power. Early GT-500s retained the 428, albeit re-rated to 360 bhp. However, some later cars got ordinary 390s when a plant strike created a spot shortage of 428s. Oddly for straight-talking Shel, customers weren't told of the substitution, though it was very hard to spot. And mid-model year brought redress in a replacement GT-500KR ("King of the Road," a title likely taken from a hit tune of the time). Also offered in fastback and convertible form, the KR packed the Cobra Jet engine, muscled up with big-port 427 heads and larger intake manifold and exhaust system. Horsepower was 335 advertised but was probably closer to 400 actual, as torque was a thumping 440 lb-ft at just 3400 rpm. Shelby also tossed in wider rear brakes and special exterior trim. Transmissions and rear-end ratios carried over from the GT-500, but the KR was quicker, generally matching the peformance of CJ-equipped non-Shelby Mustangs.

Though inflation was pushing up prices on most cars, the Shelbys didn't go up much for '68. The GT-350 fastback started at $4117, the 500 version at $4317, the KR at $4473. Ragtops listed at $4238 to $4594. Partly as a result, Shelby volume rose for the fourth straight model year, hitting 4450 units. But it would

go no higher. Increasingly potent regular Mustangs were fast eroding the performance aura of Carroll's ponycars. And Ford was now calling all the shots, fast morphing the Shelbys from no-nonsense racers into fast but cushy cruisers. In a telling development, Ford shifted '68 Shelby production from California to Livonia, Michigan (not far from Dearborn), where contractor A. O. Smith Company carried out the conversions. From now on, Ford alone would handle Shelby-Mustang promotion and development.

Times were indeed a-changin' for both Mustang and Ford Motor Company. As if to hint at things to come, Ford showed a wild Mustang-based concept at 1968 auto shows. Dubbed Mach 1, this low, sleek, and muscular fastback took familiar styling cues to extremes. Its enlongated nose was very aggressive, with a slim-section grille thrust ahead of pointy front fenders and rectangular headlamps. A louvered twin-scoop hood led back to a radically raked windshield matching a severe "chopped top" with much "faster" rear glass. Bodysides bore Mustang's signature character line, but fenders and wheel openings were prominently bulged to snug tightly around low-profile racing rubber on wide GT-40-style five-spoke aluminum wheels. A "ducktail" spoiler loomed over wall-to-wall taillamps and twin center-mount exhaust outlets. Other racing-inspired touches included a large, bright quick-release fuel filler behind each door window (the door glass was fixed) and working rear-brake cooling scoops. The rear window was combined with the trunklid, and the unit could be opened or closed by an electrohydraulic mechanism by flipping an interior switch.

Designers must have had fun creating this one-of-a-kind showstopper, which looked for all the world like a Shelby-Mustang on steroids. But did it also forecast the next showroom Mustang, which would have been mostly locked up when the Mach 1 was designed? And if Ford was mulling a bolder, brasher ponycar, how would people take to it? No one could know, of course—those pesky lead times again.

Still, we're pretty sure that Ford was well aware of one vital fact. Mustang was no longer the only horse in the stable, so future models would have to be even more carefully considered for the original to stay out in front. The ponycar stampede might be slowing as 1969 beckoned, but the race was far from over.

Convertibles joined the Shelby-Mustang stable for 1968 and shared a moderate facelift with fastbacks. Sold in both GT-500 (shown) and GT-350 trim, the ragtop included a structural roll bar with built-in shoulder harnesses. Ford was now in full control of the Shelby-Mustang program and shifted production from California to Michigan, where a contractor converted regular Mustangs. The '68 Shelbys were thus less "special" than earlier models, if still plenty exciting.

LEFT, RIGHT, AND ABOVE: Shelby's '68 GT-500s, coupe and new convertible alike, had a revised nose and, at first, a 428 "Cobra" V-8 uprated by five horses to 360. As before, hood and bodyside scoops were functional, as were those in the fastback's roof. Interiors, though, were becoming as plush as those in any regular Mustang. BELOW: At mid-model year, the GT-500s gave way to GT-500 KR models with the new Cobra Jet engine boasting ram-air induction. KR meant "King of the Road," and although horsepower was downrated to 335, mainly for drag racing, the CJ was noticeably faster in most any situation. Shelby built 1251 KRs and 1542 regular GT-500s for the model year.

Chapter Four:
1969-1970

More pizzazz! More performance! More ponycars to choose! Mustang had it all for 1969—except more buyers. And 1970 sales were lower still. Was Mustang losing its magic? Dearborn wondered. The question was particularly important to a new company president, recruited from a surprising source, who immediately made his mark with two of the greatest cars in performance history.

Success has many fathers, the old adage says, but Mustang had only one—or so the public was told. We know better now, but there's no question that the Mustang's instant phenomenal success was a huge career boost for Lee Iacocca. By 1968 he had been moved up to executive vice-president of Ford's North American Operations.

But successful leaders usually have strong wills and egos to match, and one suspects that sudden fame encouraged Iacocca to push that much harder for the job he had always wanted: president of Ford Motor Company. There was just one problem. Iacocca was a brash outsider in a family-owned enterprise, and the head of that family didn't like being upstaged. As designer Gale Halderman told Collectible Automobile® magazine many years later: "Iacocca was credited in the press as the father of the Mustang and the savior of the company, which caused [chairman Henry Ford II] to start thinking to himself, 'This guy's trying to take over.'"

Such was the background on February 6, 1968, when Ford announced that its chairman had selected a new president: veteran General Motors executive Semon E. "Bunkie" Knudsen. Detroit was astonished. Here was probably the most startling managerial shift since 1922, when Bunkie's father, William S. Knudsen, left Ford for Chevrolet after an argument with Henry Ford I. "Big Bill" quickly built Chevy into a Ford-beater, and his son made Pontiac number-three in the late Fifties before taking command at Chevrolet. Now Bunkie aimed to remake Ford. Ironically, he accepted HFII's invitation after being passed over as GM president in favor of Ed Cole.

Author Gary Witzenburg observed that "Knudsen, like Iacocca, was a hard-charging, dynamic, ambitious leader who…arrived at Ford amid a tornado of press and public attention and [was] full of big ideas on how to attack his former employer in the marketplace." Rumors of a management shake-up were flying even before Bunkie moved into Ford's "Glass House" headquarters. Though he did make some changes, there was no wholesale cleanout. But several Ford execs did resign after Knudsen came in, and Iacocca reportedly threatened to. Knudsen, for his part,

was content to work with the Mustang's celebrated papa, but their relationship was uneasy at best, the two men clashing on several occasions.

Knudsen was too late to influence the Mustang's planned 1969 redesign, which had been pretty much locked up for a year before he arrived. But he *was* able to add two very hot mid-season models while laying the groundwork for bigger, bolder future Mustangs. Knudsen loved burly high-performance cars, especially low, sleek fastbacks. He also loved NASCAR stockers and Trans-Am racers, perhaps because they resembled showroom wares.

Mustang sales had been waning since 1966, but Bunkie didn't seem concerned. "We are comparing today's Mustang penetration with [years] when there was no one else in that particular segment of the market," he explained. And he had thoughts on how to fire up sales. "The long-hood/short-deck concept will continue," he promised, but "there will be a trend toward designing cars for specific segments of the market." He also assured the press that Ford would continue in NASCAR and Trans-Am.

Bunkie, Larry, and "The Ultimate Mustang"

Almost immediately, Knudsen decided that Ford needed to develop "*the* killer street car," to use Witzenburg's term—and that it should be a Mustang. To help create it, he hired designer Larry Shinoda away from GM and teamed him with Dearborn talents like Harvey Winn, Ken Dowd, Bill Shannon, and Dick Petit. With engineering assistance from Ed Hall, Chuck Mountain, and others, Shinoda's crew whipped up a bevy of eye-opening concept cars like the King Cobra, a slicked-down Torino fastback designed for high-speed stock-car racing, while feverishly working on Knudsen's ultimate Mustang.

Shinoda and Knudsen were old friends by now. They'd first met at Daytona Beach in 1956, when Bunkie took note of a very "trick," very fast Pontiac that Shinoda was working on. Shinoda, a teen-age hot-rodder in his native Southern California, knew how to shape a car for top straightline speed—and how to tune a chassis for top cornering speed. He came to Ford after working closely with GM design chief William L. Mitchell on various exper-

imental projects and production cars including the 1963 Corvette Sting Ray and its '68 "shark" replacement. With all this, Shinoda's hiring was no less shocking than Bunkie's.

Styling: One Way and Another

Work toward the '69 Mustang had begun long before in the Ford Division studio, still captained by Gale Halderman. Joe Gilmore was now chief product planner, replacing Ross Humphries. From the very first studies in October 1965, designers seemed determined to blow up the ponycar into a little Thunderbird, contemplating billowy contours, hidden headlamps, knife-edge fenderlines, and other luxury-car cues. By early 1966 they had been told to work in some "Thunderbird influence"—which sounded like Iacocca talking. Regardless, the directive led to more large rectangular grilles, boxy rear ends, and some fairly desperate detailing. Judging from the photographic record, we might be grateful the designers changed course.

Indeed, they did a fast "180" toward an all-out muscle car. This reached fruition by October 1966 in a full-size clay fastback with a short wheelbase, a bulky cropped tail, a high rear "shoulder" leading back from a prominent scoop, a lengthy hood, gaping grille—and a cramped cockpit. "We went through a period where we were chopping about six inches off the back," Halderman told Witzenburg. "But then we went to two inches and finally back to

where we started, because we still had to package a spare tire, fuel tank, and some luggage room back there." Though a dead-end detour, this mockup prompted a less radical design that led to the '69 fastback, renamed "SportsRoof."

Wagons, No!

Ford again toyed with additional Mustang body styles during the '69 program. By mid-1966, designers had done full-size tape drawings of a "breadvan" wagon with near full-length side windows and a targa-top convertible with integral rollover bar (previewing the ragtop '68 Shelbys). The wagon had a tall "Kamm" tail like the short-chassis fastback, plus a long, tapering roofline and extreme rear-fender hop-up. The targa's lower body was curvy, almost GM-like. Though the targa was abandoned, the wagon design was refined into a full-size fiberglass mockup with slightly different treatments on each side. Photographed in November, it was an attractive, sporty thing with lots of side glass and elegant proportions. Rear fenders terminated in slim vertical taillamps arched gracefully upward from a thin U-section bumper. The front-end profile predicted production '71 styling. But with all that had gone before, a Mustang wagon remained a non-starter. "That one was pretty well liked," Halderman lamented. "I think we could have sold it."

Mustang Grows Up

Save last-minute details like taillights and trim, the '69 styling package was basically settled by early 1967. The result was a more impressive Mustang in both size and appearance. Though wheelbase stayed at 108 inches, overall length grew to 187.4 inches, up 3.8 inches, most of it in front overhang. Width swelled to 71.3 inches overall, while height came down slightly to 51.2. Base curb weight rose to just over 2800 pounds.

Dimensional gains were evident inside, too. Thinner doors improved front shoulder room by 2.5 inches, hip room by 1.5 inches. Modifying a frame crossmember upped rear leg room a whopping 2.5 inches. Trunk capacity increased "13 to 29 percent," according to bubbly Ford press releases, but that didn't amount to much because there'd been so little space before. And at a quoted 9.8 cubic feet, even this larger hold could still manage a two-suiter and little else. At least driving range *was* usefully increased via a fuel tank enlarged from 17 to 20 gallons.

Though recognizably Mustang, the '69s somehow looked more "adult," more serious. Surprising many, the galloping horse and "corral" were gone from the grille, replaced by a small pony tricolor on the port side. The grille itself was visibly vee'd and made broader to cradle high-beam headlights at its outboard ends—the first "four-eye" Mustang. Low beams nestled in the trademark flanking "sugar scoops." The hood was also vee'd and slightly domed between newly peaked front fenderlines leading to a more exaggerated hop-up. Instead of the signature bodyside sculpturing, hardtops and convertibles wore a more subtle "character" line trailing back and slightly downward from the nose to end just behind the door, with a slim, reverse-facing dummy air vent below. SportsRoofs capped the side line with a simulated scoop faired into the hop-up, an echo of the discarded shorty fastback. Taillights again grouped into two clusters of three vertical lenses, but the back panel reverted from concave to flat.

Rooflines changed too, with more steeply raked windshields and, for hardtops and convertibles, wider "formal" rear-roof quarters. The SportsRoof sported a "faster" roof sloping down to a vestigial spoiler, plus first-time rear-quarter windows, which flipped out instead of rolling down. All models lost front vent windows, adopting a new forced-air ventilation system with hidden extractor outlets. A big, round Mustang medallion replaced roof louvers on fastbacks.

The instrument panel was naturally redesigned, still a "twin

OPPOSITE PAGE: Design work toward the '69 Mustang began in October 1965. Efforts immediately focused on much greater size and luxury-car styling cues. Ford managers encouraged this direction in early '66 by ordering "more Thunderbird influence" be worked in. Typical of the results was this January hardtop workout (top) with an extended hood, large "loop" bumper/grille, upswept beltline, and thick rear roof quarters. Big square grilles, busy side sculpturing, and hidden headlamps were tried in May (bottom). THIS PAGE, ABOVE LEFT AND RIGHT: A March 1966 mockup anticipates the final '69 side treatment and general shape, but the front is a cautious evolution of 1967. RIGHT: Designers favored high "hanging" grilles for a time. This model explores ideas on headlamp placement.

THIS PAGE: A sampling of mockups from mid-1966 show just a few of the many ideas rejected for '69, including boxy tails (top) and Buick-style bodyside "sweepspears" (above right). OPPOSITE PAGE: Though recognizably Mustang, the '69s were markedly different in size and appearance. Two new models arrived, including the Grande, a $2866 upscale hardtop with standard vinyl roof, wire-wheel covers, special cloth/vinyl upholstery, and convincing faux-teakwood interior trim.

cowl" affair, but the cowls were more prominent. Lower surfaces on either side of the console were angled forward, which at least gave the illusion of extra leg space. Gauges sat ahead of the driver in four large, round recesses; a fifth hole ahead of the front passenger was used to house the clock. A debatable new extra was the "Rim-Blow" steering wheel ($66). Instead of pushing the wheel hub to sound the horn, you simply squeezed anywhere on the rim. Though supposedly a—ahem—blow for convenience, the device worked a bit too well. Fast wheel-twirling was often a comically noisy affair.

More Models, More Engines

Besides a more expansive package, the '69 Mustangs offered the widest choice of models and powertrains yet, with some introduced after the late-August 1968 showroom debut. The stalwart 200- and 250-cubic-inch sixes returned with 115 and 155 horsepower, respectively. The base 302 V-8 option remained at 220 bhp, but the big-block 390 was back to 320, down five from '68. In between these was a pair of important new 351 small-blocks, more of which shortly. Again topping the list was the muscular Cobra Jet 428, available with and without ram-air induction but conservatively rated either way at 335 bhp. Transmissions were the usual three- and four-speed manuals and Cruise-O-Matic, but Ford actually used two different four-speeds and three different automatics depending on engine.

Knudsen's comment about "models for specific segments of the market" only parroted a previous Ford decision to expand the Mustang line. The model year opened with two additions. One was the Grande, a personal-luxury hardtop pitching the same buyers as cousin Mercury Cougar and the Pontiac Firebird. Priced about $230 above the $2635 standard issue, the Grande featured a vinyl-covered roof with identifying namescript; pointy color-keyed "racing" door mirrors; wire wheel covers; two-tone paint stripes beneath the beltline; and bright wheelwell, rocker panel, and rear-deck moldings. The interior was upgraded with

standard clock, convincing imitation teakwood accents on the dash and door panels, and seats with "hopsack" cloth inserts and vinyl bolsters. Appropriate for its upscale character, the Grande got a slightly softer suspension than the base hardtop and an extra 55 pounds of sound insulation.

"Street Cred" to Spare

More exciting by far was a new $3139 intruder into Shelby-Mustang territory, the Mach 1 fastback. This packed a 351 V-8 with dual exhausts, handling suspension with styled-steel wheels and white-letter Goodyear Polyglas tires, reflective i.d. striping along the bodysides and around the tail, pop-off gas cap, and a matte-black hood with simulated air scoop and NASCAR-style tiedowns. A separate rear spoiler was available. So was a new "shaker" hood scoop, so-called because it attached directly to the air cleaner through a hole in the hood, vibrating madly for all to see. Also on the standard-equipment list were racing mirrors, high-back bucket seats, center console, the Rim-Blow steering wheel, and the Grande's psuedo-teak interior accents. Ford said all '69 Mustangs were "The Going Thing," but the Mach 1 had "street cred" to spare.

Most other '69s could be optioned to approximate a Mach 1—or a Grande. The GT Group was less promoted this year but included the Mach's stiff competition suspension (which was also a separate $31 option with 428 V-8s) and wheel/tire package, plus specific trim. A less aggressive handling option (also $31) was available with any V-8 except 428s. Also returning for regular models were an Exterior Décor Group ($32) and standard and deluxe Interior Décor Groups ($88-$133). Intermittent ("interval") windshield wipers were a new individual extra. Hardtops again offered an incongruous front bench seat option.

The Mach 1's 351 V-8 claimed 250 standard horsepower via two-barrel carburetor or 290 optional via four-barrel and elevated compression (10.7:1 vs. 9.5:1). These, too, were available for other '69s. Developed to fill a yawning displacement gap in Ford's

corporate engine lineup, the 351 was directly descended from the original 1962 small-block. Essentially, it was a 302 with a half-inch longer stroke (3.50 inches) on the same 4.00-inch bore. As author Phil Hall noted in his book *Fearsome Fords,* actual displacement was 351.86 cid, but Ford used "351" to avoid any confusion with its 352 Y-block V-8 of the 1950s.

Windsor vs. Cleveland

Note that we're talking here about about the 351 "Windsor" V-8, not the vaunted "Cleveland" unit. The Windsor got its nickname from the Canadian plant that began building it in fall 1968, a full year before the Cleveland entered production (in Ohio). Both had the same bore/stroke dimensions and 4.38-inch bore spacing, but the Windsor boasted extra bulkhead strength, a 1.27-inch higher deck, and a different crankshaft with larger main and crankpin journals. It also used a drop-center intake manifold and "positive-stop" studs for the valve rocker arms. Once the Cleveland came along, the Windsor was relegated to mainstream Dearborn models, typically with two-barrel carburetors and mild compression.

Ford spent about $100 million to tool up the Cleveland V-8, which would power most of the company's 1970-74 high-performance cars. This 351 used a unique block cast with an integral timing chain chamber and water crossover passage at the front, plus an inch-higher deck than on the 302. Cylinder heads differed dramatically from the Windsor's, as valves were canted 9.5 degrees from the cylinder axis to form modified wedge-type combustion chambers. In addition, the intakes were angled 4 degrees, 15 minutes forward and the exhaust valves 3 degrees rearward for larger port areas that improved gas flow and efficiency. Toward the same ends, the valves themselves were made as large as possible. Intakes had a 2.19-inch head diameter, while the forged-steel exhaust valves had aluminized heads measuring 1.71 inches across.

Ford sixes got their own performance tech for '69, including

TOP: Renamed "SportsRoof," the '69 fastback looked faster even in the standard trim shown here. Small front-fender badge proclaims a big 390 V-8 is under the hood. ABOVE: As ever, the '69 Mustangs could be optioned for a happy blend of performance and luxury. This ragtop is outfitted with the available 302 V-8 and Deluxe Interior Décor Group.

continued on page 75

Mustang Mach I...
new power play.

Mustang's other mainstream newcomer for '69, the $3139 Mach 1 fastback embodied youthful high performance and thus got most of the year's advertising emphasis. Ford's new 351 V-8 was standard, but the potent Cobra Jet (left) was optional. So was a novel "shaker" hood scoop (above and below). The racy basic package featured handling suspension, upsized wheels and tires, unique exterior, and a surprisingly posh cockpit.

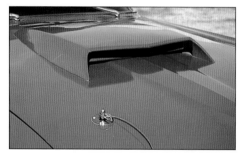

TOP: The most thrilling '69s were the mid-year Boss 429 (foreground) and Boss 302 fastbacks, low-volume hot rods built to meet racing rules. ABOVE: Boss 302 was a street version of Ford's all-out Trans-Am racer. Its small-block V-8 was rated at 290 bhp but made close to 400 actual. LEFT AND BELOW: Boss 429 was ready-made for the dragstrip and enabled Ford to qualify an exotic new "semi-hemi" V-8 for stock-car racing. Big-block mill was a very tight fit. The 429 was a bit more stealthy outside than the Boss 302, but both came with competition-style hood pins.

Larry Shinoda: In his own words

Ford's Gene Bordinat gave Larry Shinoda his first automotive design job, in 1954, only to see the new graduate of L.A.'s Art Center School leave Dearborn within a year. After a brief stint at faltering Packard, Shinoda was hired by GM design boss Harley Earl and was soon working with Bill Mitchell, who soon succeeded Earl, on futuristic concept designs—and future Corvettes. Shinoda followed GM president and longtime friend Semon E. "Bunkie" Knudsen in jumping to Ford, in 1968, but both were fired after less than two years in a widely publicized shake-up. Even so, both left their mark on Mustang, the designer most famously with the fast, tight-handling Boss models of 1969-71. Shinoda and Knudsen went on to form RV maker Rectrans, then parted company in mid-1975, when Shinoda opened his own design business. Shinoda died in late 1997 at age 67.

One of the first things I did on coming to Ford was straighten out the Boss 302. They were going to call it the SR2. They had all this chrome on it. They were going to hang big cladding on the side, big rocker moldings. It was going to be more garish than the Mach 1. They had a big grille across the back and a great big gas cap and fake cast exhaust outlets and big hood pins and a really big side scoop. I took all that off, went to the C-stripe decal and painted out the hood, did the rear spoiler and the window shades and front airdam. That vehicle ended up being a profit-improvement program. They only built a few, but they made money on each one.

Bunkie Knudsen and I knew that to capture some of the youth market you had to have street machines that would run like your race cars. Ford had never done that before, and obviously Knudsen wanted to beat the Z-28 Chevrolets at their own game. So that was my first task coming in there, doing show cars, and getting the Boss going. I knew what kind of horsepower the Z-28 had, where its strong points and weak points were. So I had to find out quickly what the Mustang was all about and what the new developments were.

And what they were working on was pretty much wrong. They had an engine with high horsepower but enormous ports, so the power was very, very peaky. They needed something with a much flatter torque curve. And they needed better

vehicle dynamics. They were saying, "All it has to do is go fast." I said, "That's not really where it's at. The Z-28 gets through corners well because it handles well. And it accelerates well off the corner because it got through the corner faster, so you think it's got more horsepower than it does. Another reason it's going through the corner faster is aerodynamics. It has enough downforce in front, balanced with downforce at the rear. Your car has some downforce at the rear with a little built-in spoiler, but not in the front. And the suspension isn't quite right."

They said, "What do you know about it? You're a designer." I said, "I'm a designer, but I've also got common sense, and I know a little bit about vehicle dynamics." Ford at that point had never used their skidpad to check out dynamics. Their skidpad at the Dearborn test track was all torn up at the time. I got an appropriation to repave it.

I took some people in a company plane and flew them over the GM Proving Grounds. I said, "See that? It's Black Lake." "What's it for?" I said, "You'll see." Sure enough, here's Roger Penske's Trans-Am Camaro, the Sunoco Camaro, running on a skidpad. I said, "That's what you need. You play with aerodynamics, suspension, roll stiffness, and tires, and you find out what's going to get around there the fastest. Of course, you'll have to do some adjustments at the race track." In those days, most of the people in Ford's performance department didn't understand vehicle dynamics, which was kind of sad. The people at Chevrolet and, basically, Frank Winchell, wrote the book on that.

And as I said, I removed all the inappropriate things they were going to put on the Boss, including the interior. I think it saved quite a few dollars when we counted it all up. Don Petersen, who was in product planning at the time, got a big kick out of that. He said, "You trying to do our job for us?" I said, "No, just trying to do the job, period."

But there was only so much he could support. Unfortunately, I made bold statements. When someone asked me, "What are your ambitions?," I said to be the first Japanese-American vice-president at Ford Motor Company. I don't think Gene Bordinat liked that.

TOP: Carroll Shelby flashes the usual Texas-size grin in posing with three of "his" Mustangs for 1969. Actually, the cars were conceived and built entirely by Ford. ABOVE AND LEFT: The '69 Shelbys were the tamest yet, just regular Mustangs with a specific big-mouth fiberglass front, scoops and scallops all over, and more wide taillamps. As in the '68, the ragtop GT-350 was the least popular of the four models. This is one of only 194 built, not counting a dozen or so "1970" leftovers.

continued from page 70

"center percussion" (forward sited) engine mounts for smoother operation. But competition manager Jacque Passino wanted to go much further: "We've been putting out [six-cylinder Mustangs] kind of artificially since '64 to fill up production schedules when we couldn't get V-8s. I think there is a real market for an inexpensive hop-up kit for the 250-cubic-inch engine." But that never happened, nor did a fuel-injected six he also favored. A pity. Either would have been very interesting. But neither was as interesting as the mighty Cobra Jet.

Driving With "CJ"

Developed by Ford's Light Vehicle Powertrain Department under Tom Feaheny, it made Mustang one of the world's fastest cars. Even saddled with automatic, *Car Life* magazine's CJ Mach 1 took just 5.5 seconds 0–60 mph and flew through the standing quarter-mile in 13.9 seconds at 103 mph. "The best Mustang yet and quickest ever," said the editors, who also declared it "the quickest standard passenger car through the quarter-mile we've ever tested (sports cars and hot rods excluded)." Yet *Car Life* found the CJ Mach 1 to be "a superb road car, stable at speed, tenacious on corners, with surplus power and brakes for any road

situation…. By choosing the optimum combination of suspension geometry, shock absorber valving, and spring rates, Ford engineers have exempted the Mach 1 from the laws up momentum and inertia up to unspeakable speeds."

That last statement partly references a new suspension wrinkle for big-block Mustangs devised by chassis engineer Matt Donner. Starting with the 1967 heavy-duty setup, he mounted one shock absorber ahead of the rear axleline and the other behind it, which reduced axle tramp in hard acceleration. Though gunning hard around corners still induced the same hairy oversteer as in previous high-power Mustangs, the '69 was more easily controlled with steering and throttle. "The first Cobra Jets we built were strictly for drag racing," Tom Feaheny recalled. "The '69s had a type of the competition suspension we offered in '67. Wheel hop was damped out by staggering the rear shocks. It was not a new idea, but it worked. Another thing was the [Goodyear] Polyglas tire. I really can't say enough about this…. In '69 every wide-oval tire we offered featured Polyglas construction."

The Boss Takes Command

Car Life notwithstanding, the Chevrolet Camaro Z-28 handled even better—and captured another Trans-Am championship in 1969. But Knudsen and Shinoda's "killer" fastback was ready by

TOP: To publicize Mach 1 performance, new Ford president Bunkie Knudsen had famed drag racer Mickey Thompson prepare three cars for a late-1968 assault on Bonneville. Thompson and three other drivers set nearly 300 new speed and endurance records. LEFT: Ace pilot George Follmer pits his Mustang in a 1969 Trans-Am race. Follmer and Parnelli Jones drove for Bud Moore, but neither they nor a two-car Carroll Shelby team could keep Chevy's Camaro from winning the season title.

March and out to even the score, at least on the street. They were going to call it "Trans-Am" until Pontiac grabbed the name for its hottest '69 Firebird, so they settled on Boss 302. Trans-Am rules required 1000 copies be built for sale to qualify as "production," but Ford ended up turning out 1934 of the '69s. Despite even that low number, the Boss brought people into Ford showrooms like no Mustang since the original.

Racing With the Wind

Shinoda's expertise in of "airflow management" showed up in the Boss 302's front and rear spoilers, effective from as little as 40 mph (unlike many such appendages). The four-inch-deep front air dam was angled forward to direct air around the car. The rear spoiler was an adjustable, inverted airfoil. Optional matte-black rear window slats did nothing for airflow but looked terrific. Without increasing power, engineers discovered the aero aids trimmed lap times at California's Riverside Raceway by about 2.5 seconds, a huge improvement.

Of course, there *was* an increase in power, and it was huge, too. Though the Boss's high-output 302 V-8 was said to produce 290 bhp at 4600 rpm, actual output was estimated at closer to 400 (in prevailing SAE gross measure, not today's more realistic net horsepower). Ford spared no expense to ensure this would be a Trans-Am-worthy powerplant, installing new "dry-deck" Cleveland-style heads with 2.33-inch intake valves and no head gaskets, solid lifters, an aluminum high-riser manifold, super-high-flow Holley four-barrel carburetor, high-capacity dual-point ignition, four-bolt central-main-bearing caps, cross-drilled forged crankshaft, and special pistons. To prevent accidental over-revving, an ignition cutout interrupted current flow from the coil to the spark plugs between 5800 and 6000 rpm.

THIS PAGE, TOP LEFT: The Mach 1 rated grille-mounted driving lamps for 1970 and a close-up on that year's brochure cover. LEFT AND BELOW: Among 1970 Ford concept cars was the vividly violet Mustang Milano with a Shelbyesque schnoz, flowing lines a la big brother Torino, a predictive rear liftgate—and lots of luggage space. OPPOSITE PAGE, TOP AND CENTER: Looking quite ritzy in 1970 advertising photos was the Grande hard-top wearing a new part-vinyl "landau" roof treatment. BOTTOM: 1970 brochure implied the Boss 302 was now a mainstream Mustang.

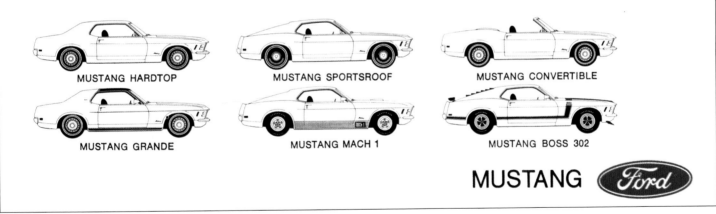

MUSTANG HARDTOP

MUSTANG SPORTSROOF

MUSTANG CONVERTIBLE

MUSTANG GRANDE

MUSTANG MACH 1

MUSTANG BOSS 302

MUSTANG Ford

For what amounted to a street-legal Trans-Am racer, the Boss 302 was an incredible value at just under $3600 to start. It basically came one way, though buyers could chose from close- or wide-ratio four-speed gearboxes at no charge. Power assist was recommended for the standard, ultra-quick 16:1 steering ratio. Another option involved Detroit "No-Spin" axles geared at 3.50, 3.91, or 4.30:1. The standard final drive was a shortish 3.50:1, available with or without Ford's Traction-Lok limited-slip differential (also offered with a 3.91 gearset). Like the engine, the chassis was loaded with premium hardware: power brakes with 11.3-inch-diameter front discs and heavy-duty rear drums, high-rate springs, heavy-duty Gabriel shock absorbers (also staggered at the rear), and fully machined axle shafts with larger splines and nodular-iron centers. All '69 Mustangs boasted wider tracks, but they were even broader on the Boss: 59.5 inches at each end. Shinoda radiused the wheel wells to snug around F60 × 15 Polyglas tires—or racing rubber. Not functional but visually arresting were the matte-black paint on hood and headlight scoops, bold bodyside C-stripes with i.d. lettering, and eye-watering paint colors including bright yellow, Calypso Coral, and Acapulco Blue.

The *Other* "Ultimate Mustang"

The Boss 302 was a stunning car—but so was the other "ultimate Mustang" that Knudsen cooked up, the Boss 429. This big-block brute was born of Ford's desire to certify a new "semi-hemi" 429 V-8 for stock-car racing. NASCAR required at least

Mustang styling was visibly cleaner for 1970, especially on standard-trim models like this convertible. Highlights included the return of dual headlamps in a new thin-bar grille, tinsel-free bodysides, and recessed taillamps. With buyer tastes changing, ragtop sales fell to an all-time low of 7673 units.

500 production installations, but didn't specify which models. So although Torinos showed up at the track, Ford qualified the engine by selling it in Mustangs.

Beside semi-hemispherical combustion chambers—"crescent-shaped" in Ford parlance—the Boss 429 engine employed thinwall block construction, aluminum heads, beefier main bearings, and a cross-drilled steel-billeted crankshaft. There were two versions of this "820" engine: a hydraulic-lifter "S" fitted to the first 279 cars, and an improved "T" version with different rods and pistons and either mechanical or hydraulic lifters. Both were nominally rated at 360 bhp in street tune or 375 bhp in full-race trim. But as with the H.O. 302, these were low-ball numbers to avoid raising the ire of insurance companies that were now fast hiking premiums on all performance cars.

Shoehorn Job

The semi-hemi was too large for even the wider '69 Mustang engine bay, so Knudsen ordered engineer Roy Lunn to find a solution. Lunn turned to Kar Kraft, the Brighton, Michigan, specialty shop that built many of Ford's racing cars at the time. Together they found just enough space by modifying the front suspension, front wheel openings, and inner fenders and moving the battery to the trunk. For all that, front track increased only 0.8-inch. To resist body flex in hard acceleration, diagonal braces were added between the wheelhouses and firewall. Kar Kraft set up a special mini-assembly line for the Boss 429, but the engine installation was a time-consuming shoehorn job and production was slow to get rolling. Even so, a creditable 852 examples were built between mid-January and July.

Outside, the Boss 429 was a bit more subdued than its small-block brother despite wearing a similar rear wing and the same F60 × 15 Polyglas tires on seven-inch-wide Magnum 500 wheels. Its front spoiler and large functional hood scoop were unique, as were the discreet i.d. decals on the front fenders. Power steering and brakes were standard here, as were engine oil cooler and a 3.91:1 Traction-Lok differential. Detroit No-Spin axles were available. Automatic and air conditioning were not offered, but the big Boss was surprisingly lush for a factory drag racer, as the Exterior and Deluxe Interior Décor packages were standard. Ford also threw in the Visibility Group consisting of glovebox lock, parking-brake warning lamp, and lights for luggage compartment, ashtray, and glovebox.

At $4798, the Boss 429 was the costliest non-Shelby Mustang to date, which partly explains why the model was killed after only 505 more were built to 1970 specs. Then again, neither Boss was meant to make money; they were "homologation specials" that had to be sold to meet racing rules.

Boss Meets Boss

How lucky for us. *Car Life* tested both and found the little Boss quicker to 60 mph—6.9 seconds vs. 7.2—though it trailed in the quarter-mile at 14.85 seconds and 96.14 mph vs. the 429's 14.09

at 102.85. Top speed for both was reported at 118 mph. The 429 was obviously potent, but its chassis was simply overwhelmed in full-bore acceleration. Not so the Boss 302, and it's interesting to note that *Car Life*'s example turned in the same quarter-mile time as a test Camaro Z-28. *Car and Driver* pronounced the Boss 302 "the best handling Ford ever.... [It] may just be the new standard by which everything from Detroit must be judged...It's what the Shelby GT-350s and 500s should have been, but weren't."

Trouble in Shelbyville

That's probably because the '69 Shelbys were Ford's work, not Carroll's, reduced to just a custom styling job carried out on stock fastbacks and convertibles at Ford's Southfield, Michigan, plant. The main distinction was a new fiberglass nose with a big loop bumper/grille that added three inches to overall length. Shelbys had only two headlamps but bristled with air intakes—five on the hood alone. Wide reflective tape stripes ran midway along the flanks. Said *C/D*'s Brock Yates: "I personally can't think of an automobile that makes a [better] statement about performance.... "

But the sad fact was that the '69s were the tamest Shelbys yet, hobbled by more weight and less power. The GT-500 was no longer "King of the Road," but retained that '68 model's CJ 428. Horsepower remained at 335 advertised but was down 25 actual

by most estimates. The GT-350 graduated to the new 351 Windsor but claimed no more horses than before—or the more affordable new Mach 1—leading Yates to call it "a garter snake in Cobra skin." Adding insult to these injuries were record prices ranging from $4434 for the GT-350 fastback to just over five-grand for a GT-500 ragtop.

With the Mach 1, the dynamic Boss duo, and four Shelbys in the '69 stable, some wondered whether Ford had *too* many hot Mustangs. The Bosses cost as much to build as the Shelbys, yet struck Yates as "a curious duplication of effort.... The heritage of the GT-350 is performance," he asserted, "and it is difficult to understand why the Ford marketing experts failed to exploit its reputation." Regardless, Shelby model-year production fell by fully 25 percent to 3150 units.

A Thoroughbred Fades Away

After seeing his cars win only one Trans-Am race in 1969, Carroll Shelby decided to leave the car business (though he would return) and asked Ford to put the Shelby-Mustang out to pasture. Ford agreed but not before exploring an interesting in-house proposal to salvage part of the '69 car. This envisioned a "1970 ½" replacement for both the Shelby-Mustangs and the Boss 429. Dubbed "Composite Mustang" by those involved, it was basi-

Like other 1970 fastbacks, the Mach 1 lost its upper-bodyside scoops but gained the Boss 302's rear-window louvers as a new option. The Mach still wore lots of matte-black paint, but in different places, and got a "pony tri-color" grille emblem like other models. Mach 1 production totaled 40,970 units.

cally the big-engine Boss with a Mercury Cougar interior and a '69 Shelby front end with the scoops filled in. The intended result would be quicker than a CJ Mach 1, cheaper to build than a GT-500, and more distinctive than the existing Boss 429. Kar Kraft ran up two prototypes, but what came to be called the "Quarter Horse" was left at the gate. One likely reason was the unsold '69 Shelbys piling up around Southfield—some 600 in all. To move 'em out, Ford made them "1970" models by applying new serial numbers, Boss 302 front spoilers, and black hood stripes—a real "distress sale" tactic.

Slipping Into 1970

Meanwhile, Ford bean-counters tallied another decline in total Mustang sales. Though the model-year loss was modest—only 5.5 percent vs. '68—it looked ominous after all the money spent on the '69 program. Interestingly, of 184,000 cars delivered in the first half of calendar '69, the Grande accounted for only about 15,000 sales while the Mach 1 ran close to 46,000. On cue, division general manager John Naughton promised "heavy emphasis on performance" with "hardware to meet the action requirements of buyers everywhere."

But after the '69 overhaul, Mustang could not be changed very much for 1970. Designers did tidy up the face, filling each "sugar scoop" with two simulated air vents and reverting to dual-beam

Still looking every inch the streetable Trans-Am racer, the Boss 302 was the only 1970 Mustang to record higher model-year production—6319 vs. 1934 of the inaugural '69s—though a full model year helped. "Hockey-stick" tape striping provided instant visual i.d. Sad to say, Ford bailed out from all forms of racing after 1970, Trans-Am included, so the Boss 302 would not return for a third season.

headlamps within a grille switched from mesh to thin horizontal bars. The tri-color emblem moved to the grille center except on Mach 1, where it was left off. Ornamention was shuffled. Bodyside scoops were erased. The posh Grande got a part-vinyl "landau" roof, but the previous full covering was now a $26 extra. The Mach 1 picked up rectangular driving lights inboard of the main beams, plus ribbed rocker-panel appliqués, "honeycomb" back-panel trim, twist-type hood locks, and revised striping. The Boss 302 traded C-stripes for "hockey stick" decals, and its rear-window louvers were newly optional for any fastback. All 1970s got recessed taillamps, standard high-back bucket seats, and, as Washington now required, three-point lap/shoulder belts, tamper-proof odometer, and steering-column ignition lock.

Engine choices expanded with the addition of a four-barrel 351 packing 300 bhp on tight 11:1 compression, and four-speed transmissions added a Hurst linkage with T-handle shifter. The separate GT option was dropped, but Mach 1s retained most of its features. They also added a rear stabilizer bar, which allowed

BOSS 429

Like its small-block brother, the Boss 429 would not return after 1970. In this case, though, the reason had less to do with Ford's decision to leave racing than with falling demand for performance cars in general, aggravated by period price inflation and inflating insurance premiums. Since then, a combination of low production, high performance, and historical interest has made every 1969-70 Boss Mustang a modern collector classic worth many times its original price, even adjusted for inflation.

lower spring rates for a more comfortable ride with no increase in cornering roll. The Boss 429 roared back with a little-changed 820T engine, then substituted an 820A unit with minor adjustments in the Thermactor emissions-control system—a sign of the times. A newly available Drag Pack fortified any 428 engine with stronger con rods, heavy-duty oil cooler, and other upgrades for quarter-mile duty.

Mustang reclaimed the Trans-Am manufacturer's trophy in 1970 but sagged in the sales race, now even more competitive. A beefy new Dodge Challenger and a companion Plymouth Barracuda arrived to do battle, followed at mid-season by a handsome second-generation Chevrolet Camaro and Pontiac Firebird. With this, plus softening demand for ponycars in general, Mustang model-year sales fell an alarming 36.4 percent to 190,727 units. Hardtops plunged 35 percent, fastbacks and convertibles by around 40 percent each. While the Mach 1 still accounted for a solid proportion of fastback sales, it was being overshadowed by other performance models at Ford and rival manufacturers. A small bright spot was the Boss 302, which soared to 6319 sales despite its specialized nature, limited availability, and stiff price.

On September 11, 1969, Bunkie Knudsen was abruptly fired after less than two years as Ford president. Larry Shinoda fast followed his patron out the door. Henry Ford II would only say "things just didn't work out," though he never elaborated on that in line with his longtime motto, "never complain, never explain." But insiders suggested that Bunkie, like his father, had stepped on too many toes. "Knudsen moved in and started doing things his way," wrote analyst Robert W. Irvin of trade weekly *Automotive News*. "Knudsen was almost running the company and [some said] he had alienated many other top executives. Others said Knudsen's departure was an indication of how the

The Shelby GTs reached the end of their road in 1970 after Carroll Shelby decided to cease being a car manufacturer and asked Ford to end these once-special Mustangs. Some 600 leftover '69s were reserialed as "1970" models and given black hood striping and Boss 302 front airdams, as shown on this GT-500 coupe.

Fords don't like to share power." Tellingly, Irvin wrote that in July 1978 on the firing of Lee Iacocca. To soothe ruffled feathers, Ford's chairman set up a presidential troika of R. L. Stevenson for International Operations, R. J. Hampson for Non-Automotive Operations, and Iacocca for North American Operations. But that lasted less than a year. Iacocca was named sole company president in 1970, finally snatching his long-coveted brass ring.

Mustang fans will forever thank Knudsen for the legendary Boss 302 and 429. All things considered, they were an amazing achievement for his brief tenure. Yet how ironic that the "father" of the ponycar would be left to preside over the new Mustang breed that Knudsen also rushed through, but wouldn't be around to introduce. Though Lee Iacocca was no doubt happy to see Knudsen dumped so unceremoniously, Bunkie would exact a sort of unintended revenge when his big new '71s proved the most controversial Mustangs yet.

Horse Racing:
The Trans-Am Series

In its early years, the Trans-American Championship—Trans-Am for short—was home to some of America's most exciting, hard-fought automobile racing. Inaugurated in 1966, it was conceived by the Sports Car Club of America as a professional series for sports cars and Detroit's popular sporty compacts, though initial publicity referred only to "sedans." Mustang's huge sales success in 1964-65 was key factor in launching the Trans-Am, which was staged on demanding road courses from coast-to-coast. But people love a good fight, so attendance and media interest didn't really take off until rival ponycars appeared to chase Mustang on the racetrack as well as in the showroom.

At first, there were two classes based on engine size. Most foreign models ran in the under-2.5-liter category, while larger cars like Mustang were allowed engines between 2.5 and 5.0 liters. Rules mandated safety roll cages, minimum racing weight, fuel tank size, and other requirements but allowed liberal tinkering with the stock suspension and powertrain. SCCA specified minimum production of 2500 units for a given model, at least 500 for basic engines, and only regular-production body modifications like speed-enhancing spoilers. In other words, to run a car in Trans-Am, you had to make a street version to sell the public. Like NASCAR in those days, SCCA knew it could move more tickets if the cars on the course looked a lot like cars people could actually buy.

With hardly any competition on or off the track, Mustang was the easy first-season champion in its class, with Jerry Titus the winningest driver. Ford bagged a second class crown in '67, spending bigger bucks for a squadron of teams with big-name pilots running race-prepped Mustangs and Mercury Cougars, though Titus again took home the driver's trophy.

The next two years belonged to archrival Chevrolet and its purpose-engineered Camaro Z-28s. But Ford's prospects got a huge boost when Bunkie Knudsen came over as president, determined to regain the title from old employer and new corporate foe, GM. Sparing no expense and marshaling all available resources, Knudsen fast-tracked the Boss 302 as Dearborn's new warrior, and gave veteran team manager Bud Moore virtually unlimited funds for testing, prep, mechanics, and drivers. Ace pilots George Follmer and Parnelli Jones re-upped for a season that saw most every ponycar in the lists. The battles were fierce, as the Boss had to take on factory-backed Dodge Challengers and Plymouth Barracudas as well as the formidable Z-28s, Pontiac Firebirds, and even some Javelins from little American Motors. It was the ultimate in "horse racing." When it was all over, Mustang was back on top again, scoring six victories, five at the skilled hands of Parnelli Jones.

Amazingly, Ford then quit all forms of racing, and interest in the Trans-Am began to wane along with the ponycar market. Eventually, the series was put to rest. Though SCCA has lately revived the name, today's Trans-Am cars are much less stock than the original racers, and the series draws less manufacturer support and public notice.

Chapter Five:
1971-1973

A bigger, brawnier Mustang looked a sure winner in the late 1960s. Unhappily for Ford, this all-new car galloped in for 1971, when buyers were moving on and the ponycar market was shrinking fast. But despite the bad timing and a herd of challenging new federal regulations, Mustang still offered high style and—with the right options—great performance.

Depending on your point of view, the 1971-73 Mustang is either a decent car that's been misunderstood down the years or a symbol of everything wrong with Detroit. In its day, this fourth-generation series was roundly criticized as oversized, overweight, and overwrought. Then again, it was undeniably the biggest, heaviest, most "styled" Mustang ever. Sales were the lowest of any Mustang to that point, yet the three-year total was nearly 410,000, a more than respectable figure for the time, and one that Ford Motor Company in 2004 would probably be delighted with. Go where vintage Mustangs gather today and you'll see far more of the 1965-70 and post-1978 models. Yet like some other period Detroiters, these "Clydesdales" are at last getting their due, being gathered in and preserved by those who grew up with them, fans who have the same affection for "their" Mustangs as older folks have for the Sixties cars of their youth.

In short, times change and all things are relative, to use two old clichés. But these Mustangs also demonstrate how every car is a product of its particular era, shaped by prevailing social and economic forces and especially the personalities of those who design and build it. They also remind us again of the auto industry's perennial problem with lead times—really "lag" times. Like the ill-fated Edsel, the ponies might have been a real success had they born three years earlier.

Changing Times

Like its contemporaries, the '71 Mustang was created in the heady atmosphere of the late Sixties. U.S. car sales hit a new all-time high in 1965—Mustang, of course, had something to do with that—and though the market had since cooled a bit, it remained plenty strong through late decade. Buyers were flush in a booming economy, and with each passing year they seemed to crave more size, more power, more luxury, and more gadgets. The Pontiac GTO had touched off a mania for "muscle cars" that had Detroit racing to stuff most every model—ponycars included—with the largest, most potent engines possible. That's why Ford made room in the 1967-68 Mustangs for a big-block 390 and 428 V-8 options.

But all too soon, the go-go good times came to a screeching halt. As Gary Witzenburg observed in his authoritative Mustang history: "The horsepower race that had been going on since the automobile was invented was just about over by the time the 1971 Mustangs were introduced on August 20th, 1970. The federal government's mushrooming mountain of safety and emissions and damageability requirements, over-reactions to legitimate concerns, had caused a massive rethinking of priorities in Detroit. Motor City was a fortress besieged by regulatory Huns. The drawbridge was up and the moat loaded with crocodiles.

"There would be no more racing for Ford…and, indeed, few more suitable cars to be raced. As the country and the industry struggled to recover from a mild recession, the federal testing and the certifications and the paperwork necessary to appease the ravenous bureaucratic beast effectively ruled out, at least for the moment, any further thought of automotive excitement, performance, or fun. It was the beginning of a new Dark Age for the American automobile, and in August of 1970, everyone in Detroit knew it."

Buyers Change Horses

The industry could certainly see by then that the ponycar was losing its appeal. Mustang sales had been sliding since 1966. The Chevrolet Camaro and Pontiac Firebird were holding up (aided by a handsome 1970 redesign) but were not gaining. American Motors' Javelin was a mild success, but no blockbuster. Neither were Plymouth's bulked-up 1970 Barracuda and its new Dodge stablemate, the aptly named Challenger, neither of which brought in the pile of orders Chrysler expected.

A big reason was that a new wave of economy imports had caught America's fancy, including some fast-improving Japanese cars wearing unfamiliar names like Toyota and Datsun. The threat seemed minimal, and most people still couldn't conceive that the world might run short of oil some day. But Detroit evidently remembered the European small-car invasion of the 1950s, because this time it counterattacked right away. Besides mustering new compacts like the Ford Maverick, Chevy Nova, and AMC

Hornet, the industry spent vast sums to bring out even smaller, cheaper *sub*compacts led by the Ford Pinto, Chevrolet Vega, and AMC Gremlin. By 1971, ponycars were fast losing sales to these and other sensible wheels—down to almost half of where they'd been at their 1967 peak.

The changing market also presented a stark reality unique to Ford: "Total Performance" was no longer that important to sales. Besides, Ford had little left to prove in competition after dominating stock-car and drag racing for much of the Sixties, not to mention winning the prestigious LeMans 24 Hours four times in as many years.

An Eerie, Accurate Prediction

With many more ponycar models chasing fewer and fewer buyers, *Motor Trend* began to think the breed was headed for extinction. In fact, the magazine began an October 1971 ponycar comparison test with a "pre-mortem." While admitting that fierce competition was doing no one any good, *MT* blamed "the auto makers themselves" for withering ponycar demand: "You see, selling cars is not really a very profitable enterprise. It's what you sell *with* the car that makes the whole venture worthwhile. If you can take, say, a $2500 Plain Jane Mustang and talk the buyer into loading it up…[then] you've got a *sale*. In that $1000 worth of options is…the *profit*. That's why the original six-cylinder Mustang sat at the back of the showroom while the salesmen pushed the optional V-8…. The escalation derby gathered momentum as time went on, until by the late Sixties you could buy…engines that originally had been developed for the 200-mph straightaways

of Daytona. And the prices of these overbuilt ponycars rose pretty well out of sight, too—in the $5000 bracket rubbing elbows with Buicks and T-Birds. Option overkill."

Answering a rhetorical "where will it all end?" *MT* made a remarkably accurate prediction: "We figure the ponycars will all fade out into the sunset by 1975…. Oh, at least one auto maker might keep his ponycar nameplate alive…as a sort of nostalgic reminder of When Things Were Good. But there are all sorts of tides running against the ponycar now…." Sure enough, most of the Mustang's imitators were either killed off or turned into something else by mid-decade, leaving only Ford, Chevrolet, and Pontiac to carry the torch—and some would judge the coming Mustang II as anything but a traditional pony.

Knudsen Talked, Ford Listened

Just as important as the late-Sixties *zeitgeist* in shaping the '71 Mustang were the personalities of short-time Ford president Bunkie Knudsen and designer Larry Shinoda, the GM guys who shocked the industry by jumping ship in 1968. Both loved hot cars, but while the expansive fourth-generation certainly reflected that, it was also something of an ego trip. Remember that Knudsen went to Ford after being passed over as GM president,

After evolving in the last half of 1967 through numerous large, heavy-looking proposals, all rejected, '71 Mustang styling got firm direction from new Ford president Bunkie Knudsen. The basic shape and proportions were largely settled by September 1968, when these hardtop workouts were photographed in the Ford Design Center courtyard.

Knudsen chose a January 1968 fastback mockup as the basis for '71 Mustang styling, and it was quickly refined with an eye to manufacturing cost and feasbility. These workouts, also from September 1968, show various thoughts on body details like scoops and sculpture lines.

a key reason he accepted the Dearborn job from chairman Henry Ford II. It's therefore reasonable to assume that Knudsen was determined to show by his labors at Ford that GM had made the wrong choice. Also, like his new Dearborn rival, Lee Iacocca, Knudsen knew a thing or two about automobiles and how to sell them. He was arguably even more a "car guy" than the jilted Iacocca, though Shinoda shaded them both.

In any case, Knudsen wasted little time in looking over Ford's near-term product plans, especially those involving icon models like Mustang. The key thing is, he did so with full knowledge of what General Motors was planning for those same future years. Knudsen's management skills were beyond doubt—after all, he'd come to Ford after doing a bang-up job as general manager at Chevrolet—but his insider knowledge of GM's plans gave Ford a golden opportunity to outdo its crosstown foe. Indeed, one suspects this loomed large for HFII in offering the president's post to Bunkie instead of Iacocca. As a result, Knudsen wielded unusu-

ally heavy influence for an outsider. Sure, he had his own opinions, but they were informed by what the competition was planning, so Ford listened when Bunkie talked. We can also be pretty sure that Ford (and GM as well) had a good idea of what Chrysler would be doing around the turn of the decade. (When it comes to spies, the CIA has nothing on Detroit.)

Marketer Machinations

A final factor in shaping the '71 Mustang was Ford's vaunted marketing department, ever a powerful influence on company decision-makers. After analyzing sales trends, customer comments, intelligence reports, and other piles of data, product planners concluded the next Mustang, to use Witzenburg's words, "would have to be bigger...longer wheebase, wider treads, beefier chassis, suspension, driveline, and brakes, and larger wheel openings to take the bigger tires. At the same time, it would have to be quieter, roomier, more comfortable, [softer-riding], and more

A convertible mockup from early 1969 is very close to the '71 ragtop that greeted buyers in Ford showrooms, but the "crosshair" grille was rejected and the taillamps would be tweaked. As usual, designers debated such details almost until the last minute. Wheel design here would be preserved for optional wheel covers.

luxurious to satisfy the other end of the market. Of the so-called 'three faces of Mustang,' the profits were clearly generated by the luxury face as much as the macho face, and the expectations of small luxo-car buyers were also increasing every year."

All perfectly logical, but how to pull it off? Witzenburg quotes Ford design chief Eugene Bordinat on that very topic: "You [always] run into the problem…of how to make the car all things to all people, and I think that over time, the greatest fights we had with the Mustang were to keep the compromise package. The product planner's idea of how to increase the sales volume of a car is to make it accommodate more people and to add creature comforts. But the minute you begin to fool with compromises in that sort of package, guess what? You end up with a two-door sedan. And then they wouldn't understand why it didn't look quite the same, and you have to explain that you…can't make [one car] serve two masters."

More Big Ideas

Nevertheless, Gale Halderman and his Ford Studio designers tried to do just that. They began work around May 1967, just as the '69 Mustang was wrapping up. Once more, they immediately thought big. "The first clays looked monstrous," Witzenburg notes. "And they were ugly!" Though the long-hood/short-deck profile remained a given, most workouts through the fall of '67 were visually massive and awkward, with puffy lower-body contours, high beltlines, thick rear roof quarters, pouty Thunderbird-like noses with massive bumper/grilles, and willy-nilly sculptures and humps. Evidently, designers still felt management wanted some T-Bird "influence" in the Mustang, but they now tried to marry that with "performance" cues like Shelby-style scoops and pop-open gas caps. For all the false starts and misdirection, several early ideas would survive to the showroom, such as a simple, straight character line high on the bodysides and, for the hardtop, a "flying buttress" rear roofline with upright "tunneled" backlight, perhaps prompted by intelligence on '68 Dodge Charger styling.

Fortunately, designers stripped away most of the flab by autumn, opting for crisp creases, swoopy fender shapes, and kicked-up "ducktails." More protruding fronts were tried, but also flat faces, and trapezoidal nose shapes were favored for a time. As usual, there were many experiments with dual, quad, and hidden headlamps, plus "floating" grilles and—as a new signature for the fastback—a set of vertical air slots just behind the door. For a time, the fastback was also planned for a "tunnelback" roof, with and without rear-quarter windows.

By mid-January 1968, the fastback had acquired a sharp belt-line kickup aft of the doors and an almost flat roofline with a near-horizontal rear window. When Knudsen came to power a few weeks later, he took one look at this fiberglass model and looked no more. As Halderman related: "He approved that '71 right in the studio. We asked if he didn't want to take it outside…and he said, 'No, I like it right here.' We said, 'Well, there are a couple more being done, wouldn't you prefer to wait and see how they turn out?' He said, 'No, I like this one.' We had never had approvals like that before."

Even so, designers worked up several alternatives in full-size

ABOVE AND LEFT: The Mach 1 fast-back would remain the raciest regular Mustang for '71. This full-size fiberglass prototype from March 1969 is production-correct except for its inner grille and hood scoop. Body-color front bumper covered with polyurethane plastic would be a new standard Mach 1 feature. BELOW AND BOTTOM: Grande hardtop and a standard SportRoof fastback pose for their official styling "sign-off" photos in late January 1970. By that point, production tooling was on the way and plans were being laid for refitting plants to build the new models. The new Mustangs went on sale along with other '71 Fords on August 20.

drawings during April even as Knudsen's choice was being production-engineered with an eye to cost and feasibility. The car was more or less finished by mid-June, but tinkering with grille inserts, taillamps, trim, and other minor stuff continued for another year. When Carroll Shelby decided to leave the car business in 1969, management briefly considered a "Cobra" version of the '71 to replace the Shelby-Mustang. Based on the hardtop, not the fastback, it ended up looking aggressive but contrived. We might be glad it went no further.

Tales of the Tape—and Scales

The Mustangs that did reach showrooms reprised base and Grande hardtops, a convertible, and Sportsroof fastbacks in regular and Mach 1 trim, plus a new Boss 351 version. Stylists didn't try to hide the expanded dimensions that Knudsen and his product planners ordained. If anything, the new look seemed to emphasize the sudden growth spurt. Though wheelbase was stretched just an inch to 109 inches, overall length tacked on 2.1 inches to 189.5. More significant was a near three-inch gain in overall width, to 74.1 inches, matched by broader front/rear tracks of 61.5/61.0 inches. Height was fractionally reduced to 50.1 inches on SportsRoofs, 50.8 on other models. Though each of these changes was hardly colossal in itself, they collectively helped fatten the '71 Mustangs by some 500-600 pounds over comparable 1970s, with the heaviest models flattening the scales at over 1.5 tons. All very different from the lithe compact Ford started with just seven years before, which author Brad Bowling pointed out was some seven inches shorter and narrower, plus a good deal lighter.

A Tasteful New Look

If the '71s were heavier by design, at least they were quite tasteful per Mustang tradition. All models wore a higher beltline swept up behind the door, rounded bodysides relieved by a simple half-length creaseline, and neatly cropped tails with the trademark triple taillamps, albeit squashed a bit and rounded at the corners. Bumpers were slim U-shaped beams snugged close to the body. Grilles were blunted and full-width, with a dual-beam headlamp at each end. Base models and the Grande capped hoods and fenders with a bright inverted-U molding curved down to meet the bumper ends as a sort of frame. Within the grille was a bright, broad rectangle bisected by a chrome horizontal bar carrying a coralled running horse—back after a two-year absence. The Mach 1 and Boss 351 had their own face, with a black, honeycomb-texture grille insert, a small "pony tricolor" emblem in the middle, and flanking "sportlamps"—amber running lights wired in with the headlamps. All models wore more steeply angled windshields, and hoods were extended back over the cowl to hide the windshield wipers, a dubious GM idea doubtless decreed by Knudsen and Shinoda. Hardtops wore bulkier "buttressed" rear-roof quarters and shared a higher rear deck with convertibles. Luggage space, however, actually decreased to 8.1 cubic feet on those body styles. Exterior door handles shifted from pushbutton grips to a flush-mount pull-up style. Grande retained a standard

Car Life magazine called Mustang's '71 fastback a "flat back" because the rear window was pitched only 14 degrees from horizontal. It looked very racy but played hob with visibility, as most road testers complained. The Mach 1 version in this bird's-eye view wore specific i.d. and trim, including simple flat-face hubcaps and bright wheel rings.

vinyl roof covering (available in five colors), twin "racing" mirrors keyed to body paint, bright wheel-lip and rocker moldings, and bodyside pinstripes. Convertibles were upgraded to a standard power top with glass rear window and color-keyed boot, plus tinted windshield.

The Mach 1 borrowed another contemporary GM styling gimmick: a front bumper covered in body-color polyurethane plastic (with matching upper grille frame). Though not as "squashable" as the similar Endura-covered noses of recent Pontiacs, the plastic wrap did ward off dings while lending a purposeful look appropriate for the model. Mach 1s also carried an angled chin spoiler; domed hood; honeycomb back-panel appliqué; bold bodyside tape stripes in black or argent (silver); and contrasting perimeter lower-body paint, again black or argent depending on main paint color. A freestanding Boss 302-type rear spoiler was available. A double-dome hood with simulated air scoops was a no-charge option. The scoops were functional when ordered with one of the top-power engines.

The Inside Story

Yet more GM influence was evident in a new reverse-angle instrument panel. Like recent Camaro dashboards, it had three large rounds ahead of the driver and a central "stack" housing radio, climate controls, air vents, and optional oil pressure, coolant-temp, and ammeter gauges. For price competitiveness,

the Mach 1 "Sports" interior became a $130 option that was also available for other Mustangs (bar the Boss, where it was included). This comprised woven-vinyl seat inserts, the problematic "Rim-Blow" steering wheel, molded door panels with front armrests, clock, and bright pedal trim. The Grande came with many of these items but retained vinyl/Lambeth-cloth upholstery. The base interior was fairly plain despite including full carpeting and a new mini floorshift console. Standard lap and shoulder belts returned, but new "Uni-Lock" buckles allowed linking the upper webs to the lap belts for cinching as a unit, a convenience that presumably encouraged seatbelt use.

Another new safety feature was required by Washington: a longitudinal steel beam in each door to absorb side-impact energy. It proved its worth when the occupants of a '71 Mustang prototype emerged unscathed after being broadsided by another car during a public-road shakedown run. Chief program engineer Howard Freers was pleased that this "actual test" confirmed "all the lab testing done by body engineering."

Colorful New Options

Not surprising for Mustang, the '71s offered several new options. Leading the list were power windows, electric rear-window defroster ($48), and a good-sounding AM/FM stereo radio (a stiff $214, but worth it). A vinyl roof option was added for fastbacks but was aesthetically debatable. Ford got into hot "Grabber" paint colors for several of its '71 model lines. Mustang listed a vivid blue, green, yellow, and lime under that name, plus a dozen more-conventional hues. Interiors were color-keyed in black, white, green, blue, red, and ginger.

As ever, standard Mustangs for '71 offered all sorts of dress-up options to enhance their sporty styling. Visible on this nicely equipped convertible are Magnum 500 styled-steel wheels, rear-deck spoiler, and the $97 Decor Group with bold bodyside stripes, bulged hood, and high-back front bucket seats. But ragtops were falling out of favor, and the convertible was the least popular '71 Mustang, with just 6121 built.

Mach 1 looked meaner than ever for '71 but packed less standard power, demoted from a 351 V-8 to a mild 302. This one, however, is optioned the way most enthusiasts would, packing the big 429 Cobra Jet V-8 that arrived to replace the previous big-block 428 CJs. Twin-scoop hood with racing-style twist-locks was a no-charge option. Functional scoops were included with one of the available ram-air CJ-R engines. Profile view (top) shows Mach 1's standard "chin" spoiler. Rear spoiler (top and right) cost extra. Other options shown here include Magnum 500 wheels, two-tone hood paint, and folding "sport deck" rear seat.

After several years of wooing customers with extended war-ranties, the Big Three called a truce to save themselves some money. Ford's coverage reverted from one-year/unlimited miles to the tradtional 12 months/12,000 miles. To *make* money, Ford began the model year by hiking prices five percent across the board, then adjusted some models in early October to account for equipment changes and competitors' moves. When the dust settled, six-cylinder models started at $2911 for a hardtop, $2973 for a SportsRoof, $3227 for a convertible, and $3117 for a Grande. A two-barrel ("2V") 302 V-8 added $95 in each case.

Mach 1 Meets a New Boss

The Mach 1 was not what it was in '71 guise. First, base price went up a sizable $200 to $3268, and that bought only a stan-dard 302, not a 351. Worse, retuning for this year's stricter emis-sions standards robbed the 302 of 10 horses, leaving it at 210 bhp on unchanged 9.0:1 compression. The new Boss 351 listed at $4101 on its belated debut at the November 1970 Detroit Auto Show. Save model i.d. and a chrome front bumper, it looked much like the Mach 1 but was much stronger, thanks to an exclusive High-Output (HO) 351 Cleveland with four-barrel (4V) carb, soar-ing 11.0:1 compression and 330 bhp. Milder 351s were available

for Mach 1 and other models: a 240-bhp 2V ($45) and a 275-bhp 4V ($93). With vehicle weights up so much, the base 200-cubic-inch six was sensibly scratched, leaving the torquier 250, though it, too, lost 10 horses, dwindling to 145.

Big-Block Intrigues

Mustang's big-block was now a 429—which raised a few eye-brows—but it wasn't the exotic semi-hemi of 1969-70. While this new Cobra Jet did have the same cylinder dimensions, it was essentially a short-stroke version of the Thunderbird/Lincoln 460 V-8, with wedge-type combustion chambers and conventional construction. It began the model year in regular (CJ) and ram-air (CJ-R) versions. Both had 4V carburetors, hydraulic lifters, and a nominal 370 bhp, though most observers thought the cold-air ducting put the CJ-R at 380-385 bhp. A solid-lifter Super Cobra Jet (SCJ) arrived a few weeks later at 375 bhp, again with or without ram-air. All 429s could be ordered with 3.91 and 4.11:1

Though less fiery than the Boss models it replaced, the Boss 351 fastback was the quickest, most roadable '71 in the Mustang stable. A special High-Output 351 V-8 with premium internals delivered a solid 330 bhp through a four-speed manual gearbox with Hurst shifter, good for 0–60 in under six seconds. Alas, hot-car demand was waning fast, and Ford fired this Boss at midseason after build-ing only 1806.

rear axles, but the SCJ required those ratios and the optional Drag Pack with locking differential. None of these brutes was inexpensive at $372-$493, which likely explains why initial orders were so weak—and why Ford decided to drop all three by mid-season. Most probably went into Mach 1s, though they were technically available for any '71 Mustang.

The Boss 351 could have been badged "Mach 2," as many of its standard performance goodies were available for the more affordable Mach 1. For example, though both included the stiff competition suspension, the Boss came with F60-15 tires instead of E70-14s, plus power front-disc brakes ($70 otherwise), wide-ratio four-speed gearbox with Hurst linkage, 3.91:1 Traction-Lok axle ($48), functional hood scoops, dual exhausts, heavy-duty battery and cooling system, rear spoiler, electronic rev limiter, and gauge package.

Less, But the Best

Though touted as "the best all-around performer in Ford pro-duction-car history," the new Boss was necessarily less muscular than the cars it replaced. Still, it was the fastest of the '71 breed—and the most roadable right out of the box. Chuck Koch, who tested a trio of Mustangs for a January 1971 *Motor Trend* review, clocked the Boss at 5.8 seconds 0–60 mph, with a stand-ing quarter-mile of 13.8 seconds at 104 mph. By contrast, a 429 Mach 1 took 6.5 seconds and did the quarter in 14.5 at 96.8

mph, though it might have been hampered a bit by its Cruise-O-Matic. Koch's third '71 tester, an automatic 302 hardtop, posted comparative tame numbers: 9.9 seconds 0–60 mph and 17.5 seconds at 78 mph in the quarter-mile. And where the Boss topped out at 100 mph and the big-block Mach 1 at nearly 114, the 302 managed only 86 mph with the standard 2.79:1 axle. Then again, it scored the best fuel economy by far: 15.2–17.1 mpg on regular fuel vs. 10–11 for the burly Mach 1 and just 9–10 for the speedy Boss, both on pricier premium gas, of course.

Make Room for a "Monster"

According to Howard Freers, the 429 with its canted-valve heads "was a much wider engine than the 428, and that's why the car got wider"—ironic in view of the engine's short tenure. "It took a [wider track] to get those monsters in there." But engineers took advantage of that to optimize handling for all models, which was "a major problem objective," Freers recalled. "I think we [improved] it...on the base model as well as the big-engine jobs." A key decision was fitting staggered rear shocks with any 351 or 429 engine. The chassis wizards also recalibrated the base sus-pension to suit the bigger, heavier '71 package, revamped front-end geometry, and redesigned the steering gear. Cars with the comp suspension got variable-ratio power steering, allegedly bor-rowed from GM. Its chief advantage was needing fewer turns lock-to-lock, appreciated on fast, twisty roads.

Mixed Reviews for the Boss

The Boss 351 seemed tailor-made for that sort of driving, and *Car and Driver* had lots of good things to say about it in a February 1971 road test. For starters, the "HO engine performs admirably.... It produces a generous quantity of power for its size and yet is remarkably tractable and docile." *C/D* explained this by waxing poetic about premium internal features like Boss 302-type "staggered valves the size of manhole covers and ports like laundry chutes. It makes the [Camaro's] Z-28 look like a gas-mileage motor.... [C]amshaft lobes lift the Boss' valves to rare heights for a street engine. In fact, only registered extremists like the L88 and aluminum-block ZL-1 Chevys have more valve lift than the Boss 351 engine." Topping it off was "a 750-cubic-feet-per-minute Autolite carbure-tor the size of an electric typewriter."

C/D judged the variable-ratio power steering as "not particularly quick on center" but "remarkably precise—certainly as good as the best from Detroit—and small steering corrections can be easily and accurately made." But despite Freers' claims, the editors had "serious doubts about the suspension. The car just doesn't handle well enough to be worth the punishing ride. It feels like all of the suspending was done by

Hoping to spur lagging Mustang sales, Ford added a "Sports Hardtop" in April 1971 with Boss/Mach 1-style hood, grille, body-color bumper, side stripes, and wheel coverings, plus a "halo" vinyl roof and thin-stripe whitewall tires. Though value-priced at just $97 over the regular hardtop, the package failed to impress, and only 500 or so were sold, perhaps because it didn't have performance to match the looks.

Mustangs looked much the same for 1972 save revised badging and standard (vs. optional) wheel-lip and rocker trim. Repeal of the federal excise tax allowed Ford to trim base prices. This standard hardtop came down $182 to start at $2729.

short lengths of oak two-by-fours…. [S]tylists should share part of the blame…. They demanded a low car, which means the engineers had very little room for suspension travel. Consequently, the spring rates had to be very stiff to avoid bottoming out. The Boss has what feels like cement springs, but it still bottoms readily—a situation that deals your hind end a healthy whack." On the other hand, "it doesn't roll much and it will generate high cornering forces in situations where you can use plenty of power to keep the tail out. Without power it understeers fiercely…. [And if] the space available is really tight, [the driver] dare not apply power suddenly because the car will understeer even more. We prefer something with more nearly neutral-steer characteristics like the Firebird Trans-Am."

"Sabotaged" by Styling

But the Boss's biggest faults in *C/D*'s view stemmed from the racy fastback styling that had so fast captivated Bunkie Knudsen. While conceding it "generally attractive," the editors thought it "sabotaged" the car in a number of ways. "It's like sitting in a bunker. You can hardly see out. The windows are gun slits, the beltline comes up almost to your chin, and the nearly horizontal rear deck and wide roof pillars block off all but a shallow field of vision directly to the rear…. The long, level front fenders and the bulged-up hood block off an enormous area immediately in front of the car, and right turns, particularly those onto a section of road that falls away, are virtually blind." In addition, the editors criticized the instrument panel as "a triumph of symmetry over function. [Main gauges] are well located…but other small gauges are so low in the center of the panel as to be well out of the driver's line of sight. Even worse are the heater controls…just above the tunnel…. To perform any adjustments, you have to lean well forward from the normal driving position—a move which is entirely unnecessary."

Lest you think *Car and Driver* was unusually critical, rival *Car Life* had similar issues with the SportsRoof. "[The '71 fastback] is actually a flat back. The roof angle is only fourteen degrees. The rear window would make a good skylight. A glance in the rearview mirror provides an excellent view of the interior with a small band of road visible…." Dragstrip-oriented *Cars* magazine allowed that "you do become used to this after awhile," but com-

plained that, exterior dimensions considered, "there isn't *that* much interior space. A big guy can get awfully cramped behind the wheel, even with the bucket [seat] in its rearmost position."

In fairness to Ford as a whole, and maybe Knudsen in particular, almost no one in those days bought a ponycar for passenger room, trunk space, fuel thrift, or even visibility. Style and performance were usually all that mattered, and the '71 Mustangs offered those in abundance. Besides, if you couldn't come to terms with the SportsRoof environment, you could always opt for a hardtop or convertible that might accommodate you much better. Indeed, *Motor Trend*'s lanky Chuck Koch judged his test 302 hardtop just fine "creature-comfort-wise," though he did think the driving position could be improved. "It would be as simple as offering a telescopic steering column, lowering the foot pedals and allowing for more seat travel." Koch also echoed *C/D*'s gripe about needing overly long glances from the road to see controls and readouts in the center stack.

Reviewing all the road tests leaves little doubt that Ford's ponycar had drifted far from its original concept—maybe too far. "While the Mustang is bigger than it has any business being, snorted *Car and Driver*, "it's certainly not the [aircraft carrier U.S.S.] *Forrestal* it would appear from the driver's seat. In reality, it's about the same size as the Camaro—1.5 inches longer and slightly narrower. [But] at least half our disenchantment…is based on poor visibility and an optical illusion of size…. Logically, the Boss 351 should be an American equivalent to Europe's high-performance GT cars…but lacking the feeling of lightness and agility as it does, it's not even close."

Koch provided a more balanced perspective, and maybe a more helpful one, in summing up *Motor Trend*'s comparison test: "When considering the price and relativity of these three cars, you have to admit that, as much fun as the performance Mustangs are to drive, the plain hardtop with its 302-2V engine is the best buy. It exemplifies what Ford started out to do in 1964 with the first Mustang: build an inexpensive car that is still stylish and pleasing to drive."

Second Thoughts

Running changes—updates made during a model year for various reasons—would become a vexing Detroit routine in the Seventies, and Mustang saw several more before closing the '71 campaign. Besides dropping big-block options, Ford fired the Boss 351 around midseason. Sales were only 1806 to that point, evidently too few to satisfy Dearborn bean-counters. But then in April came a pretender of sorts, a "Sports Coupe" hardtop decked out like the Boss and Mach with a similar grille, twin-scoop hood, striping, and color-keyed front bumper, all for just $97 extra. "This may have sold a few cheap hardtops," Witzenburg huffed, "but it was also one more nail in the *real* high-performance Mustang's coffin." Exact production is unknown, but many experts estimate 500—not exactly a barn burner.

Another telling sign of the times appeared in May with a so-called "351 CJ" option. This was basically the HO V-8 with hydraulic instead of mechanical lifters, plus compression drastically lowered to 8.6:1 for knock-free running on the low-lead and unleaded gasoline then coming on the scene—another response to government emissions standards. Even so, horsepower checked in at a respectable 280, channeled to a mandatory 3.50:1 rear axle through automatic or four-speed transmission. The competition suspension was a mandatory option.

In retrospect, the '71 Mustang probably deserved the bad press it got, but that's only because buyers had moved on in ways that no one could have predicted in 1968. Ford showed far better timing with its compact Maverick, which rang up close to 579,000 sales in a long debut model year and nearly 272,000 more for sophomore '71. Mustang, meantime, again suffered right along with its peers, model-year sales dropping nearly 21.5 percent from 1970 to 149,678 units. Hardtops plunged to around 83,000, the convertible sank to a bit over 6000, and fastbacks did about 60,000, of which Mach 1 accounted for a healthy 36,500. At least Ford could still truthfully advertise Mustang as the most popular car of its type, as the archrival Chevy Camaro finished a distant second with 114,630 model-year sales, though admittedly with just coupes.

Press On Regardless

There was nothing Ford could do with its yearling but keep to plugging and hope the market might swing back Mustang's way. Predictably, the '72s didn't look very different, but there were plenty of changes underneath.

The most discouraging alterations occurred under the hood. First, stricter emissions standards dictated reduced compression for all engines to accommodate low-calorie 91-octane fuel. Second, Ford and other automakers now switched from quoting horsepower in SAE gross measure to the more realistic SAE net method—which had the unhappy effect of making the actual power losses look even worse on paper.

With this, compression on the 250 six was dropped a full point (to 8.0:1), resulting in 95 net bhp. A half-point drop (to 8.5:1) left the 2V 302 V-8 at 136 bhp. Among 351s, the 2V unit claimed 168 net bhp on looser 8.6:1 compression, while the 4V was down-rated from 280 to 275 bhp (and no longer called "CJ"). Performance fans cried in their beer, but Ford made amends at midseason by reinstating an HO 351 option, albeit decompressed to 8.8:1 and 275 bhp. As before, three-speed manual was the standard transmission for the six and two-barrel V-8s, with four-speed and Cruise-O-Matic optional. Four-speed was otherwise standard and Select-Shift automatic available—except in

Though Mustang's optional big-block V-8s were also gone by '72, an emissions-tuned 351 HO arrived midyear to offer muted Sixties-style excitement on regular gas. It was a good choice for the Mach 1 (shown), but was optional for any '72. Alas, it would be Mustang's last performance V-8 for quite a while.

Ford built 50 special Mustang convertibles with the new Sprint Decor Group available for 1972 hardtops and SportsRoofs. The option came two ways. A basic "A" package comprised white paint with color-matched plastic-covered front bumper, broad blue hood, and rear-end accents edged in red, racing mirrors, wheel-trim rings, and bold "U.S.A" flag decals on the rear fenders. Interiors were color-coordinated in vinyl with blue cloth inserts for the seats. A second package bundled all this with Magnum 500 wheels, F60-15 white-letter tires, and firm competition suspension. Sprint orders apparently weren't tallied, but were probably low.

California, where even stricter emissions levels mandated automatic with all V-8s. "California versions" would be another yearly burden for automakers in the Seventies.

A Final Fling

At least the HO was clean enough to be sold in the Golden State, "a feat many other manufacturers (Chevrolet with its 454s, for example) haven't been able to accomplish," as *Car and Driver* noted in March 1972. The magazine got an early drive in an HO fastback, and though the thrill factor was inevitably lower than with the short-lived Boss 351, there was still a certain magic at

work. "[This car] is no Little Lord Fauntleroy out to play," *C/D* reported. "It's big and it's self-assured. Everything is massive. When you lean on the Hurst lever…you can feel about 10 pounds of brass synchronizer rings and steel hubs sliding into position…. There is little demand for finesse, only *machismo*…. The HO doesn't really feel like a high-performance engine at all. You don't have to wait for the good part of the torque curve. It's there all the time—flat rather than peaky like the old Boss 302s." Of course, performance was down thanks to the lower compression and a less radical solid-lifter camshaft, but the '72 HO wasn't exactly sleepy, *C/D* reporting 6.6 seconds 0–60 mph and a stand-

ing quarter-mile of 15.1 seconds at 95.6 mph. And more go was readily available for determined hop-up artists with a Ford parts catalog. "Just change the camshaft (the adjustable rockers are already there) and raise the compression ratio back up where it belongs," *C/D* advised. "And if you are really serious you'll bolt on a higher-capacity intake manifold and carburetor."

Best of all perhaps, this HO was available in any '72 Mustang. And it looked amazingly cheap at $119, though it required other equipment that added up to a fairly stout delivered price. Among these mandatory options were the comp suspension ($29), F60-15 tires on wide wheels ($92), power front-disc brakes, 3.91:1 rear axle with Traction-Lok ($56), and heavy-duty battery and radiator. "But you need that stuff anyway," *C/D* asserted. "And when you get it all you find that the 351 HO drives just like last year's Boss [351]. It rides like a Grand National stocker [and] understeers—plenty. Ford apparently likes its cars that way."

C/D spoke for many performance fans in summing up this Mustang: "The idea of paying more [over $4000 delivered] for a slower car is irritating, but that's the way it is in 1972. Still, the HO does have some potential. Which is more than can be said about most of the competition." Sad to say, this would be Mustang's last performance V-8 for a long while.

More Grooming

HO aside, the '72 story mainly involved revisions to trim and features. Examples include fixed rear-quarter windows on fast-backs without optional power windows, unique wheel covers for the Grande, restyled nameplates, and standard bright wheel-lip and rocker moldings. Prices came down a bit after Congress

For 1973, all Mustangs wore a color-keyed front bumper that was redesigned to meet the government's "5-mph" impact standard, taking effect that year. Parking lamps moved up to the grille from under the bumper. A grille insert with enlarged eggcrates further freshened the Grande hardtop (shown) and base models. The Grande interior was still quite posh considering the model's $2946 base price.

repealed the federal excise tax, hoping to boost car sales amidst "stagflation." Ford reduced its dealer discount at about the same time. Together, these moves saved consumers an average of $200.

Star-Spangled Sprint

In February, Ford again hauled out the Sprint name for another cosmetic package—two, actually. The basic $156 "A" option sported white paint set off by broad blue hood and decklid accents edged in red, plus star-spangled "U.S.A." shield decals on the rear fenders and a color-keyed Mach-style nose. Also included were matching two-tone cloth/vinyl upholstery, color-keyed hubcaps with bright trim rings, whitewall tires, and racing mirrors. A more functional $347 "B" version added "mag-type" wheels, F60-15 white-letter tires, and the comp suspension. Either way, a Sprint was hard to miss. But author Gary Witzenburg deemed it just one more marketing ploy dealing "another heavy blow to what remained of the macho Mustang's ego" because a similar treatment was also available for "limp-wristed Pintos and Mavericks." Ostensibly, the Mustang Sprint package was available only for base hardtops and SportsRoofs. However, Ford ran off about 50 convertibles for a parade in Washington, D.C., and it's possible that a few more were built for customers who were able to sweet-talk their local dealer into placing a special order.

By now, Ford's San Jose, California, and Metuchen, New Jersey, plants had switched to building the popular Pintos and Mavericks, leaving the company's big Dearborn complex as the sole home for Mustangs. It was more evidence of the ponycar's declining fortunes—which dipped again for '72, model-year sales falling another 20 percent to just over 125,000. Only the slow-selling convertible maintained its previous level.

A Welcome Award

On March 6, 1972, *Popular Hot Rodding* magazine announced that it had chosen Mustang as "Car of the Decade." Though the award did nothing for sales and seemed rather odd on its face (why 1962–72?), Ford appreciated the thought. Yet the praise was not totally unalloyed, as the magazine's press release spoke mostly in the past tense. To wit: "The Mustang was one of the finest cars (for its price) ever to roll off a Detroit assembly line.... No single car model ever captured the public fancy as did the Mustang.... It was Mustang that broke the ice (in the pony car field) and its tremendous and continued popularity is one of the reasons [it is] 'Car of the Decade.'" Perhaps the enthusiast editors were trying to send a message.

Author Witzenburg found one much later: "How ironic to have such a performance-oriented magazine heap praise on [the] car in the very year the last vestige of real performance was taken out of it." Then again, the award "did serve to point out just how strong the Mustang image remained even during the worst years of its history." You can bet Lee Iacocca knew that already.

If not quite a case of flogging a tired horse, this 1973 Mustang ad certainly strained to portray a sense of excitement about a three-year-old design. Though Mustang scored its first year-to-year sales gain since 1965, the market was now fast tiring of ponycars in general.

What makes Mustang different is the way it looks, handles, and makes you feel.

For eight years now, the Ford Mustang has been the top-selling car in its class.
There are at least three reasons why.

The way it looks.
Sporty, sexy, sleek. You can choose from 5 models: Mach I, SportsRoof, Grandé, Hardtop, and Convertible.
New for 1973, you also get a rugged color-keyed front bumper and a dramatic grille design.
But not all the good looks are on the outside. Inside the cockpit, you sit back in a bucket seat while your hand drops to a floor-mounted shift console and you look out over a deep-set instrument panel.

The way it handles.
The Mustang's low silhouette and compact size make its handling as beautiful as its looks.
A smoother independent front suspension with anti-sway bar helps take the bumps of rough roads and the twist out of twisting turns.

Giving you decisive sporty-car handling with a comfortable passenger-car ride.

The way it feels.
The feeling of control and balance you get from driving a Mustang adds up to a statement of personal style. Like when you do something very well, and know exactly how you did it.
It's a very different experience.
You can ask any of the 1½ million people who own a Mustang. Or you can find out for yourself. At your Ford Dealer's.

FORD MUSTANG
FORD DIVISION

One More Time

Mustang remained its hefty self for 1973, but sales somehow picked up to nearly 135,000. The convertible, now the only one in the Ford line, soared a resounding 85 percent to 11,853 units, perhaps because Ford announced that it would not return the following year. As we know, the ragtop Mustang would be back, but not for another decade.

Washington now required front bumpers to sustain low-speed shunts without damage. Though Ford and other automakers met the rule with some pretty awful-looking cowcatchers, Mustang fared quite well, as body-color bumpers were now standard for all models and stuck out only a little more. The bumpers absorbed energy through an I-beam mounting bar with a box-section bracket attached to two longitudinal rubber blocks that gave way on impact, then bounced back to original position.

Elsewhere, base models and the Grande got a grille insert with larger eggcrates, and parking lights on all '73s migrated from beneath the bumper to within the grille, where they were stood on end to resemble running lamps. The usual trim shuffles occurred, and Grabber colors were dropped in favor of quieter "Ember Glow" metallics. The Sprint package was forgotten, but base models could now mimic Mach 1 via an optional Decor Group ($51) and,

Though most engines lost a few more horses for '73, Mustang could still be dressed to thrill. This convertible sports two options offered that year: polished aluminum wheels and Mach-style twin-scoop hood. A useful Intrumentation Group (above) was still available.

for the first time, a twin-scoop hood. Two-tone hood paint in matte-finish black or silver was again sold separately ($35). A functional ram-air hood remained optional with the 2V 351 only (at $58). Steel-belted radial tires joined the options list, where snazzy polished aluminum wheels ($111–$142) replaced the familiar styled-steel Magnum 500s. Fastbacks now offered an optional vinyl covering for the front ¾ of the roof ($52). The Mach 1 got a revised honeycomb grille texture and new lower-body striping. The uptown Grande hardtop now included a useful parking-brake warning light. As it had since '71, the Grande came with a "halo" vinyl roof, so-called because the covering left a slim band of body color around the side windows.

To meet new limits on oxides of nitrogen (NOx), all '73 Mustang engines got a revamped emissions-control system with positive crankcase ventilation and exhaust-gas recirculation. The EGR routed gases from the exhaust manifold through a vacuum valve into the carburetor to be diluted by the incoming fuel/air mixture. This permitted leaner carburetor settings but also diminished horsepower except on the 302 V-8 and 250 six. The 2V 351 sunk to 173 net bhp, the four-barrel version to 259. As noted earlier, the HO got the heave-ho, a victim of weak demand and too much required finagling to satisfy the federal air marshals. Equally disheartening, four-speed manual was now limited to the 4V 351, and automatic was mandatory with the 2V unit (though most buyers ordered that anyway).

In other technical news for '73, power front-disc brakes were newly standard with either 351 V-8 and for all convertibles, and both disc and drum brakes were enlarged for cars without power assist. Interiors adopted flame-retardant materials to meet a gruesome new federal "burn rate" standard (four inches per minute), and some hardware was redesigned to be less injurious.

Prices went up a bit for '73. With six-cylinder engine the hardtop started at $2760, the fastback at $2820, the ragtop at $3102, Grande at $2946, and Mach 1 at $3088. Mach excepted, the 302 V-8 added $87.

Time to Start Over

Thus endeth "Bunkie's Mustang, the one that looked like it hit the wall," as Ford marketing exec Hal Sperlich derisively termed it. Knudsen, of course, was long gone by 1973, but many in Dearborn were still mighty unhappy with the Mustang he left behind. Said design vice-president Eugene Bordinat: "We started out with a secretary car and all of a sudden we had a behemoth." Lee Iacocca was even more displeased. "I've said it a hundred times and I'll say it again. The Mustang market never left us, we left it," he declared years later. "If we hadn't gone nuts and put the Boss 429 engine in, the car never would have grown in size. That was what triggered it out of the small-car world—performance, performance, performance!"

But Mustang was about to rejoin the world of sensible sportiness, thanks to Iacocca's push for an entirely new car in the spirit of the original mid-Sixties blockbuster. Though this one would be no less contoversial in its way than the 1971–73 models, Iacocca's new brainchild, for better or worse, was going back to basics for a brave but battered new automotive world.

TOP AND ABOVE: New bodyside striping and a bolder honeycomb texture on the back panel, hood scoops, and grille were the main visual differences unique to the '73 Mach 1. BELOW: This period photo shows a '73 Mach 1 gunning through a wide turn at Ford's Dearborn Proving Ground. Though 1971–73 Mustangs are often critcized for excessive nose-plowing understeer, especially in tight corners, sportier models like the Mach 1 could be reasonably agile for their size and heft.

Chapter Six:

1974-1978

With Lee Iacocca back in the saddle, Ford's ponycar revisited its roots. A dramatically smaller, lighter design marked a fresh start for Mustang and a refreshing return to rationality. Iacocca just knew the market was ready for Mustang II, but even he couldn't have wished for better timing with the car he conceived as a "little jewel."

Success often stems as much from common sense and dumb luck as from cleverness and hard work. The Mustang II is a case in point. As the smallest, lightest Mustang since the original, it was a fresh start for Ford's ponycar and a refreshing return to rationality. And it couldn't have been better timed, introduced just two months before the first "Energy Crisis" upended America. People came in droves to see the Mustang II—and to buy. First-year unit sales were a smashing 385,993, within 10 percent of the original Mustang's 12-month production record of 418,812. Of course, the Mustang II was in the works long before the Organization of Petroleum Exporting Countries (OPEC) decided to squeeze world oil supplies. That it appeared at virtually the same time was mere coincidence, though a lucky break for Ford.

In several ways, the Mustang II shows how history repeats itself in the automotive world. For starters, Lee Iacocca just knew the market was ready for it in the same way he suspected the original Mustang was the right car for its time. As we've seen, ponycars were falling from favor by 1970, with many buyers turning to lower-priced, fuel-efficient compacts like Ford's own Maverick—a huge first-year success itself. But Americans were also turning *on* to sporty 2+2 import coupes like Ford's own British/German Capri, which bowed in April 1970 to good reviews and strong initial demand. Another "captive import," GM's German-built Opel Manta, was selling well, and the Toyota Celica was more popular still. In 1965 such "mini-ponycars" attracted fewer than 100,000 sales, but by 1972 were up to around 300,000—and expected to go above 400,000 by '74. Mustang II's mission was to capture a big slice of this sizable new pie.

Ford design v-p Eugene Bordinat gave full credit to Iacocca for the Mustang II: "[He] was the first guy to come along [at Ford] who had the feeling for cars that had existed in General Motors for some time." For his part, Iacocca observed: "When I look at the foreign-car market and see that one in five is a sporty car, I know something's happening. Look at what the Celica started to do before the two devaluations [of the dollar] nailed it! Anyone who decides to sit this out just ain't gonna dance!"

But Ford didn't start out to start over. The Mustang II program actually dates from around the middle of 1969, when work began on what was then simply the next Mustang. With muscle-car mania still raging, first thoughts inevitably centered on larger, heavier-looking designs, reflecting Ford's belief that buyers would still want roomy, "impressive" ponycars in the mid-Seventies. In fact, early proposals were even more hulking than the '71 Mustang then nearing completion. But by the time Iacocca became Ford Motor Company president in 1970, the bottom had dropped out of the ponycar market, and the imported Capri—which Iacocca said was more like the original "than any Mustang we have today"—was doing solid business at Lincoln-Mercury dealers.

Iacocca had never liked Bunkie Knudsen's '71 Mustang, and it wasn't just because the man who backed it had been favored with the president's chair. Iacocca had been troubled by Mustang's course since 1966. He wasn't alone. As author Gary Witzenburg related, the grumbling had been going on at least since 1968. At that year's stockholders meeting, one Anna Muccioli, who owned a '65 Mustang, rose to ask Henry Ford II: "Why can't you just leave a small car small?...[Y]ou keep blowing them up and starting another little one, blow that one up and start another one...[W]hy don't you just leave them?" To her likely surprise, the chairman said he agreed. "Hopefully we will keep in mind what you say here and, hopefully, we will have a product that will be satisfactory to you."

Thinking Small

In November 1969, less than two months after HF II fired Knudsen, Iacocca voiced his own concerns to a group of top-level Ford executives at the toney Greenbrier Resort in West Virginia. According to Witzenburg, this meeting quickly led to "top-priority plans to build a new sporty small car for the 1974 model year based on...the Maverick shell. A second program, codenamed 'Arizona,' was to investigate an upmarket variation on the upcoming '71 Pinto subcompact for 1975."

Both programs were turned over to Nat Adamson, manager of advanced product planning, who recalled that the Maverick-based car, code named "Ohio," was initially favored. "[The

Maverick] then seemed like a very small car to us," he told Witzenburg, "especially when we compared it to that year's much bigger and longer Mustang. And the Maverick was selling very well at the time." But the smaller Arizona got priority when three concept models "tested" well against contemporary sports cars in two Southern California consumer showings. It was the first sign the public might go for something even smaller than the original Mustang. But neither of these programs produced anything that satisfied Iacocca, Bordinat, or Advanced Design chief Don DeLaRossa. Ohio proposals ended up blowsy and staid, while initial Arizona designs looked like the restyled Pintos they were.

An Assist From Ghia

But then, in November 1970, Ford acquired a controlling interest in Ghia of Italy, and Iacocca wasted no time in asking the famed coachbuilder to submit concepts for his new small sporty car. With typical dispatch, Ghia sent over a running prototype in just 53 days, a sloped-nose red-and-black fastback that Iacocca himself drove to and from work. It greatly accelerated the drive toward the eventual Mustang II. "Aside from the new slant on styling that it gave us," Iacocca said later, "the quick delivery of that real, live, driveable sample...coalesced our thinking and gave us something tangible to look at and argue about early in the game, an experience that I had never had before in my career in the company.... It was a great early boost for the whole program." Several months later, Ghia offered a second running prototype, a trim notchback with an airy "pagoda" roof *a la* Mercedes SL and bodyside sculpturing like that of the first Mustang. This, too, would stimulate Dearborn design thinking.

Raising Arizona

Around July 1971, management decided to abandon the Ohio car and moved up Adamson's preferred Arizona to 1974. These were key decisions, because they effectively ruled out using Ford's long-serving straight-six. Bordinat recalled that DeLaRossa "put his studio to work on a clay model showing how big the Mustang would have to be to accommodate that big I-6 engine. He got me to call Lee over for a look at it. Don became, shall we say, very forthright and told Lee that if we really wanted to make a smaller car, we had better start with a smaller engine because this one with this engine in it was getting bigger even before it was designed. Lee agreed with us and that was the end of the I-6. The next thing we heard was that the choice of engines would be a new small 2.3-liter four-cylinder and a larger-displacement version of the German Capri V-6, so we were able to get down to making the rest of the car smaller too."

Still, there was no early consensus on how *much* smaller the new Mustang should be, though it obviously had to shrink from 1971–73 size. There was also debate over whether to offer a notchback, a fastback, or a blend of both. In another echo of the original Mustang program, Iacocca staged an intramural design competition to get things rolling. "Lee thinks that pitting our guys against each other breeds our best stuff," Bordinat told Witzenburg. "I've tried to disagree with him, but every time we do it, we get an exceptionally good car." This contest, begun in August 1971 and ultimately lasting three months, pitted the Ford and L-M production studios against DeLaRossa's Advanced Design group and the Interior Studio under L. David Ash. Talk about "back to the future." Even many of the key players were the same as 10 years before.

OPPOSITE PAGE, TOP AND UPPER CENTER: Mustang II didn't start out as a much-smaller ponycar but as an even-bigger next Mustang. The program kicked off in mid-1969 amid "muscle car mania," so first thoughts like these were big and ultra-racy. LOWER CENTER AND BOTTOM: Workouts through mid-1970 continued to assume a large package a la 1971–73. THIS PAGE, RIGHT: This September 1970 proposal looks like a re-roofed version of the 1971–73 hardtop. BELOW: An October 1970 idea looked more mid-size than ponycar. Covered rear wheels would likely have been rejected as too impractical for most buyers.

"Little Jewel"

Once again, rival teams worked from an idea clearly defined by Iacocca: "The new Mustang must be small, with a wheelbase between 96 and 100 inches. It must be a sporty notchback and/or fastback coupe; the convertible is dead and can be forgotten. [He'd later think otherwise at Chrysler.] It must come as standard with a four-speed manual gearbox and a four-cylinder or small six-cylinder engine. Most important, it must be luxurious—upholstered in quality materials and carefully built." At one point, Iacocca declared "the 1974 Mustang will have to be…a little jewel."

According to Ben Bidwell, then chief program product planner (he became Ford Division general manager in 1973 and was later Chrysler president under Iacocca), high quality was a must for Ford's president: "He will be out there in the showroom and he'll run his finger around the molding, and if it so much as scrapes him, some poor son of a gun will get it."

Of course, Iacocca also took a keen interest in Mustang II styling. As corporate planning chief Hal Sperlich recalled: "He was planning an entirely new kind of domestic car for a different kind of customer, so naturally he wanted it to look different from other cars on the market; different from the Mustangs of 1971, 1972, and 1973; different from the Pinto and different from the Capri, too."

All this ultimately came down to a late-November management review of five full-size clay models, one notchback and four fastbacks. The easy winner was a fastback from the Lincoln-Mercury group under Al Mueller. Like Joe Oros before him, he painted his clay—in an eye-catching persimmon, not white—so it would stand out and improve his team's chances. As Mueller recalled for Witzenburg: "Mr. Iacocca's procedure at these showings usually is the same. He walks around the cars a few times and listens to the comments of others. Then he says exactly what he thinks—either pro or con. He really flipped over our fastback. His cigar must have rolled around three times."

But though surprisingly little altered for production, the design got mixed press reviews, and some critics felt that the notchback derived from it was a hodge-podge. The fastback was considered more handsome, though it wasn't a "classic" shape like the '65 Mustang. It was, however, more practical by dint of its European-style lift-up rear "door," a first for a Mustang and another boost for the popularity of hatchback body styles in America.

Two is Better Than One

The notchback almost didn't make it. The one such car at the November executive showing, submitted by DeLaRossa's troops, had been nicknamed "Anaheim" after it bombed at a September consumer clinic in Disneyland's hometown. But Iacocca, suspecting researchers had missed something, decided to give it one last chance at a San Francisco session in February 1972. Reaction was positive, so it was decided to do a "trunked" version of the approved fastback—this with barely 16 months left before production was scheduled to start. "It seems we go through that with every Mustang program," said Jack Telnack, who later replaced Bordinat as company design chief. "We always start with the fastback…. Then we find out the surveys still say fifty-fifty [preference] and we have to add the notchback."

DeLaRossa long maintained the Anaheim should have been chosen as the theme model. As he later told Witzenburg: "[If] we wanted to design a modern second generation of Mustangs, why not recapture some of the flavor of the famous original model of 1965? That was a notchback. The fastback Mustangs were offshoots that came in later." He could have added that the notchback had always outsold the fastback, something that may have occurred to Iacocca too. In any case, Iacocca certainly knew the

BELOW: June 1969 "Apex" was one the earliest attempts at a downsized Mustang. OPPOSITE PAGE, TOP: Italian coachbuilder Ghia submitted two prototypes that helped focus Ford designers. This later model revived Mustang's original bodyside sculpturing. CENTER: Trim "Anaheim" convinced Iacocca to offer a notchback as well as a fastback. BOTTOM: This September 1971 fastback wasn't Ghia's, but showed Italian influence.

sales necessity of having two body types, and he'd liked the Anaheim from the first, though maybe not as much as the Mueller fastback. Interestingly, Ford also investigated a cut-down two-seat fastback in February '72, but it was never seriously in the running.

First-Class Cabin

Interior design was less debated, though no less involved. Forsaking usual design practice, studio chief Dave Ash decided to make his "seating buck" unusually realistic to convey a sense of being in a real automobile. He even attached exterior sheet-metal and four wheels. "It was a time-consuming thing to build," he said later, "but it served its purpose very well. We didn't have to go through an elaborate series of meetings to determine everything. It was all approved right here. We were on a crash basis to get it done, and it was very enthusiastically received."

Ash later confessed that his team was partly inspired by the likes of Jaguar, Rolls-Royce, and Mercedes. "We put everything in that we could conceive of that connotes restrained elegance, plus the get-up-and-go that says Mustang—something of a fire breather.... It's a kind of a mini T-Bird."

Unlike the massive, heavily sculptured twin-cowl instrument

panels of 1969–73, the Mustang II panel was dominated by a simple large oblong directly ahead of the driver. This put all controls close at hand, yet still had room for all necessary warning lights and instruments. Surprisingly, the latter included a standard tachometer, temperature gauge, and ammeter. Seats were initially covered in pleated cloth, vinyl, or optional leather—unusually plush for a small car. They had no rake adjustment, cited as a literal sore point by some road-testers, but were definitely more comfortable than previous Mustang seats. Rear legroom was limited, but the new car was seen as being used primarily by one or two adults who would sit in the front. Back-seat room would be sufficient only for a couple of small children or for an adult passenger to be comfortable for a short time. Another echo of Ford's first ponycar.

Ford PR paired a Mustang II with a '65 hardtop as the background for a series of press photos to drum up public interest ahead of the August 28, 1973, on-sale date. In the foreground here is Lee Iacocca, of course, looking somewhat low-key. However, he enthusiastically declared that the Mustang II would "turn the small-car market on its ear."

FORD MUSTANG II CAR SELECTOR

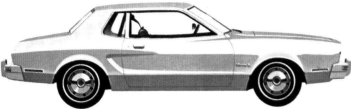
Mustang II Hardtop. Light Blue (Code 3B).

Mustang II 3-Door 2 + 2. Medium Yellow Gold (Code 6C).

Mustang II Ghia. Ginger Glow (Code 5J).

Mustang II Mach 1. Dark Red (Code 2M).

Ford Mustang II. A new class of small car: First Class.

TOP: Mustang II offered four basic models, shown here as pictured on the back cover of the 1974 sales brochure. ABOVE: Inside the catalog was this view of the posh Ghia notchback interior with its wood-tone dash accents and luxury carpeting and door trim. Iaccoca wanted every Mustang II to be a "little jewel," and ad types made sure buyers didn't miss premium small-car features like the standard tachometer, European-style pull-up central handbrake, and more comfortable, new-design bucket seats. RIGHT: Mustang II sales got a lucky boost from the OPEC oil embargo and resulting "gas crunch," so the headline here is quite truthful. Note new "cantering" horse logo alongside the Ghia notchback.

FORD MUSTANG II. The right car at the right time.

TOP AND CENTER: Mustang II styling came from a fastback theme model by the Lincoln-Mercury studio, which was little altered for production. "Mouthy" grille, C-shaped side sculpturing, and other elements linked the new mini-ponycar to the '65 original. Bumpers were now body-color front and rear. ABOVE: Sportiva II concept previewed the Mustang II at 1973 auto shows, but in a "targa" convertible style that would not see production. Iacocca had already nixed another ragtop Mustang.

Less Is More

Though it retained the signature long-hood/short-deck proportions, Mustang II was visibly smaller than the original. The real target was sporty import coupes. Against the '65 it was nearly six inches shorter in wheelbase (at 94.2 inches), 6.6 inches shorter overall (at 175.0), two inches slimmer (68.2), and 1.1 inches lower (49.9). There were dramatic differences against the 1971–73 models, the II being some 20 inches shorter overall, nearly 13 inches trimmer between wheel centers, four inches narrower, an inch lower, and—the important part—lighter by a whopping 400–500 pounds. The increasingly popular Toyota Celica had a 1.3-inch longer wheelbase than Mustang II but was 11.1 inches shorter, 5.2 inches slimmer, and 2.5 inches taller.

To prepare the public for Mustang II, Ford ran up a lightly disguised concept version as a 1973 auto-show attraction. Called Sportiva II, it was essentially the production car recast as a "targa" convertible, with a fixed rollover bar between removable roof sections. It would have been a great showroom lure, but the ragtop market had collapsed and Iacocca had ruled out a new open Mustang—another break with the past. This left a base-trim notchback and fastback, a sportier Mach 1 fastback, and a vinyl-topped Ghia coupe, replacing Grande as the luxury model. All were fixed-pillar styles, not pillarless designs. Fastbacks offered flip-out rear-quarter windows as a $29 option.

Not Just a Sporty Pinto

At announcement time, some observers suggested Mustang II was just a sportier Pinto. Of course, that *was* how it started. And sure enough, a good many components were shared. Even wheelbase was the same. But the Pinto was actually upgraded for '74 to take advantage of components and features designed for Mustang II. For example, both models employed unit construction—still another first for the ponycar—and shared a basic coil-spring front suspension with unequal-length upper and lower arms. For the Mustang, however, the lower arms as well as the drivetrain were cradled by a U-shaped rubber-mounted subframe; the Pinto's front suspension bolted directly to the main structure. The subframe, a brainstorm from program engineers Bob

Negstad and Jim Kennedy, greatly reduced road shock and drive-line vibration reaching the cabin. It also contibuted to more precise steering and a smoother ride vs. Pinto. Stingy company accountants approved the added expense in light of the Mustang's planned higher selling price. Witzenburg notes the "toilet seat" (as the subframe was known internally) "came to be regarded as the single most important component of the Mustang II chassis."

There were other differences, too. For example, Mustang II shared the Pinto's rack-and-pinion steering but mounted it differently, again to minimize shock, and offered optional power assist (which Pinto did not at the time). At the rear, Mustang leaf springs were two inches longer than Pinto's, and shock absorbers were staggered as in previous high-performance Mustangs. Spring rates were computer-calculated to match each particular car's equipment and weight. The Ghia notchback, for example, came with very soft settings, while the optional competition suspension had the stiffest springs, along with a thicker front antiroll bar, a rear bar, and Gabriel adjustable shock absorbers.

European Hearts

Per Iacocca's edict, engineers gave no thought to a V-8, yet another break with Mustang tradition—and something Ford would soon regret. Initial engine choices comprised a new 2.3-liter (140-cubic-inch) single-overhead-cam inline four and a 2.8-liter enlargement of the Capri's overhead-valve V-6. The four, sometimes called the "Lima" engine after the Lima, Ohio, plant that supplied it, was the first American-built engine designed to metric dimensions. That wasn't surprising. Originally slated for some of Ford's larger European cars, it was actually a bored-and-stroked version of the Pinto 2.0-liter. A novel feature was "monolithic engine timing." After each engine was assembled, an electronic device hooked to a computer was connected to two engine sensors, an indicator point at the rear of the crankshaft and an electrical terminal between the distributor and coil. The computer compared readings from each sensor, then set timing automatically by means of a distributor adjustment. The computer's high degree of precision made this technique very useful for meeting increasingly tough emission standards.

The V-6 was basically the same engine offered in U.S.-market Capris from 1972. It used the same camshaft, valvetrain, pushrods, and distributor as its European parent but was bored and stroked for American service, capacity increasing from 2.6 liters (155 cid) to 2.8 (171 cid). At the same time, Ford switched from siamesed to separate exhaust ports for improved performance and thermal efficiency. Supplied only with dual exhausts, the V-6 was optional for any Mustang II save the Mach 1 hatchback, where it was standard. Like early 2.0-liter Pinto fours, it was imported from Ford's West German subsidiary in Cologne.

The Mustang II's standard four-speed gearbox was basically

Don DeLaRossa: In his own words

After several years at GM, designer Don DeLaRossa jumped to Ford in 1947, where he spent the next decade working on numerous cars and other projects. By the early Sixties he headed the Corporate Advanced Studio that produced the first design proposals for what became the Mustang, including the now-famous Allegro and Stilletto design series. DeLaRossa also contributed to the later Mustang II program, then followed Lee Iaccoca to Chrysler in 1979. He retired 10 years later after establishing Chrysler's Pacifica design outpost in Southern California.

We had the original Mustang, and then we got into ruining it by getting it so overweight [for 1971–73]. Bunkie Knudsen and Larry Shinoda came in. They were competition-oriented people and really seemed to eat, sleep, and breathe big engines and bigger cars. So that was not a happy course for Mustang.

Then we finally started addressing the next generation, the Mustang II. I did a candidate design that came to be called "Anaheim" after the city in Southern California where some of the market research was done. When we started the Mustang II, I said to Lee Iacocca that we should not forget the original Mustang was a notchback—that was followed with a fastback—so let's not do a fastback first. Let's do the notchback first. My recollection is that that made sense to him. So I got to work on a notchback right away at Ghia, and a version of it in Dearborn.

When Lee saw the "Anaheim" he said to me, "It's terrific, but it doesn't have enough 'Mustang' in it. It's almost like it's too modern, too much of a departure." And much to my chagrin, there was a young designer, Fritz Mayhew, who embarks on doing a fastback. It was very attractive. And damned if Lee didn't buy it. A 180 degrees from what we had talked about. So then all hell broke loose trying to make a notchback out of that car. There was no way, and that accounts for the strange look of the Mustang II notchback. It never looked right. The C-pillar looked like a tree trunk growing out of the quarter panel.

The Mustang II was a mild success and just hung around. I had trouble adjusting to that. I think the car I did would have been gangbusters, but that's life in the creative business.

the four-speed unit from the British Ford Cortina as used in the Pinto but strengthened to handle the Mustang's more powerful engines. Of course, SelectShift Cruise-O-Matic was available (at $212). Brakes were usefully upgraded to standard 9.3-inch front discs and 9 × 1.75-inch rear drums.

American Soul

Predictably, most Mustang IIs exhibited "American" ride and handling characteristics. The Mach 1 was both more capable and entertaining with its standard V-6 ($299 extra on other models), but no '74 Mustang II was Sixties speedy. The car was heavy for its size (curb weight was a porky 2650–2900 pounds), so a V-6 with four-speed would do 0–60 mph in a lackluster 13–14 sec-

onds and reach only about 100 mph, a far cry from the Boss and big-block days. As if to signal the reduced performance, the trademark running-horse emblem became a less muscular steed that seemed to be cantering. It was created by interior designer Charles Keresztes, inspired by the work of noted Western artist Frederic Remington.

Early Miscue

Despite its terrific first-year sales (and winning *Motor Trend*'s 1974 "Car of the Year" award), the Mustang II wasn't an instant hit. With the economy still beset by "stagflation," early buyers favored low-priced models with few frills, whereas Ford production planning had assumed just the opposite.

OPPOSITE PAGE, TOP: As usually happens in the car business, Ford considered additional Mustang II models and trim variations after the car was launched. This late-1974 study envisioned a luxury fastback with Ghia-level appointments, rear-quarter "opera" windows, and vinyl roof, but the idea was rejected. OPPOSITE PAGE, BOTTOM: Grilles on all '75 models wore large eggcrates, a change made partly to accommodate that year's revived 302 V-8 option. Luxury Ghias added slim "opera" windows, as shown here. THIS PAGE: Small front-fender emblems identified V-8-equipped cars like this lovingly maintained Mach 1.

ABOVE AND LEFT: Purists blanched when Ford added the Shelby-like Cobra II package for '76 fastbacks, but the option proved quite popular even though it did nothing for acceleration. BELOW LEFT: Neither did the Stallion package, another new '76 dressup kit, but it, too, arguably made the fastback look faster. BELOW RIGHT: Open-air fiends welcomed a T-top roof with twin liftout glass panels as a new 1977 option.

Demand picked up pace once the oil embargo hit and long lines formed at gas pumps. Ford fast adjusted the model mix, but some sales were probably lost anyway because Mustang II looked to some people like less car for more money.

More for Less?

The price escalation was certainly dramatic, even allowing for the "little jewel's" extra standard equipment. The base coupe started the year at $3081, up $321 from its '73 counterpart—

which came with a six-cylinder engine, not a four. The fastback was up $455 to $3275, the $3427 Ghia was $481 costlier than the last Grande, and the V-6 Mach 1, at $3621, was up $533 from its V-8 predecessor. Though prices would go even higher, sales held up quite well through end-of-the-line '78.

Options were fewer than in recent years, but more than sufficient. Besides air conditioning ($383) and various radios and tape players, the '74 list showed power steering ($106), power brakes ($45), tilt/takeout sunroof ($149), antitheft alarm ($75), console

Trim options aside, Mustang II styling was unchanged after 1974. This well-cared-for Mach 1 wears non-stock driving lights ahead of a Cobra II-style front airdam. Factory options here include the desriable 302 V-8 and the Rally Performance Package with raised-white-letter tires on styled-steel wheels, plus three-spoke sports steering wheel and brushed-aluminum dashboard accents. By this time, all fastbacks came with a fold-down rear seat, which enhanced the cargo room and carrying versatility of the practical hatchback body style.

($43), electric rear-window defroster ($59), rocker-panel trim, protective bodyside moldings, fold-down rear seat ($61), and "Glamour Paint." A $100 Luxury Interior Group for base cars and Mach 1 delivered most of the Ghia's upscale appointments; its extra noise insulation was available for other models in a "Super Sound" package ($22). All models offered a Convenience Group (dual door mirrors and such), a Light Group (courtesy lamps and extra warning lights), and a new Maintenance Group ($44) with a shop manual, basic tools, fire extinguisher, and other items for roadside emergencies. Tempting enthusiasts were Traction-Lok differential ($45) and the comp suspension (only $37) with adjustable shock absorbers, wider tires, and rear antiroll bar. These items were also part of a V-6 Rallye Package along with heavy-duty cooling, chrome exhaust tips, raised-white-letter tires on styled-steel wheels, twin remote-adjustable door mirrors, leather-rim steering wheel, and quartz digital clock.

The V-8 Returns

For 1975, the Ghia added a flip-up glass "moonroof" ($422) and a $151 Silver Luxury Group with cranberry-color crushed-velour upholstery, silver paint, matching half-vinyl top, and standup hood ornament. At the same time, Ghia rear-quarter glass was abbreviated into "opera" windows, a popular luxury-car styling fad of the day. A fold-down rear seat was now standard for fastbacks, and cast-aluminum wheels and steel-belted radial tires were newly optional across the board. So was an "extended-range" (17-gallon) fuel tank ($18), a tacit admission that even these radically "downsized" Mustangs were rather thirsty. Mid-model year brought partial relief in a special "MPG" notchback and fastback with catalytic converter, which eliminated the need for some add-on emissions hardware and allowed engine retuning for better mileage and driveability. The MPG models then vanished, though not their "cat con."

But the big news for '75 was the return of V-8 power, answering customer pleas for more performance. Optional through '78, this was, of course, the familiar small-block 302, initially tuned for 122 net horsepower, then 139. Unlike many second-year updates, this one was quite involved. As product development v-p Harold McDonald told historian Witzenburg: "We had a very difficult time…because there hadn't been provision made for [a V-8]…The hood had to be much longer and a half-inch higher for clearance, we had to change the radiator support and move the radiator forward three inches, change things along the firewall, beef up [the frame] and mount the engine differently…but we didn't have to move the tread or change suspension mounting points." However, springs, brakes and other components were beefed up to handle the heavier V-8, and all models regardless of engine wore larger grille eggcrates.

Mustang II Meets Monza

Others were bound to follow Ford's lead, and Mustang II got new competition for 1975 in Chevy's Monza 2+2, a sporty version of the bow-tie brand's subcompact Vega. Monza's optional 4.3-liter (262-cid) V-8 looked no match for Mustang's "5.0," and in straightline acceleration it wasn't. Yet after a two-car shootout, *Road & Track* recommended the Chevy for its fresh, Ferrari-like styling and comfort, ride, handling, and fuel economy that were all judged superior to the Ford's. A year earlier, reporting on a four-speed Mach 1, *R&T* said "it would be unrealistic to expect

Cobra II cosmetics changed a bit during the 1977 model run, as a small chrome snake was added to each rear side window and the nonfunctional hood air scoop was reshaped. Though dorsal racing stripes now cost extra, the package price was hiked $220 to $535. Cobra IIs were converted by contractor Motortown at its small plant near the Dearborn Mustang factory. Note T-top roof on this "late" '77.

Ford of Dearborn to produce a European-type sporty car. Instead they've come up with a distinctively American interpretation of a sporty compact…[T]he car's great weight and poor balance make some [functional] options virtually necessary…[But] if you're not bothered by such considerations, [Mustang II] is solid, well-built, quiet and plush—and not at all unpleasant to drive…as long as you don't ask too much of it."

Though gas started flowing freely again in March 1974, a slow economic recovery depressed auto sales into model-year '75. Mustang II was not immune, volume dropping over 50 percent to 188,575. Yet even that was far more encouraging—and profitable—than the tepid pace of 1971–73.

With Mustang II styling so little changed each year, marketers increasingly pushed for new paint-and-tape options to keep customers interested. These Ford Design "record" photos show a sample of ideas considered for 1977, including a tamer "Stallion II" package (lower right) and a rather gaudy multi-hued treatment (below). None of these made the cut, however, partly because many outside "aftermarket" companies were already offering similar dressup kits to Ford dealers, many of whom eagerly snapped them up as easy profit-boosters.

Shelby Spirit

Deliveries totaled 187,567 for bicentennial '76, which introduced a trim option evoking the late, great Shelby-Mustangs. Called "Cobra II" and available for fastbacks only, it was suggested by Jim Wangers, the advertising whiz who'd helped create the legendary GTO for Pontiac in the early Sixties. Wangers sold Ford on the Cobra II idea with the understanding that a company he owned, Motortown, would manufacture most of the package's styling add-ons and install them at its small plant near the Dearborn Mustang factory.

The Cobra II debuted as a $325 option, but another $287 was required for a "Cobra II modification package" to ready the stock fastback for all kinds of extra stuff. Immediately apparent were louvered covers on the rear-quarter-windows, a front air dam, a rear spoiler, and a simulated hood air scoop. Also included were a "blackout" grille, styled-steel wheels with trim rings and radial tires, and bold model i.d. Broad Shelby-style racing stripes were applied to the hood, roof, trunklid, and rocker panels in either blue against white paint or gold over black. Other color combina-

The somewhat surprising popularity of the Cobra II package prompted Ford itself to offer an even more arresting option for 1978. Though arguably over the top, the King Cobra wasn't entirely for show, as the 302 V-8 and handling-oriented suspension were included in the $1253 asking price. A giant snake decal on the hood seemed rather "Seventies pyschedelic," but interior decor (left) was tasteful and included aluminum accents, console, and sports steering wheel.

tions were added for '77. The interior was spruced up with a sports steering wheel and brushed-aluminum accents, plus dual remote-control door mirrors. Purists laughed at the Cobra II, especially with the stock four-cylinder engine, but Witzenburg observed that "properly equipped, the thing actually performed pretty well by 1976 standards." Incidentally, the option was available for the Mach 1 as well as the base fastback, making a car so equipped a Mustang II Mach 1 Cobra II.

Nobody laughed when road racer Charlie Kemp ran a wildly modified fastback in the International Motor Sports Association (IMSA) GT class during 1976. Though far from stock and not blessed by Ford, it looked enough like a Cobra II to cheer Blue Oval partisans. Unhappily for them, Kemp's car was competitvely fast but unreliable and often ended up in the DNF (did not finish) column. It scored no victories in one of the Mustang II's few attempts at competition.

No less subtle than the Cobra II was the Stallion, another all-show/no-go 1976 package that was also offered (in slightly different forms) for that year's Pintos and Mavericks. Again restricted to fastbacks, it delivered acres of black paint on hood and roof, silver elsewhere, and forged-aluminum wheels, all set off by snorting horse's-head front-fender decals. One other bit of '76 news involved the Ghia moonroof, which was now optional for other models and with either silver or brown tint.

For 1977 came a Ghia "Sports Appearance Group" keyed to black or tan paint. This featured many color-keyed items including console, three-spoke sports steering wheel, cast-aluminum wheels with chamois-color spokes, and a trunk luggage rack with hold-down straps and bright buckles. All models now offered optional "lacy spoke" aluminum wheels in chrome or with white-painted spokes and red trim rings. A Corvette-style T-top roof with twin lift-off glass panels arrived as a fastback option. Two-toning was now available on most models. But all this was just gilding a familiar lily, and Mustang II model-year sales skidded to 153,173 units. Another 8481 were built to '77 specs but sold as "interim" '78s to get around a temporary emissions-related regulatory snag.

All Hail the King Cobra

Ford apparently didn't track Cobra II installations, and in retrospect the package symbolizes the dreary "paint-on performance" that was about all Detroit could offer in the Seventies. Even so, the Cobra II proved quite popular and was continued. Moreover, its success prompted Gene Bordinat to set his designers working on an even more hard-core fastback package. It arrived with the "real" '78s as—what else?—the King Cobra. Priced at $1253, the ensemble put a huge snake decal on the hood and tape stripes on the roof, rear deck, rocker panels and A-pillars, around the wheel wells, and on the standard front air dam. "King Cobra" was writ large on each door, the air dam, and a standard rear spoiler. Grille, window moldings, headlamp bezels, and wiper arms all got the "blackout" treatment, while the dash got another dose of brushed-aluminum trim. Happily, Ford also threw in the 302 V-8, plus power steering, the handling-oriented Rallye Package, and Goodrich 70-series T/A radial tires. It was only fair, given all that bold advertising. The result was eye-catching if nothing else. The typical King needed about 17 seconds in the standing quarter-mile, hardly "high performance" in the traditional sense, but about as hot as you could get at the time.

TOP: Road racer Charlie Kemp ran this much-modified Mustang II in the IMSA GT series during 1976. The car was fast when healthy but often didn't finish and scored no victories. Still, it gave Ford racing fans something to cheer for the first time since 1970. ABOVE: Jim Wangers, who'd sold Ford on the Cobra II option, proposed this "IMSA Cobra" for 1978. Patterned on the Kemp IMSA racer, it was even wilder than the King Cobra (note the bulged fenders). Ford, however, said no thanks.

The King Cobra was chosen over an "IMSA Cobra" package suggested by Wangers and patterned on the Charlie Kemp racer. Instead, Ford added a stealthy $163 Rallye Appearance Package that adorned fastbacks with gold accents against black paint, plus color-coordinated cloth upholstery.

All '78s benefited from a standard electronic voltage regulator and, with optional power steering, variable-ratio gearing (replacing fixed-ratio). The Ghia adopted "Wilshire" cloth seating. A new Fashion Accessory Package spruced-up the standard notchback by adding door pockets, striped fabric upholstery, lighted vanity mirror, and four-way manual driver's seat, all clearly aimed at women buyers. Fortunately, such sexist appeals were on the way out. Otherwise, 1978 was a quiet year for Mustang II. It was also the last, yet sales jumped to 192,410, helped by an economy now fully recovered from the gas crunch.

Despite its popularity when new, the Mustang II has few fans today. Its styling has not aged gracefully, and many find its "less ponycar" nature an unhappy reminder of an unhappy era for American automobiles. But the Mustang II kept the ponycar spirit alive in the face of those very rough times, thus paving the way for even better Mustangs. That's no small achievement and reason enough to respect Iacocca's "little jewel."

Chapter Seven:
1979-1981

Mustang began a second revolution with the handsome, sophisticated "New Breed" of 1979. It was clearly a new kind of Ford ponycar, yet in its sporty elegance and affordable versatility, it was every inch a Mustang, as appealing for its time as the original was for the Sixties. Not surprisingly, it scored big on the sales chart—and in the hearts of car lovers everywhere.

Ford marketers had put a Roman numeral on the Mustang II to emphasize just how different it was from previous Mustangs. For the same reason, they removed the suffix for the new 1979 generation—*and* plunked on a running horse that looked more like its muscular old self.

The car attached to it looked nothing like any Mustang before. Clean, taut, and crisp, it combined the best of American and European design thinking, yet had a uniquely "Mustang" kind of sporty elegance. Admittedly, some old shortcomings remained: problematic handling, a less-than-ideal driving position, limited passenger room, and workmanship that didn't compare well with that of European and Japanese cars like the BMW 3-Series and Toyota Celica. But no car can be faultless, especially one so affordable. By almost any standard, the '79 Mustang marked a second revolution for Ford's ponycar.

This basic design would be good enough to continue without fundamental change for no less than 14 years, an eternity in the auto business. Even more remarkable, a subsequent retooling enabled it to ride on another 11 years—and outsell its two remaining rivals along the way. By 2003, Ford again had America's only ponycar...but we're getting ahead of ourselves.

Dearborn Changes Course

The '79 Mustang was the result of a bold decision taken a good six years earlier. Even before the Middle East oil embargo, Detroit began to realize that many of its cars had simply grown too big. With Washington's endless stream of safety and emissions rules, the Big Three began to wonder if fuel-economy standards wouldn't be next. Indeed, April 1973 ushered in a new mandate for vehicle window stickers showing mileage figures for city and highway driving as calculated by the recently established Environmental Protection Agency (EPA). The numbers weren't very accurate at first, but the implication was clear. Then the gas crunch hit. "Almost overnight," records historian Gary Witzenburg, "fuel-efficient cars were in and gas-hogs were out, maybe forever as far as anyone knew, and Detroit wasted little time in formulating future plans for a newly fuel-conscious America."

As it happened, General Motors was already planning to "downsize" its cars, starting with 1977 full-size models. Chrysler, with far less capital, would bank on updating its popular compacts and offering smaller "captive imports" from overseas partners. Ford had different ideas. In public at least, chairman Henry Ford II staunchly defended tradition. The gas crunch was an aberration, he said. Once it passed, most Americans would again want big cars with big engines and "road-hugging weight," just as they always had. He was right—to a point. The oil embargo *was* short-lived, and much of the public *did* swing back to big size and power. Unfortunately, the oil barons would deliver another shock even as the '79 Mustang was reaching showrooms.

Enter The Fox

Yet even as HFII promised to push the latest economy imports "back into the sea," his company was embarking on a bold new project intended to serve fuel efficiency in the United States and save big bucks on a global basis. Code named Fox, it was initiated in early 1973 with the aim of devising a single foundation or "platform" suitable for a variety of future Ford models in the U.S., Europe, Latin America, even Australia. The idea was "a new corporate worldwide sport/family four/five-passenger sedan" with "imaginative packaging and component application," plus adaptability to both rear-wheel drive and the space-saving front-wheel-drive powerteams long familiar in Europe. In October 1974, project responsibility was shifted from Ford's Production Planning and Research office to the Product Development Group at North American Automotive Operations in Dearborn. Two months later, company president Lee Iacocca green-lighted a 1978 Fox-based replacement for either the little Pinto or the compact Maverick—and a new Mustang for 1979 or later. Though a "world car" was soon deemed incapable of satisfying the diverse needs of Ford's many global markets, the Maverick-replacing Fairmont and the new Mustang were in the works by April 1975, now with top-priority status in the wake of the oil embargo. Per recent Dearborn practice, each would have a Mercury sister, respectively the Zephyr and a new domestically built Capri.

Mustang First

The key thing, as Witzenburg notes, is that Fox development "was tailored around the Mustang's needs as a sporty, agile, European-style product...." He then quoted Gordon Riggs, planning manager for light and midsize cars, who was put in charge of the overall effort on special assignment: "We said, okay, we're going to have a series of cars off of a platform as yet undefined, and what should that platform be? We decided first-off that it was going to be a sporty platform, because we knew the focal point of it was really Mustang. Anything we did...to help the Mustang would probably benefit any other car we took off of it. It was not planned just for the Mustang, but the whole platform was designed to accommodate it."

Though the mass-market Fairmont/Zephyr would bow a year ahead of Mustang, designers initially worked on both models

more or less together under light-car design chief Fritz Mayhew and corporate design vice-president Gene Bordinat. Because Mustang was first seen as mainly just a sporty Fairmont, early proposals were sedan-like and slab-sided, not very "Mustang" at all. But April 1975 also ushered Jack Telnack into the program after a tour of duty as design v-p for Ford Europe. From his new post as executive director for North American Light Car and Truck Design, he would soon put his stamp on the emerging ponycar.

ABOVE: A sampling of early "concept" sketches by Fritz Mayhew that pointed the way toward 1979 Mustang styling. Note the persistent use of low slim noses tapered sharply down from the windshield, plus glassy rooflines and traditional long-hood/short-deck proportions. BELOW: A clay model from very early in the program shows a roofline perhaps inspired by that of Chevy's soon-to-appear 1975 Monza 2+2.

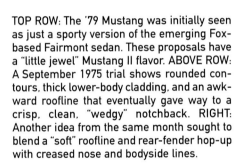

TOP ROW: The '79 Mustang was initially seen as just a sporty version of the emerging Fox-based Fairmont sedan. These proposals have a "little jewel" Mustang II flavor. ABOVE ROW: A September 1975 trial shows rounded contours, thick lower-body cladding, and an awkward roofline that eventually gave way to a crisp, clean, "wedgy" notchback. RIGHT: Another idea from the same month sought to blend a "soft" roofline and rear-fender hop-up with creased nose and bodyside lines.

Another Styling Showdown

But not before another of Iacocca's intramural design contests. This one pitted Advanced Design and two other Dearborn studios against Ford's Ghia operation in Italy, where Don DeLaRossa was now in charge. All were given the same package parameters or "hard points" including length, width, wheelbase, and cowl height as the basis for sketches, clay models, and fiberglass mockups. This time, however, quarter-scale clay models were tested for up to 136 hours in wind tunnels. That's because aerodynamics was increasingly recognized—actually rediscovered from the lessons of Thirties streamlining—as crucial to maximizing fuel economy, a key program goal. That, in turn, meant engineering with a keen eye on weight.

In addition, the program aimed at improved space-efficiency—meaning more interior room for a given external size—plus lower manufacturing costs through careful engineering and maximum component sharing among the various Fox-based models. Planners said the platform could be shortened somewhat for Mustang, and it was: by 5.1 inches in wheelbase, to 100.4. Mustang II engines—2.3-liter overhead-cam four, 2.8-liter over-

head-valve V-6 and 5.0-liter/302-cubic-inch V-8—would be retained. Recalling 1965, curb weight was pegged at a comparatively lean 2700 pounds. The interior would be larger than Mustang II's but still planned for comfortable seating in front and "occasional" seating in back for children or smaller adults.

Like the original Mustang but unlike the II, stylists were directed to do a notchback first, then a fastback version of it. After reviewing several full-size fiberglass models, management chose the distinctive offering from Telnack's group. Remarkably, the only changes made for production were substituting an eggcrate grille insert and adding simulated louvers behind the rear side windows. The fastback ended up with a vestigial rear deck instead of a full-sweep roofline. This shortened the hatch to reduce maximum opening height and make it easier to pull down.

Besides Mayhew and Telnack himself, the winning team included pre-production-design executive David Rees and pre-production designer Gary Haas. The shape they evolved was a subtle wedge: slim in front, with the hood sharply tapered from a rather high cowl—actually an inch taller than that of the Fairmont/Zephyr.

ABOVE: Many '79 Mustang mockups wore "7X" i.d. in Design Center record photos. Here, a trial fastback and a Mustang II lead a parade of proposals for what was likely an unrelated small-car program (note production Pinto behind proposed Mustang). The venue was Ford's Dearborn Proving Grounds. LEFT: Yet another September 1975 mockup shows the basic form and feel of the eventual '79 notchback.

Breaking the Rules

"We were supposed to hold the Fairmont cowl...and radiator support," Telnack told Witzenburg, "which really stiffened the hood...made it much straighter. Bob Alexander was in charge of engineering at the time, and he had just come back from Europe, too. We had a lot of people who had just come back from Europe and who had a different feel for this type of car. [We decided] to pivot the hood around the air cleaner and actually raise the cowl to get the front end down. No Detroit designer ever asks to make anything higher, but we felt it was important aerodynamically to get the nose down lower. Of course, this would require a new radiator support [and inner fender aprons] but Gene Bordinat said to go ahead and try it."

Though all this added a sizable $1.4 million to total program cost, all involved agreed it was justified. Witzenburg noted another advantage of Telnack's change: Drivers could see four-feet closer to the nose than in a Mustang II. Also helping "aero"—and looks—were a modest lip on decklids, a curved rear window on the notchback, a small spoiler built into front bumpers, and Mustang's first rectangular headlights (newly allowed by Washington), a quartet that also helped slim the nose.

Out with the Old

"Normally we get the package hard points and adhere to them," Telnack recalled, "but we weren't accepting anything on this car as gospel." That included traditional Mustang styling signatures like the galloping grille pony and C-shaped side sculpturing. The latter was abandoned for smooth, slightly curved sides, while the horse was maintained in a small "pony tricolor" logo for a circular hood medallion just above the grille. "Jack really wanted this car to have the impact of the original Mustang," said Fritz Mayhew, "so we [tried] to do a car that would look as different on the road as the original had. We felt, as management obviously did, that it was time for a change. We had done about as much as we could with those [1964] design cues."

Lower Cd = More MPG

The applied rear-roof slats hindered over-the-shoulder vision, but they weren't Telnack's idea. Indeed, he directed his team to always be mindful of the "form follows function" ideal. "We want-

As with past Mustangs, '79 styling was chosen from proposals submitted by competing teams—three in Dearborn, plus the Ford-owned Ghia studio in Italy. Each group had its own ideas, but all worked from the same set of "hard points," most of which reflected the planned sharing of chassis and some inner structure with the new compact Fairmont sedans and wagon. These workouts highlight various lines of thinking as of February 1976.

ed to be as aerodynamically correct as possible before getting into the wind tunnel. In the past we have designed cars and then gone into the tunnel mainly for tuning the major surfaces that have been approved....With the Mustang, the designers were thinking about aerodynamics in the initial sketch stages, which made the tuning job in the tunnel much easier. Consequently, we wound up with the most slippery car ever done in the Ford Motor Company: a drag coefficient [Cd] of 0.44 for the three-door fastback, 0.46 for the two-door notchback. [Aerodynamics is] probably the most cost-effective way to improve corporate average fuel economy. We know that a 10-percent [reduction] in drag can result in a five-percent improvement in fuel economy at a steady-state 50 mph....That's really worthwhile stuff for us to go after."

It's worth noting that the drag figures Telnack cited were good for the time but would soon seem mediocre. The Fox-based 1983 Thunderbird, for example, arrived with an altogether more impressive Cd of 0.35. While the difference may not seem dramatic, it represents a reduction of more than 20 percent, and shows just how quickly standards can change. Incidentally, Telnack directed that effort too.

Less Weight, More Space

For performance as well as fuel economy, engineers used lightweight materials wherever feasible, including plastics, aluminum, and high-strength/low-alloy (HSLA) steel. A significant new plastics technology appeared in color-keyed bumper covers of soft urethane made by the reaction-injection molding (RIM) process. HSLA steel was used for rear suspension arms and the number-three frame crossmember, while aluminum featured in drivetrain components and the bumpers of some models. Slimmer-section doors saved more pounds. So did thinner but stronger glass (even though there was more of it), a lower beltline, and taller "greenhouse" allowing much larger windows. With all this, the '79 Mustang was some 200 pounds lighter on average than Mustang II despite being slightly larger in every dimension—quite an accomplishment for the age of downsizing.

Interior design received equally careful attention. Total volume rose by 14 cubic feet on the notchback and by 16 cubic feet on the hatchback. The thinner doors opened up 3.6 inches of front shoulder room and two inches of hip room. Back-seat gains were even more impressive, with five inches of added shoulder width, six more inches of hip room, and more than five extra inches of leg room. Cargo volume expanded too, adding two cubic feet in the notchback and four in the hatch.

New Features, New Function

Telnack's European experience also showed up in standard full instrumentation including trip odometer, tachometer, ammeter, and oil-pressure gauge. Another "foreign" touch was the use of steering-column stalks to control wipers/washers and turn signals/headlight dimmer/horn; these came from the Fairmont/ Zephyr, as did the basic dashboard and cowl structure. A third lever (on the right) adjusted a tilt steering wheel, one of several new extras. Among other new options were an "ultra fidelity" sound system with power amplifier and, for hatchbacks, a rear-window wiper/washer. Still another first-time convenience option was a console-mounted "vehicle systems monitor." This used a Honda-style graphic display with warning lights placed on an overhead outline of the car to signal low fuel, low windshield-washer fluid, and failed headlights, taillights, or brake lamps. A pushbutton allowed checking that the display itself was working. The console also housed a quartz-crystal digital chronometer showing time, date, or elapsed time at the touch of a button.

Planners decided on three trim levels for the two body styles: standard, Sport option, and Ghia. The Mach 1 was history, but lived on in spirit with a new $1173 Cobra package for the hatchback that was virtually a separate model. Recalling the late King Cobra, this "boy racer" kit featured black-finish greenhouse trim and lower bodysides, color-keyed body moldings, and an optional snake decal for the hood, plus sportier seats and cabin appointments—and a new engine that we'll get to shortly.

Classy Chassis

Also for broadest possible market appeal, the '79 offered three suspension setups: standard, "handling," and "special," each designed for and issued with its own set of tires. As planned, basic hardware came from the Fairmont/Zephyr, which meant switching the front end from upper A-arms to modified MacPherson-strut geometry. Unlike similar layouts in many contempory European and Japanese cars, the coil spring here did not wrap around the strut, but mounted between a lower control arm and the body structure. This eliminated the need for an expensive spring compressor when replacing shocks. A front antiroll bar was standard across the board, with diameter varied to suit engine weight and power. At the rear was a new "four-bar link" system, also with coil springs, lighter and more compact than Mustang II's leaf-spring Hotchkiss arrangement. V-8 cars included a rear antiroll bar that was more for lateral location than controlling sway, but it effectively lowered the car's roll center, allowing commensurately softer rear springs for ride comfort.

The basic chassis was tuned for standard 13-inch bias-ply

TOP: A Mustang II look evidently still had a chance well into 1976, as suggested by this full-scale model photographed in early March. ABOVE: A Ghia idea, also from early '76, shows a different take on the "formal" look ultimately rejected. BELOW: Once approved, '79 styling was refined in the wind tunnel to trim air drag and thus enhance fuel economy.

ABOVE: Mustang's basic '79 styling was the work of a team headed by Jack Telnack. Note the applied vertical slats aft of the rear side windows on this Sport Option hatchback, one of the few changes made before production. Note, too, the vestigial rear deck, chosen over a full-sweep roofline so the hatch door would be easier to pull down when fully opened. LEFT: Unlike Mustang II, the '79 was designed as a notchback. It's shown here in base-trim four-cylinder form. Rear window was modestly curved to reduce wind resistance, one of several decisions approved by management despite higher cost.

tires. The mid-level "handling" package (just $33) came with 14-inch radials, higher-rate springs, different shock valving, stiffer bushings, and, on V-6 cars, a rear stabilizer. The "special" suspension was engineered around Michelin's TRX metric-size radial tires, which Ford had been offering in Europe for several years on its large Granada sedans. These tires had an unusual 390mm (15.35-inch) diameter and so required matching wheels, which ended up as forged-aluminum rims with a handsome three-spoke design done in Dearborn. Priced at $117–$241 depending on model, the TRX suspension came with its own shock-absorber valving, high-rate rear springs, a thicker (1.12-inch) front stabilizer bar, and a rear bar. It was the best choice for handling, engineered "to extract maximum performance" from the 190/65R390 rubber according to puffy press releases.

Precise rack-and-pinion steering continued, but housings for both the manual and power systems were changed to weight-saving die-cast aluminum. As before, a variable-ratio rack was included with optional power assist. Brakes were again front discs and rear drums, but of slightly larger size.

A New Engine Blows In

The '79 powertrain chart showed an intriguing new engine option. The heart of the racy new Cobra package, it was a turbocharged "Lima" four rated at 132 SAE net horsepower against only 88 bhp for the unblown version. Though common now, turbos were pretty exotic in the late Seventies, especially for a mass-market Detroit product. With four-speed gearbox, the blown-four was good for a claimed 8.3 seconds in 0–55-mph acceleration (Detroit wasn't quoting 0–60s with a "double nickel" national speed limit still in force), plus mid-20s fuel economy—an excellent compromise overall.

Turbocharging, of course, was nothing new. Like the similar supercharger, it's a simple bolt-on means to improve volumetric efficiency. A small turbine plumbed into the exhaust manifold uses exhaust gases to turn an impeller that drives a pump near the carburetor. In normal running, the turbine spins too slowly to boost exhaust-manifold pressure or affect fuel consumption. But as the throttle is opened and the engine speeds up, so does the flow rate of the exhaust gases. The increased flow spins the tur-

John J. Telnack: In his own words

Designer Jack Telnack was born to be a Ford man. Not only did he enter the world at Dearborn's Henry Ford Hospital, his father was a power-plant worker at Ford Motor Company's giant River Rouge factory complex. As a boy he met old Henry Ford himself when the legendary mogul visited a neighbor family. He also remembers many youthful hours spent gazing at the shiny new cars on display in the old Ford Rotunda—and being shooed away from unauthorized visits to the company proving grounds. Eventually, the love of cars led Jack to study automotive design at the Art Center School in Los Angeles. On graduation he was plucked by a Ford recruiter and joined the company in 1958, where he would remain for 39 years. Though various assignments would take him to all parts of the global Ford empire, Telnack spent plenty of time in Dearborn contributing to various Mustangs. In fact, he worked on the very first ponycar as an enthusiastic twentysomething in Joe Oros' Ford Studio. His first big U.S. design coup came with the sleek 1979 Mustang that so reflected his European experience. Partly on the basis of its sales success, he was promoted to head Ford's North American design operation, where he masterminded the successful "aero look" exemplified by the 1983 Thunderbird and 1986 Taurus. He then went on to craft Ford's "New Edge" theme. He retired from Ford in 1997.

I was in and out of Mustang programs pretty much my whole career. I left for Australia in '66 and returned in 1969 to be in charge of the Mustang studio. We did the first soft bumpers front and rear, the urethane bumpers for '71, which was a breakthrough. I'm not sure anybody else was doing them then, but it was a pretty dramatic change for us.

I consider the '79 Mustang a breakthrough car. It was the first project I worked on when I returned from Europe [as design vice-president in 1973–76]. It was such a departure from anything we were doing here. It had the first slantback front end we had done in Ford U.S. That was big news because we had clear direction from our vice-president of design at that time, Gene Bordinat, saying "thou shall never do a slantback front end. Henry Ford II only wants vertical front ends, and he'll show us the door if we ever try anything like it."

I can remember showing the first European Granada slantback front end to Henry Ford in London. He said he was a little uncomfortable with it. And I said, "Well, Mr. Ford, if you would just think about it, but we'll do some variations." We did,

and on his next visit to England he said, "Boy, I've got to tell you, it really works. Let's go with this."

The '79 Mustang seemed extemely European at the time to most people around here, including Gene Bordinat. We had other designs in competition with that car. The next preferred model was very, very American, very boxy. I just thank God we didn't go that way. I don't think it would have lived as long. We would have been into some fairly major sheetmetal rip-ups.

But the car we did had a lot of support from management, and, fortunately, made it through market research and just squeaked ahead of this very traditional American Mustang being proposed at the same time. And I mean *squeaked* ahead in terms of general acceptance, overall image. But today it's normal design. I like to think of it as normal good design, but you don't hear anybody refer to it as "European" anymore.

When I first came back from Europe, people seemed to be afraid to express themselves....But I really wanted our designers to tell me what they thought about various ideas, good or bad. Once they knew that and really came around...they began coming up with these new ideas. They weren't afraid to express themselves. And the '79 Mustang is a direct result of it. Because I said, "You guys are putting this stuff in sketches. You must think that way, so why aren't you doing it in full-size?" They asked me, "Are you serious?...Does he really want to break out of the boxy mold?" I said, "Yeah, I really do." I had to convince them. I think that was a significant breakthrough, because the talent was there. And we used it.

That car would have been very acceptable in Europe. So we knew there was some risk involved, but it was a calculated risk. We knew it may have a bit of a warmup period with some people, but it would have longevity, and that's important because the Japanese competition in that segment were changing about every two or three years. And yet the Mustang is still hanging in there and that's a real credit to these designers.

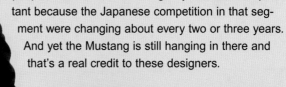

Mustang was chosen pace car for the 1979 Indy 500. Ford celebrated the honor by running off some 11,000 replica hatchbacks like this, the 65th built. The replicas looked much like the actual pace car but had a flip-up sunroof instead of a T-top, plus stock-tune engines, either the new 2.3-liter turbo-four or, as here, the tried-and-true 302 V-8. "Official Pace Car" decals were included.

bine, which speeds up the impeller to boost the density (pressure) of the air/fuel mixture, resulting in more power. To prevent damage, engineers set maximum boost at six pounds per square inch via a "wastegate" relief valve that allowed gases to bypass the turbine once that pressure was reached.

Carryover engines weren't neglected for '79. The veteran 302 V-8, now rating 140 bhp, gained a new low-restriction exhaust system, more lightweight components, and an accessory drive with a single "serpentine" V-belt for greater reliability. The German-made V-6 was down to 109 bhp—and in short supply, prompting Ford to replace it during the model year with the hoary 200-cid inline six, which now rated just 85 bhp. The V-8 and both sixes offered an optional four-speed gearbox developed specifically for them—essentially the base three-speed manual with a direct-drive third gear (1:1 ratio) and an overdrive fourth (0.70:1) tacked on. Final drive ratios were 3.08:1 for automatics, four-speed V-6, and the standard four, 3.45:1 for other combinations. Three-speed Cruise-O-Matic, also carried over with minor updates, was optional at $307.

Horses for Courses

Powerteam still determined the character of any particular Mustang. The V-8 was a drag-race engine by '79 standards, doing 0–60 mph in 8–9 seconds. A V-6 still took around 11 seconds with manual four-speed, while a like-equipped turbo-four needed 11–12 seconds. The straight-six took close to 13. Standing quarter-mile times ranged from 17 seconds at 85 mph for the V-8 to 19.2 at 75 for the 200 six.

Press reaction also still depended on engine—and who was in the driver's seat. Some writers thought the V-8 had too much power for its chassis and was out of step with gasoline prices that were starting to rise again. *Car and Driver*'s Don Sherman judged the V-6 Mustang as the best choice for handling by dint of "the best power-to-front-end-weight ratio." But he was also

impressed with two other cars he sampled for a preview report. "The lightweight revolution has arrived in performance land. Rejoice." The intriguing turbo-four naturally garnered much "buff book" attention. Said *Road & Track*'s John Dinkel: "The TRX turbo would seem to be an enthusiast's delight. I just hope that the design compromises dictated by costs and the fact that Ford couldn't start with a completely clean sheet of paper don't wreck that dream....There's no doubt the new Mustang has the potential to be the best sport coupe Ford has ever built, but in some respects [it] is as enigmatic as its predecessor."

Drop Off the Key, Lee

Another enigma came to light barely a month after reporters got their first drives in the new Mustangs. In June 1978, Ford again set industry tongues a-wagging with word that Lee Iacocca was out of a job after 32 years. Officially, he was taking early retirement (on October 15, his 54th birthday). But many observers assumed he'd be dumped before Henry Ford II's scheduled retirement as chief executive in 1980 and as chairman in 1982. As usual, the head man didn't say much, though he reportedly told Iacocca, "It's just one of those things." Iacocca wasn't bitter, at least in public. "You just surmise that he doesn't want strong guys around," he said later. "[T]hat's the only thing I can come up with, because I really don't have a good sound answer myself." Ironically, and as Iacocca was careful to note, June 1978 was the biggest single sales month in Ford history, capping a first half that netted the company its largest six-month profit on record. "They probably won't be at this peak again, so I

"New Breed" Mustang styling was little changed for sophomore 1980, but this "carriage roof" was newly available to give notchbacks the top-up look of a true convertible—right down to a simulated rear-window zip. As before, metric-size tri-spoke alloy wheels with Michelin TRX tires were part of the handling-oriented "special" suspension option.

ABOVE: The racy Cobra package for hatchbacks was updated for 1980 via a slat grille, deep front airdam, and reverse-facing hood scoop, all picked up from the '79 Pace Car Replica. A splashy snake decal for the hood remained a separate option. LEFT: The "New Breed" interior showed as much European influence as the exterior, with standard full instrumentation and handy steering-column stalk controls for wipers and lights. Optional cruise control was operated from slim buttons on the steering wheel as shown here. BELOW: Optional vinyl roof, wire-wheel covers, and whitewall tires spiff up this 1980 notchback.

guess it's a good time to go." As we know, Iacocca rode off to Chrysler, which he eventually saved from extinction, but he would have had rough going even if he had stayed in Dearborn. Though not nearly as well publicized at the time, Ford had its own financial troubles and would soon be down for the count, too.

In 1979, however, Iacocca's successor, Philip Caldwell, was happy to count a strong 369,936 sales for the "New Breed" ponycar. Though that was slightly less than the Mustang II's smashing first-year total, it bested the company's forecast of 330,000—and represented a startling 92.2-percent jump from model-year '78. Buyers must have liked the new models, because Ford charged a lot more for them. Aggravated by stubborn period inflation, base sticker prices swelled a whopping $500–$700—a 15–17 percent jump—ranging from $4071 for the four-cylinder notchback to $4824 for the Ghia hatch.

Back to The Brickyard

Highlighting the Fox Mustang's debut year was its selection as Indy 500 pace car, the first Mustang so honored since 1964. Doing the deed was a colorfully striped hatchback with a special T-bar roof and a V-8 massaged by tuner extraordinaire Jack Roush to attain the Brickyard's required 120-mph minimum track speed. As so often happens with Indy pacers, the public was offered a replica. This had the same striping, pewter/black paint scheme, unique hood and three-slat grille, and premium Recaro bucket seats, plus flip-up sunroof and a choice of turbo-four or regular V-8 engines. Race-day decals were included for dealers to apply if the customer wished. The mists of time seem to have shrouded original price, but Ford built about 11,000 of these Replicas, unusually high for the genre.

CAFE Jitters

Significantly, the '79 Mustang bowed in the second year for CAFE standards—Corporate Average Fuel Economy. A Congressional response to the energy crisis, this law mandated specific mpg targets for all automakers selling in the U.S. In brief, the EPA-rated fuel economy for all cars sold by a given manufacturer had to average so many miles per gallon for a given model year—initially 19 mpg, rising progressively to 27.5 mpg by 1985. Companies whose "fleet average" fell below a yearly target were fined a set number of dollars for each 0.1-mpg infraction—multiplied by *total* sales for that model year. Obviously, failure to comply could be costly indeed. However, the law provided credits for exceeding a given year's target that could be used to avoid or reduce penalities for non-compliance in another year, past *or* future. All rather complicated—and highly political, of course. Still, CAFE achieved its goal of spurring Detroit to develop smaller, lighter, thriftier cars in most every size and price class. The effort took on new urgency with the onset of another energy crisis in spring 1979, when the Shah of Iran was deposed by a fundamentalist Ayatollah who cut off the country's oil exports and held Americans hostage. But the ensuing oil shortage soon became an oil glut. That, plus a fairly quick economic rebound and the new Reagan Administration's more relaxed attitude toward restrictions on business, rendered CAFE almost meaningless by the mid-Eighties.

More—and Less—for 1980

But it was still very much a factor for 1980, when Ford replaced the Mustang's hallowed 302 V-8 option with a debored 4.2-liter/ 255-cid version. Though this seemed an amazingly quick, prescient response to "Energy Crisis II," it had been planned well before. Ford claimed an average 1.2-mpg improvement over the "five-point-oh," but speed freaks groaned at losing 10 bhp and being forced to take automatic. As the rest of the powertrain chart was basically a photocopy of late 1979, Don Sherman reluctantly recommended the turbo-four to *Car and Driver* readers as "the only choice...that even comes close to delivering on last year's performance promise...."

As usual, there were other sophomore-year tweaks. Base models adopted high-back bucket seats and full color-keyed interior trim, and all 1980 Mustangs came with brighter halogen headlights (replacing less-efficient tungsten sealed-beams). The options list added a roof-mounted luggage carrier ($86), a "window shade" cargo-area cover for hatchbacks ($44), and—shades of Boss 302—hatchback liftgate louvers ($141). A pricey new notchback extra was a $625 Carriage Roof, a diamond-grain full vinyl covering set off by black window frames and moldings so as

A decade after abandoning motorsports, Ford hinted at an imminent return with the 1980 Mustang IMSA concept. Named for the International Motor Sports Association, whose GT racing series was a natural Mustang playground, this one-of-a-kind hatchback looked competition-ready with fat Pirelli tires on wildly dished wheels, plus muscular fender bulges, grille-less nose, deep front airdam, loop rear spoiler, and eye-bending stripes.

to simulate the top-up appearance of a true convertible. Still available for notchbacks and newly standard on hatchbacks was the Sport Option, again comprising styled-steel wheels with trim rings, black rocker-panel and window moldings, wide bodyside moldings, striped rubstrip extensions, and a sporty steering wheel. The luxury Ghias returned with color-keyed seatbelts, mirrors, bodyside moldings, and hatchback roof slats, plus new low-back bucket seats with adjustable headrests, door map pockets, visor vanity mirror, thicker pile carpeting, deluxe steering wheel, roof-mounted assist handles, and a full complement of interior lights. Leather or cloth-and-vinyl upholstery was available in six different colors.

Cheering enthusiasts, the Pace Car Replica's Recaro bucket seats were optional for any 1980 Mustang. Though not cheap at $531 per set, they were genuine Euro-car furniture with reclinable backrests and adjustable thigh and lumbar supports—all much preferable to the fixed-back stock chairs that road-testers still

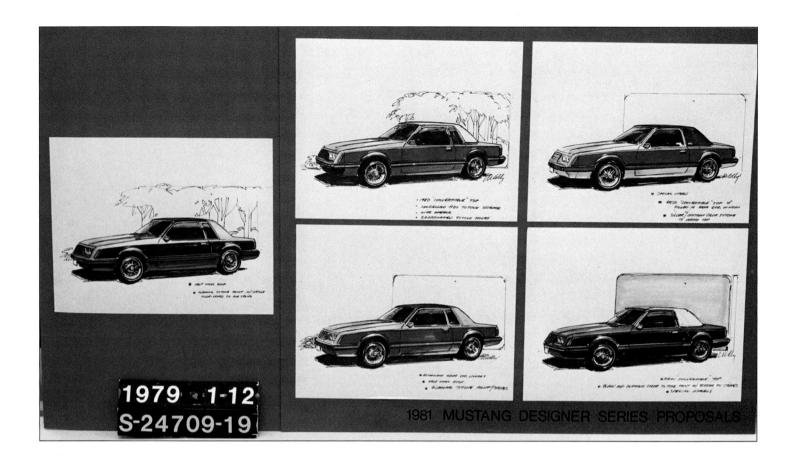

1979 1-12
S-24709-19

1981 MUSTANG DESIGNER SERIES PROPOSALS

often lamented. Last but not least, Cobra styling was updated with a Pace Car-style slat grille, rear-facing hood scoop, and front and rear spoilers. Standard foglamps and TRX suspension continued, but the package was no longer available with optional V-8 (sensible with the weaker 255 engine)—and its price was up $309 to $1482. As before, a big hood snake decal was available separately (at $88, up $10).

"Buff book" testers still paid scant attention to the base four-cylinder engine because it just didn't have the muscle to be very interesting in a car like Mustang. The 200-cid six was also widely ignored, doubtless because it was so familiar (old, in other words) and far from exotic: seven-main-bearing crankshaft, overhead valves with hydraulic lifters, cast-iron block, a simple one-barrel carburetor. Even so, the straight six still had a place in 1980, being efficient and easy to live with. It had less horsepower than the V-6 it replaced but compensated with greater displacement and torque, so "real-world" performance wasn't that different. And by Ford's "Cost-of-Ownership" formula, where required maintenance for the first 50,000 miles was averaged according to dealer parts and labor prices, the inline six cost less to operate than the V-6, an appreciated plus for inflation-weary buyers.

A Brief Look Back

As the Mustang itself was 15 years old in 1980, it was natural to compare the latest Fox model with the 1965 original. Looking at "vital statistics," it was tempting to say little had changed. Though the newest pony was 7.6 inches trimmer in wheelbase, it was only 2.5 inches shorter overall (at 179.1), about an inch wider (at 69.1), and less than 100 pounds heavier (2516 pounds at the curb). Front passenger space was about equal, but the '80 was much roomier in back, suggesting Ford had learned something about space utilization in all that time. And unlike the '65,

Marketers always fear a new car growing stale, hence these January '79 ideas for a 1981 Mustang "Designer Series." Though not approved, the likely plan was for one or more option groups created with an assist from name fashion designers, the same profit-booster already proven in Bill Blass, Cartier, and other special-edition luxury Lincolns.

the Fox was burdened with all manner of safety features mandated by the federal government, such as reinforced doors and five-mph bumpers, so Ford had apparently learned something about weight control too.

Engine comparisons were equally interesting. While the 2.3-liter four was a Seventies invention, the six was exactly the same powerplant that was standard in '65 Mustangs (save early cars with the 170-cid unit). The 255 V-8 was based on the 302, which, in turn, evolved from the 289 that itself was enlarged from the original Mustang's 260. Yet both the six and V-8 now returned much better fuel mileage than their 1965 counterparts.

What such comparisons couldn't convey was how much Mustang had changed over 15 years. As we've seen, the stylish sporty compact that won all America's heart was allowed to become too large, too unwieldy, too wasteful. Ford knew that as well as anyone, hence the far more rational Mustang II. But the Fox generation was far better, deliberately designed to be even closer to the '65 in size, if not character. And why not? Then as now, it was the original that defined Mustang for most people. Of course, the Fox couldn't be a retro copy, because automotive realities had changed greatly since the Sixties. All the more remarkable, then, that it ended up so nimble, attractive, and efficient—and with a winning charm all its own.

Racing Into The Future?

Ford gave strong indications during 1980 that it was about to get its performance act back together and put it on the road, with Mustang the star of the show. Hinting at what might lie ahead was a tantalizing "concept" attraction for that season's auto-show circuit: the Mustang IMSA. Powered by a much-modified turbo-four, this buff hatchback crouched low on ultra-wide Pirelli P7 tires hugged by outlandishly flared fenders. Also featured were a grille-less nose, deep front air dam, loop rear spoiler, and competition-inspired pop-riveted plastic covers on the side windows and taillight panel. In name and appearance, the IMSA strongly suggested that Ford was more than just thinking about a return to competition—and about the International Motor Sports Association GT series in particular.

September 1980 brought more racy news as Ford announced formation of a Special Vehicle Operations (SVO) division headed by Michael Kranefuss, summoned to Dearborn after serving as competition director for Ford Europe. SVO's stated purpose was to "develop a series of limited-production performance cars and develop their image through motorsport." The new outfit quickly got down to business with a turbo Mustang to be driven by former Porsche pilot Klaus Ludwig in selected 1981 IMSA GT events. Ford also provided direct support to other Mustang racers, backing a Trans-Am mount for Dennis Mecham and an IMSA Kelly American Challenge car for Lyn St. James.

As if to signal its return to the track, Ford introduced the McLaren Mustang in late 1980. The work of designers Todd Gerstenberger and Harry Wykes, it was another heavily modified hatchback with enough built-in potential for easy adaptation to race duty. Looking somewhat like the IMSA show car, the McLaren sported a grille-less nose above a low-riding "skirt" spoiler, plus functional hood scoops, tweaked suspension (mostly a mix of heavy-duty off-the-shelf components), massive fender flares, and premium German BBS alloy wheels wearing broad-shouldered 225/55R15 Firestone HPR radials. Power was again provided by the turbo-four, but it was newly fortified with a variable boost control having a range of 5–11 psi vs. the regular engine's fixed 5 psi. Rated output was 175 bhp at 10 psi, a big jump over the 132-bhp stock mill. A $25,000 price tag and virtual hand construction limited McLaren production to just 250 units (including the prototype)—but at least they were for sale.

An optional T-bar roof with twin lift-off panels had been offered on late Mustang IIs, but the "New Breed" did without one until 1981, when it returned as an $874 item for either body style. It's pictured here on a hatchback that's also equipped with the TRX "special" suspension and a $54 dummy hood scoop. Typical of the times, this ad is long on emotion and short on specifics, but note four-cylinder EPA mileage ratings.

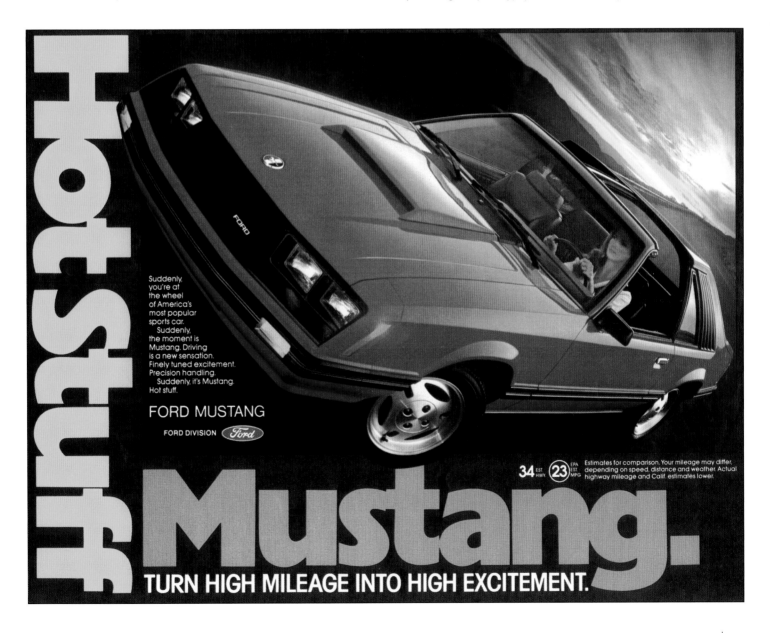

Hotstuff

Suddenly, you're at the wheel of America's most popular sports car. Suddenly, the moment is Mustang. Driving is a new sensation. Finely tuned excitement. Precision handling. Suddenly, it's Mustang. Hot stuff.

FORD MUSTANG

FORD DIVISION ⟨Ford⟩

34 EST. HWY. ⟨23⟩ EST. MPG — EPA Estimates for comparison. Your mileage may differ, depending on speed, distance and weather. Actual highway mileage and Calif. estimates lower.

Mustang.
TURN HIGH MILEAGE INTO HIGH EXCITEMENT.

A Sales Setback

With a new gas crunch triggering another sharp recession, total U.S. car sales plunged for model-year 1980. Mustang was not immune but fared reasonably well, tallying 271,322 units. Not surprisingly, demand for four-cylinder models shot up from 54 percent to nearly 68 percent of total deliveries. Sixes declined a little over a point to just below 30 percent, leaving V-8s at under three percent. These shares stayed about the same for 1981, but on much lower volume of 182,552 units. Sharp price hikes didn't help. The base four-cylinder coupe went up to $6171, the top-line Ghia hatchback to $6729.

Changes were modest for '81. Interior trim was shuffled and slightly upgraded, and an optional T-bar roof with twin lift-off glass panels was revived for both body styles at a hefty $874. The turbo engine was restricted to manual transmission, only to be quietly phased out, reportedly due to persistent drivability and reliability problems. The Cobra package was a near rerun except for a stiffer $1588 price.

Mustang's main '81 news involed full availability of an optional five-speed overdrive manual gearbox for four-cylinder models, an item that had been phased in the prevous season. Engineers sensibly specified a "shorter" 3.45:1 final drive vs. the four-speed tranny's 3.08:1 cog for better off-the-line snap. The overdrive fifth was geared at 0.82:1 for economical highway cruising. It was just what the base Mustang needed— almost. As CONSUMER GUIDE noted at the time: "Our biggest objections to the five-speed are its linkage—stiff, yet vague—and its shift pattern. As with the four-speed, first through fourth are arranged in the usual H-pattern. But fifth is awkwardly located at the bottom of the dogleg to the right of and opposite fourth, instead of up and to the right.... Why Ford did it this way is a mystery, but it makes getting into or out of fifth real work. Our guess is that the engineers wanted to prevent inexperienced drivers from accidentally engaging overdrive and needlessly lugging the engine, as well as to prevent confusion with the often-used third. If so, they've succeeded admirably." At the time, one transmission engineer told us

that Ford thought most drivers would want to downshift from fifth directly to third, bypassing fourth. A more logical reason was that putting fifth over-and-up would have entailed excessively long arm reach. The "official" explanation was that the U-shaped shift motion better emphasized the economy benefits of the long-striding fifth gear. Whatever the reason, it just didn't work.

Overall, though, the "New Breed" worked beautifully, another Mustang just right for its time. But the turn of the Eighties was another unhappy time for car lovers of every persuasion, and the future promised to be no better as far as anyone could see.

It was in this dour atmosphere that *Motor Trend* picked Mustang to kick off a series of nostalgic "Now Vs. Then" comparisons in its November 1980 issue. After driving a modestly optioned V-8 notchback against a classic hardtop of similar spec, writer Tony Swan concluded on a wistful note: "Mustang '66 is one of those automotive immortals that's earned a special niche. It is a car of distinctive character...produced in a manufacturing community blithely free of today's frequently conflicting regulations. Mustang '80 is also a car of distinctive character, an achievement made more remarkable in view of [those] regulations.... [It's] contemporary in every sense and perhaps suffers from this in contrast to its ancestor. In an age of behemoths and excess, it wasn't particularly difficult for something as trim as the original Mustang to stand out from the crowd. But in the age of the Big Shrink, it is much more difficult for a designer to achieve something truly striking. Thus, we are comparing not only two cars but two eras. On a straight point-for-point comparison, each contender scores.... But in the perspective of today's world, the 1966 Mustang is an anachronism—a collector's item. Of *course* they don't build 'em like they used to. [E]ven if they wanted to...there's this problem: They're not allowed to."

Maybe not, but that didn't rule out building 'em better—which is exactly what would happen. More immediately, performance was about to make a suprise comeback in embattled Detroit. Not surprisingly, Mustang would lead the charge.

OPPOSITE PAGE: Ford PR photographed this Mustang trio for 1981 press-kit purposes. A sunroof-equipped hatchback sits above Sport Option and T-top notchbacks. Styling was again little changed for '81, but so was the broad options list that still gave Mustang such wide appeal. THIS PAGE, TOP: The notchback's optional Carriage Roof continued for '81. ABOVE: Announced in late 1980, the McLaren Mustang teamed Ford Design with McLaren Performance of Formula 1 racing fame. Just 250 were built, all with turbo-four engines featuring a competition-style variable boost control, plus chassis and body mods clearly designed for the racetrack. RIGHT: Though not predictive, the 1981 RSX concept showed how Ford's Ghia studio in Italy might handle a Mustang. Built on a shortened stock chassis with turbo-four power, the Rally Sport Experimental boasted angular "aero" lines, vivid orange-pearl metallic paint, and simulated all-glass doors.

Chapter Eight:
1982-1986

When the going gets tough, the tough go racing—or so said the new hard chargers who took command at Ford during the rough times of the early 1980s. But they knew "Total Performance" had worked sales magic before. Why not again? In short order, Ford went back to the tracks, back to genuine performance Mustangs— and back to solid sales and profits.

The Fox generation was a happy turn of events for Mustang fans. However timely and popular, the Mustang II was not a genuine ponycar, even if it served the noble purpose of keeping the Mustang spirit alive through the dark and difficult Seventies. By the 1980s, however, Detroit had pretty much come to terms with with government-mandated emissions limits, crash-performance standards, even Corporate Average Fuel Economy. This meant they could literally afford to return to more interesting things—like head-turning style and truly vivid performance. The "New Breed" Mustang reflected this by offering many qualities of the '65 original in a more sophisticated package appropriate for challenging new times.

Actually, ponycars shouldn't have survived to the Eighties in any form—and most didn't. Mustang's Mercury sibling, the Cougar, was puffed up into a personal-luxury midsize after 1973, while the Plymouth Barracuda, Dodge Challenger, and AMC Javelin were all dumped after '74, never to be seen again. But against all odds, the Chevrolet Camaro and Pontiac Firebird managed to hold on to decade's end—and with surprisingly few changes after 1970. They even enjoyed a strong sales resurgence. The main reason, of course, was that after the first energy crisis, they were about the only American cars (other than Chevy's Corvette) offering anything like Sixties-style performance. The fact that their hottest models, the Z28 and Trans Am, also became the hottest sellers didn't go unnoticed in Dearborn.

A New Crisis and New Leaders

Ford Motor Company needed to be on its toes, because its financial situation by 1980 was almost as dire as Chrysler Corporation's. Echoing the late Forties, Ford faced another historic change of leadership at a time when its future looked anything but rosy. Chairman Henry Ford II had announced his intention to resign, and did, leaving many to wonder if his successors could turn things around.

Inspiration in the executive ranks was sorely needed. Though Ford had enjoyed good sales in recent years, its bottom line was being hurt by the high costs of a top-to-bottom product overhaul,

begun with the '78 Fairmont/Zephyr and the '79 Mustang, a necessity mothered by the ever-present need to stay competitive. When the economy and the car market tanked with "Energy Crisis II" in mid-1979, Ford suddenly found itself facing a major cash crisis.

Stockholders needn't have worried, though, because 1980 ushered in two highly experienced go-getters at the top: Philip A. Caldwell as chairman and, to replace him as president, Donald E. Petersen. A bit later, Eugene Bordinat retired after some 20 years as design vice-president, replaced by Donald Kopka, a man whose tastes closely mirrored those of North American design chief Jack Telnack. It was also in this period that a younger generation of Fords began to take a hand. Among them was Edsel B. Ford II, son of the departed chairman and a big Mustang fan, who now served as manager of market planning for Ford Division. Other rising talents included Louis E. Lataif, named division general manager in 1981, and Harold A. "Red" Poling, executive v-p of North American Operations. Edsel Ford called Poling "a quality freak," so few were surprised when corporate advertising adopted a new slogan during 1980: "Quality is Job 1."

All of this would prove very good for Ford, but the press took particular note of Petersen's promotion. After all, he was an avid, knowledgeable "car guy" (having served in product planning for years). And he had definite ideas about Ford's future, particularly in the areas of design and performance. Petersen's enthusiasm would soon be evident in a dramatic new fleet of Ford Motor Company vehicles. Meantime, he put his stylists and engineers to work on imbuing existing models with some of the old "Total Performance" flair that had worked sales magic in the Sixties. As a direct descendant of those times, the Mustang was one of the first Fords to benefit.

The Boss Returns

The first benefit appeared for 1982 in a revived Mustang GT with the most potent small-block V-8 in recent Ford history.

"The Boss is Back!" ads declared. And it was. At its heart was a new H.O. (High-Output) 302 with 157 horsepower, up a solid 18 horses from the last 302 of 1979. Contributing to this gain was a more aggressive camshaft adapted from a marine version of the long-running V-8, plus a larger two-barrel carburetor, a bigger and smoother exhaust system, a more durable double-row timing chain, and low restriction twin-snorkel air cleaner. Teamed exclusively with four-speed overdrive manual transmission, it made for the fastest Mustang in years. Claimed 0–60-mph acceleration was below eight seconds, but most magazines clocked closer to seven, and Jim McCraw reported 6.9 seconds in tests at Ford's Dearborn Proving Grounds for the September 1981 *Motor Trend*.

Torrid But Tasteful

The reborn GT was not a package but a distinct hatchback model with a top-of-the-line $8308 base price. Effectively, it replaced the Cobra package as a more "adult" enthusiasts' Mustang but retained much of its styling. "Existing body add-ons are used," noted *AutoWeek*'s George D. Levy, "but with greater discretion than in the past. The spoilers and [hood] scoop are there, for good reason, but the stomach-grabber colors and yahoo graphics are gone, replaced by a few small GT emblems. Exterior colors are limited to [dark red], black, and silver." Whatever the hue, most exterior chrome went noir, while the grille, headlamp frames, and bumpers were tastefully left in body color. The interior was resolutely black except for cloth seat inserts with jazzy op-art white striping. Bucket seats flanked a standard shift console (still housing a pull-up handbrake as well) but were more heavily bolstered than in lesser models.

Reflecting separate but parallel development tracks, the H.O. engine was not tied to the GT model, being available in other '82 Mustangs for $402 with the TRX suspension or $452 without. Those prices seemed steep, but the engine came with its own bundle of good stuff.

Beside the four-speed tranny, Ford threw in a 3.08:1 Traction-Lok differential, power steering, power brakes with enlarged front discs, and the baseline "handling" suspension, which was also a stand-alone option tagged at just $50. The TRX suspension cost $533–$583 this year except on the GT, where it added a mere

$105—another reason to choose the top horse, as most V-8 buyers did. Incidentally, the tame 4.2-liter (255-cubic-inch) V-8 was available for the GT as a $57 credit option, though few buyers were likely penny-wise and performance-foolish this way.

McCraw noted that the GT got "the nod from the highest echelon of management and [was first slated] as a 1982½ addition. But the swell of enthusiasm at the marketing and engineering levels, and the speed with which engineering problems were solved, have pushed the program up to an October 1 startup, only a couple of weeks after introduction of the 1982 Ford line." The GT was a showroom symbol of Ford's renewed commitment to competition, chiefly road racing, begun in 1981. Both were part of what McCraw termed a "new marketing strategy. Public reaction to this return to big-league racing has been overwhelmingly positive; a whirlwind of mail has told the company to start building something that's quick, fast and fun to drive...."

Ford happily lavished much attention and money on its newest H.O. V-8. For example, the intake manifold was switched from steel to lightweight aluminum, and the exhaust system was redesigned for quicker warmup—so the catalytic converter would start burning off nasty pollutants that much faster—and for less performance-sapping back pressure. Impressively, there was no muffler, yet the car was fully street-legal noise-wise. A new accessory drive reduced power losses by declutching the air-conditioning compressor and radiator fan at full throttle. The result, as McCraw relayed from engine engineer Jim Clarke, was more power to the rear wheels than most cars managed.

Most every '82 GT delivered for magazine road tests had the TRX suspension—a sensible PR ploy, even if the tires didn't like dragstrip work. "The Michelins provide superb cornering gip," said

Ford planned no big, immediate styling alterations for the Fox Mustang, but easy-change items would be redone from time to time. A Ford Design staffer snapped this August 1980 pose of two future wheel-cover ideas. The three-blade design at right would be base-model rim wear for '83. Note the shrouded 1982 Ford EXP coupe at left and, uncovered behind the Mustang, its Mercury sister, the LN7.

ABOVE: A late-August 1980 comparison of the rare and racy '81 McLaren Mustang (left) and two workouts for the production '82 GT with rejected hood-scoop and lower-valence ideas. RIGHT: '82 GT tail styling was already decided. Non-GT hatchback at right has a center filler panel with bold Mustang lettering, another no-go notion. BELOW: This interesting late-September 1981 shot appears to show a new Carriage Roof Mustang notchback with a Mercury Capri nose cap (as on white car at right), suggesting thoughts of expanding Mustang's sister lineup.

ABOVE: Mustang again listed several roof options for 1982. This advertising shot highlights the T-bar roof with twin liftoff glass panels. Its price that year was $1021. Also available: flip-up sunroof and, for notchbacks, conventional and pseudo-convertible Carriage Roof treatments. BELOW: Wheel designs and sizes were no less numerous for '82.

AutoWeek's Levy, "but they're poorly matched against the Mustang's torque. Delightful. Full-throttle acceleration is a rush job, quick and satisfying…. Braking is just as sure. A fine match. Try a turn. Brake, commit, now steer with the throttle. That's right, steer with the throttle. It works. The TRX suspension guys have been vindicated. Unlike the testy 2.3 turbo or weak-kneed 4.2 V-8, the 302 has more than enough guts to take full advantage of the suspension, and the suspension responds in kind, sticking to its *Twilight Zone* limits, then breaking away smoothly and progressively."

Buttoned-Up, Suddenly Young

McCraw reported that a GT piloted by vehicle development engineer Dan Rivard set a new course record at Ford's Dearborn track despite a still nose-heavy weight distribution of 58/42 percent front/rear. McCraw himself then took to a tight, twisty low-speed section replicating the world's worst pavement. "We simply gave up after four bone-jarring laps; [the car] didn't generate enough thump and shudder to complain about. After three years of experience with the Mustang, the engineers have managed to dial out all but a few noises and harshness sources. This GT is one buttoned-up automobile."

Both reviewers came away raving about the '82 GT. McCraw termed it "the best-balanced, most capable Mustang ever done." Said Levy: "It's as if the car's entire personality is derived from the pulse underhood. The engine makes everything all right. Suddenly the Mustang is young again."

New Steeds, Same Old Horse Race

Several months later, *Road & Track* drove a GT against a pair of redesigned 1983 Chevy Camaro Z28s—and was reminded of 1970: "For today we once again have a super-stylish new Camaro, featuring a newly refined chassis…pitted against a now somewhat dated Mustang with a chassis that's hard-put to handle its engine's generous torque. A Camaro that offers…moderate power with a manual transmission and somewhat better power only with an automatic. A Mustang that specializes in good old-fashioned straight-line performance against a Camaro that revels in curves." Though these editors ultimately picked the new over the familiar by a small margin, they admitted others might disagree. "Chevrolet has not revolutionized the Camaro, but merely updated it," *R&T* concluded. "If brute performance is a top priority, then the Mustang GT 5.0 gets the nod." Lusty H.O. aside, there was little excitement in Mustang '82. Model nomenclature was revised, with L, GL, and GLX hatchbacks and notchbacks arrayed below the GT in ascending order of price and luxury. Prices ascended greatly, ranging from the L coupe at $6345 to the GLX hatchback at $7101. And that was with four-cylinder power. The 200-cubic-inch six added $213; the 4.2-liter V-8 cost $263. At least the extra dough included a few new standard items: a larger gas tank (up from 12.5 to 15.4 gallons), wider wheels (now 14-inchers), steel-belt radial tires, and remote-control driver's door mirror. After compiling a poor reliability record, the turbo-four was withdrawn, though it would soon return. Remaining powerteams were reruns except for the 4.2-liter V-8, where the "mandatory option" automatic transmission got a fuel-saving lockup torque converter effective in all three forward gears, a device we'd see more of in the future.

The market slump that began in 1979 bottomed out in '82, when Mustang sales plunged by about a third to 130,418 units. Helped by an early sendoff that spring, Chevy sold some 179,000 of its new third-generation Camaros; Pontiac retailed 116,000 of the sister Firebirds. They cost more too, but at least they were visibly new. One bright spot for Ford was that model-year V-8 Mustang sales soared no less than five-fold over '81. Initially, the division expected to move only 20,000–25,000.

Though General Motors' new entries were formidable competition, they did not cripple Mustang's appeal. To be sure, later "buff book" comparison tests echoed Road & Track's initial verdict,

lauding the GMers for superior handling and more modern styling but usually picking Mustang as the more practical choice for day-to-day use. And where V-8s were concerned, the 'Stang was the clear performance choice. In a showdown of 1983 models, Car and Driver reported 0–60-mph times of 8.1 seconds for the GT against 8.6 for an injected V-8 Camaro with automatic and a comparatively sluggish 10.6 seconds for a carbureted V-8 Trans Am with four-speed. Writing for the magazine's August 1982 issue, technical editor Don Sherman declared that "...in terms of sheer visceral appeal, [the Mustang] is right up there with the Porsche [928]"—high praise indeed.

Consumer Guide® Weighs In

Not all was bliss, however. In testing the GT's sister ship, the RS version of the Mercury Capri (the domestic Mustang twin replacing the European Capri for '79), Consumer Guide® editors judged the power-assisted rack-and-pinion steering irritatingly vague, overly light, and lacking in feel. Wet-weather traction suf-

TOP: This good-looking L notchback was the most affordable '82 Mustang, starting at $6345 as a four-cylinder, $7062 as a six. BELOW: Mustang offered a slightly broader '82 lineup with new L, GL, and GLX titles for notchbacks and hatchbacks, plus hatchback-only V-8 GT. GLX trim and features basically duplicated those of the former Ghias.

FORD **MUSTANG GLX** SERIES INTERIOR

Clockwise: GLX interior with optional leather seating surfaces in Medium Red. GLX instrumentation. GLX 3-Door cargo area. Graphic Display Warning Module.

ABOVE AND LEFT: Announcing Ford's sudden but welcome return to hot street cars, the 1982 GT hatchback was the quickest Mustang in years. At $8308 to start, it also was top of the line, but its new 157-horsepower H.O. 302 V-8 was optional for other models at $402–$452. Functional hood scoop (shown above, along with a McLaren Mustang) cost $38. BELOW: Ford also returned to racing in '82, hiring German firm Zakspeed and car builder Jack Roush to develop Mustangs for road-course competition. One early result was this winged wonder for driver Rick Mears in the SCCA Trans-Am series.

fered from the V-8's ample torque of 240 pound-feet, peaking at a low 2400 rpm. The editors weren't able to evaluate handling fully because the test car arrived during one of the coldest weeks at their Chicago home base, and conditions were far from ideal. Even so, they found it easy to light the back tires in brisk takeoffs, accompanied at times by rear-end jitter through bumpy corners. Sherman had similar complaints: "In left-hand sweepers, the gas pedal acts as a power-over-steer switch.... That smooth two-step unfortunately turns into a jitterbug in right-hand bends, where power hop conspires to make life difficult."

But Dearborn's ponycars still had much to recommend them. Their interior was not only roomier but was more comfortable than Camaro/Firebird's. All were hatchbacks, but Ford somehow managed to provide a good deal more usable luggage space than GM. Most testers also preferred Mustang's manual gearbox for its lighter shift action vs. the truck-like Camaro/Firebird linkage. There was division over the driving position, some preferring the snug, low-slung stance of the GM cars to the more upright "vintage" openness of the Ford products.

Yet most agreed the Mustang/Capri was a far better compromise for the daily grind, where the manual-shift Camaro/Firebird could be tiring.

Speedy Refinements

Ford folks must have been stung by road-test carping, because the GT returned for 1983 with a number of changes that made it more competitive with Camaro/Firebird in the renewed ponycar performance wars. They began with wider-section tires, including newly optional 220/55R390 Michelin TRX covers, plus a slightly larger rear antiroll bar, softer rear spring rates, stiffer bushings for the front control arms, and revised shock valving. Higher-effort power steering was also included for better high-speed control.

Speaking of speed, the H.O. V-8 went to 175 bhp via a deeper-breathing four-barrel carb, plus minor valvetrain and exhaust system tweaks. Just as welcome, the motor now mated exclusively with a new Borg-Warner T-5 close-ratio five-speed gearbox, the same one available in Camaro/Firebird. This answered com-

Sun-lovers cheered the first Mustang convertible in 10 years on its early-1982 debut as an '83 model. The reborn ragtop was first sold only in luxury GLX trim (top), but a V-8 GT (below) soon followed. First-year sales way outstripped Ford's estimates.

plaints about poor gear spacing on the wide-ratio four-speed it replaced. All this plus a shorter final drive (3.27 versus 3.01:1) made for stronger takeoffs.

Elsewhere for '83, the never-impressive 4.2 V-8 was dropped, and the 200-cid straight-six was replaced as the step-up power option by the new lightweight "Essex" V-6 introduced the previous year in several other Ford model lines. A 3.8-liter (232-cid) overhead-valve design with two-barrel carburetor, the Essex arrived with a claimed 105 bhp (vs. 88 for the old straight six) and 181 lb-ft of torque (against 158). The 2.3-liter four, still standard for all models except the GT, exchanged a two-barrel carb for a more efficient one-barrel unit and adopted long-reach spark plugs for quicker combustion, a move aimed at reducing emissions while improving warmup and part-throttle engine response. Curiously, these changes boosted alleged horses by five, to 93 bhp, but the rating would fall back to 88 the following year.

Newly standard for all manual-shift '83 Mustangs was a Volkswagen-style upshift indicator light. Reflecting the fuel jitters of 1979–80, this economy aid signaled drivers when to shift to the next higher gear, based on the fact that an engine is usually most economical when running at relatively low revs on wide throttle openings. It was useful, if hardly in the free-spirited Mustang tradition.

A Smooth, Fresh Face

Nineteen eighty-three also brought the New Breed's first facelift. The most obvious change was a more rounded nose bearing a narrower, sloped horizontal-bar grille, good for a claimed 2.5-percent reduction in aerodynamic drag. The running-horse hood emblem gave way to a blue Ford oval in the grille (another graced rear decks), and taillights were revised to wrap around from the sides and hug the central license-plate "shadow box." GTs sported a wide swathe of matte-black paint on the grille and the hood's modest central bulge.

Other '83 alterations included revised seat and door trim, a

canceled standard roller-blind cargo cover for hatchbacks, more-legible gauge graphics, and less interior brightwork. The base handling suspension was canceled, while the TRX suspension was divorced from its Michelin tires to make two options respectively priced at $252 and $327–$551. The pricey Recaro seats hadn't been popular, so Ford substituted more-affordable low-back front buckets with cloth seating surfaces and mesh-insert headrests ($29–$57). Leather upholstery (with the low-back buckets) was still available at just over $400. Reflecting its new emphasis on aerodynamics, Ford deleted the hatchback's optional liftgate louvers and rear wiper/washer.

Return of the Ragtop

The notchback Carriage Roof option was also missing, but it wasn't missed because the real Mustang convertible was back after 10 long years. Since the early Seventies, a number of small aftermarket converters had been doing good business by snipping the tops from Mustang notchbacks (and other cars) to satisfy a small but steady demand for top-down motoring. Ford wanted a piece of this action for itself.

Unlike the Buick Riviera and Chrysler LeBaron ragtops announced at about the same time, the Mustang was engineered in-house and mostly built at the factory. Only top installation was farmed out, Ford tapping Cars & Concepts of Brighton, Michigan, which more or less built those other two convertibles. "[W]e decided that we wouldn't let the vendors do our job," Edsel Ford II told Car and Driver. "We would make sure that when someone buys a Mustang convertible, it lives up to our standards of quality." A small area of the big Dearborn plant was set aside for turning notchbacks into convertibles. As *C/D*'s Michael Jordan related, this involved removing the roof; reinforcing the windshield pillars and cowl/dashboard area; substituting stiffer rear-quarter panels; and adding side members (just above the rockers), a thicker taillight panel, and a stiffening crossmember between the rear wheelarches.

Like the Riviera ragtop but unlike the LeBaron, the Mustang convertible featured roll-down rear quarter windows and a tempered-glass rear window, plus standard power top operation. Any drivetrain was available save the four-cylinder/automatic combination, and any trim level at first so long as it was top-line GLX. Despite a slightly intimidating $12,467 base price, sun-loving Mustangers happily snapped up 23,438 of the new '83 ragtops. Again, Ford had underestimated itself, having predicted only about 7000 sales for a long model year starting in mid-'82.

A Turbo from T-Bird

A GT convertible was inevitable, and it bowed as a midseason '83 priced at $13,479. At the same time, Ford added a Turbo GT hatchback and convertible with a reengineered version of the

ABOVE: The H.O. V-8 added 18 horses for 1983 via internal tweaks and a deeper-breathing four-barrel carb instead of a 2V. A new close-ratio five-speed transmission further improved performance. LEFT AND BOTTOM: Recalling Mach 1 days, the '83 GT wore broad patches of black on its slicker new hose, as well as on the hood and lower bodysides.

hyperaspirated "Lima" four developed for the slick new 1983 Thunderbird Turbo Coupe. The principal changes here involved junking the carburetor for Bosch port electronic fuel injection and positioning the turbocharger upstream of the induction system so as to "blow through" it rather than "draw down" from it. Also new was Ford's latest EEC-IV electronic engine control system, which

governed injector timing, idle speed, wastegate operation, supplementary fuel enrichment, engine idle, and emissions control. Other upgrades included forged-aluminum pistons, valves made of a special temperature-resistant alloy, lighter flywheel, die-cast aluminum rocker cover, and an engine-mounted oil cooler. Per usual turbo practice, compression was lowered from 9.0:1 to 8.0:1, and premium unleaded fuel was recommended for best performance. The result: 145 bhp at 4600 rpm—only 5 bhp more than the previous version, but better than the magic "1 hp per cu. in." ideal for this 140-cube mill. Torque was 180 lb-ft peaking at a relatively low 3600 rpm.

Aside from different nameplates, Turbo GTs were visual twins to the V-8 versions. All came with black exterior moldings, beefy Eagle GT performance radials, aluminum wheels, sport bucket seats, and five-speed manual gearbox. Suspension was tuned to match engine weight and power characteristics. Despite its small

size, the turbo-four packed the same horsepower that Chevy advertised for its base Z28 V-8. With that, the revived Turbo Mustang could run 0–60 mph in well under 10 seconds and the standing quarter-mile in about 16 seconds—*and* return 25 mpg overall. But the T-Bird TC could match all those numbers, and the fortified 5.0-liter Mustang now flew to 60 in near six seconds flat.

ABOVE: Ford revived a "blown" Mustang in mid-'83, but the mechanically improved four-cylinder Turbo GT was a poor seller, being slower and costlier than the similar V-8 GTs. BELOW: The exotic Mustang GTP prototype racer of 1983–84 extracted an amazing 600–700 horses from small four-cylinder turbo engines but was less reliable and less successful than rival Porsches and Corvettes.

Tough to Drive, Tough to Sell

Although it seemed to offer the best of both worlds, the improved blown Mustang laid a sales egg. The lack of available automatic transmission and air conditioning probably cost more than a few sales, but the real problem was price. The Turbos started some $250 *above* comparably equipped V-8 GTs, yet they were slower. Also, their peaky engine was relatively weak on low-rpm torque, so it had to be caned most all the time. The V-8, by contrast, was a traditional, relatively lazy American engine with muscular low-end thrust, and it just loafed along easily at highway speeds. Ford said a late introduction and a slow production ramp-up limited Turbo GT sales, and only 483 of the '83s were built. But the real damper is best expressed by that time-worn Detroit adage, "There's no substitute for cubic inches"—not even high techology.

Swift, Sophisticated SVO

Nevertheless, Ford massaged its turbo-four even more, fearing that the latest energy crisis would get worse. (It wouldn't.) The result appeared for 1984 in a very different performance Mustang, the SVO. Engineered by Ford's recently formed Special Vehicle Operations unit (hence the name), this was basically a Turbo GT hatchback with enough modifications to satisfy the most confirmed devotees of toney European machinery. Notable was the first air-to-air intercooler in American production. This chilled the pressurized air for a denser, more powerful charge. A world first was electronic control to vary boost pressure, which could reach 14 psi, said to be the highest of any production turbo engine to that point. There was even a cockpit switch for "tuning" the engine electronics to allow running on regular or premium-

Mustang marked 20 years with a modest trim option for the 1984 V-8 GT convertible (here with a classic '64) and hatchback. Done in Oxford White with Canyon Red stripes and interior, this GT-350 package prompted a lawsuit from Carroll Shelby, who said Ford broke a promise in using the name without his permission. Ford settled.

grade fuel. With these and other racing-inspired ideas, maximum horsepower jumped by a claimed 20 percent to 175 at 4500 rpm. Torque increased some 10 percent to 210 lb-ft at 3000. Putting it to the ground was a five-speed manual gearbox with special Hurst linkage driving to a Traction-Lok limited-slip differential with 3.45:1 final drive.

SVO chassis revisions were no less thorough. The 9.0-inch rear drum brakes of other Mustangs were swapped for beefy 11.25-inch-diameter discs, and the front discs swelled from 10.06 to 10.92 inches across. New "aero-style" cast-aluminum wheels measuring 16 × 7 inches wore V-rated European Goodyear NCT radials, later exchanged for P225/50VR16 Goodyear Eagle GT50s with unidirectional "gatorback" tread (as on the '84 Corvette). Spring rates and bushings were stiffened, premium Koni adjustable shocks replaced the stock dampers, the front antiroll bar was thickened (from 0.94 to 1.20 inches), and a rear bar was added along with an extra inch of front wheel travel. The stock rack-and-pinion power steering went from variable-ratio to fast constant-ratio gearing but retained high-effort valving to optimize road feel.

Last but not least was "Quadra-Shock," a nifty idea borrowed from the T-Bird Turbo Coupe (and easily adapted from that Fox-based relative). The name referred to an extra pair of shock absorbers sitting almost horizontally astride the differential between the axle and the body structure. The idea was to minimize jittery axle "tramp" in hard acceleration, and it worked. Intriguingly, Quadra-Shock had been sort of promised for the V-8 GT back in '82 but was delayed for various reasons that are still not entirely clear.

Not Your Father's Ponycar

One thing was clear: The SVO was definitely *not* your father's ponycar. Setting it apart were a distinctive "biplane" rear spoiler made of polycarbonate plastic, a specific grille-less nose (engine air entered from below the bumper and through a small slot above). A large hood air scoop fed the intercooler, and dual square headlamps replaced the normal Mustang's smaller quads. A deep front air dam incorporated standard foglamps, and small fairings at the leading edges of the rear wheel openings helped smooth airflow around the fat tires.

Inside, the SVO boasted such driver-oriented accoutrements as a left "dead pedal" footrest, resited brake and accelerator pedals for easier heel-and-toe shifting, an 8000-rpm tachometer, turbo-boost gauge, and multi-adjustable seats like those in the T-Bird Turbo Coupe. Also included were electric rear-window defroster, tinted glass, AM/FM stereo radio with speaker/amplifier system, leather-rim tilt steering wheel, and the familiar Mustang console with graphic warning display. Only six major options were listed: air, power windows, cassette player, flip-up glass sunroof, and leather upholstery.

The SVO was an enthusiast's dream come true. Handling was near-neutral, cornering flat and undramatic, steering direct and

continued on page 153

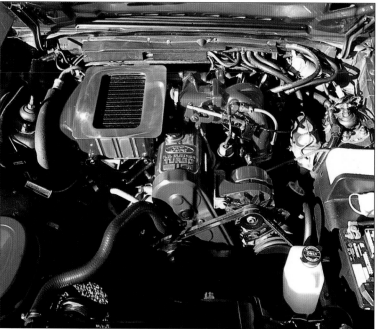

Mustang blazed a new performance trail with the sophisticated 1984 SVO. A grille-less nose and "biplane" rear spoiler mimicked the look of Ford's sporty European Sierra XR4. The interior was similarly understated. A hood scoop fed air to a high-tech four-cylinder turbo engine making 175 bhp. Great go and eager handling won purist plaudits but not too many sales.

SVO: Ford's Speed Shop

"Race on Sunday, Sell on Monday" is a Detroit adage, and no one knew the truth of it better than Ford. Even before founding Ford Motor Company, old Henry made headlines driving stripped-down flyers like the "999" to record speeds. Sixty years later, his grandson decided to pump up the company's image and sales with an all-out assault on most every major form of motorsports. This "Total Performance" initiative netted a pile of trophies and taught lessons that showed up in fast, flashy street cars like the Boss Mustangs. Indeed, many of those cars were in response to competition requirements, underscoring another industry truism: "Racing Improves the Breed."

By 1970, however, "Total Performance" was out of step with radically changed conditions, and Ford abruptly got out of racing. Over the next 10 years, fading public memories of the glory days and a procession of dull showroom models left the Blue Oval with a ho-hum image and sagging sales prospects. For Henry Ford II, there was only one thing to do: Get back into racing. Thus, before stepping down as chairman in 1980, he personally authorized the formation of Special Vehicle Operations.

It was patterned on the small, hush-hush Lockheed "skunkworks" now famous for creating amazing aircraft such as the 3000-mph SR-71 Blackbird. Unlike "Total Performance" days, when outsiders like Carroll Shelby were typically recruited for specific projects, SVO was Ford's own "speed shop," with a separate budget and lots of freedom from top-brass meddling. It had three assignments: develop and manage various motorsports programs, from NASCAR to Formula 1; expand Ford racing and high-performance parts business; and develop hot limited-edition street cars.

Within a few months, a select group of some 30 designers, engineers, and experienced racing hands was assembled under German-born Michael Kranefuss (kranna-fus), the successful competition manager for Ford Europe in the early 1970s. Later dubbed "Rommel of the Racetrack" by *Car and Driver,* Kranefuss set the team to work on a variety of projects, many straightforward, a few very exotic.

He gave priority to road-racing Mustangs for the Sports Car Club of America (SCCA) Trans-Am and International Motor Sports Association (IMSA) GT series. This was partly because the public could easily link those racers with showroom Mustangs—all the better for sales. As Kranefuss explained to *Motor Trend*'s Gary Witzenburg in 1984: "If you want to get your technical message across, where you're headed in the future, it's road racing more than anything else.... This is something that very clearly talks about the new Ford Motor Company, which is very much technologically oriented and dedicated to product integrity. It's a combined corporate effort, with some budget from Ford Design, some from Aerospace [division], and quite a bit from SVO to build the first four cars and about 15 engines."

Kranefuss was speaking of the new Mustang GTP prototype racer, for which Ford ponied up about $1 million in 1983 alone. A Mustang in name only, it had a long, low aerodynamic body. A *very* high-tech four-cylinder engine produced an astounding 600 horsepower in initial 1.7-liter form, around 700 when bumped to 2.1 liters for '84. Unfortunately for SVO, the GTP Mustang was outclassed by more-durable Porsches and Corvettes, though Ford did score one win in '83.

SVO had greater success with production-based Mustangs. In 1981, Tom Gloy won at Sears Point, Mustang's first Trans-Am victory in 11 years. By '84, SVO chassis specialist Bob Riley had teamed with engine magician and car builder Jack Roush and factory-backed Mustangs soon dominated Trans-Am, winning 17 of 34 contests in 1985–86 alone. Between 1984 and '89, Ford notched 46 Trans-Am victories, more than all other manufacturers combined. Driving talent helped, including Lyn St. James and especially Dorsey Schroeder, who won half the 14 Trans-Am events in 1989, a great way to celebrate Mustang's 25th birthday.

SVO was no less a less a power in other forms of motorsports, thanks to a talented team, the determined drive of Kranefuss, and deepening corporate pockets. *C/D* noted that in 1992, "Ford was the most diversely successful manufacturer in racing in the world. Ford drivers...finished 1-2-3 in NASCAR's final Winston Cup standings, and Ford broke a nine-year Chevrolet stranglehold on the NASCAR manufacturer's championship. Out of the box, Ford's new turbo Cosworth engine dominated the Indycar series, overpower the long-dominant Chevy Indy V-8.... And Ford, while spending only half the money Honda and Renault poured into Formula 1, finished third in the Driving Championship." And that was just one year in the life of SVO. Too bad it missed the mark with its sole production car, the arguably too-European Mustang SVO. But nobody's perfect.

Though Ford remains a motorsports power, SVO was reorganized in the early Nineties and its street-machine charge handed to a new Special Vehicle Team. SVT generated all manner of Mustang Cobras and other hot Fords, setting the standard for whatever would next carry the flag at Dearborn's skunkworks.

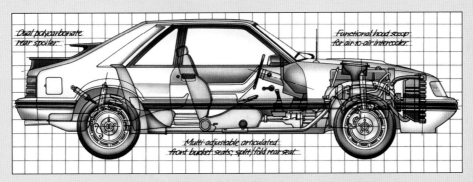

Dual polycarbonate rear spoiler. Functional hood scoop for air-to-air intercooler. Multi-adjustable articulated front bucket seats; split/fold rear seat.

Mustang got another nose job for 1985, this time with a simple one-slot grille above an integrated bumper/spoiler. Interiors were also freshened, gaining a new steering wheel and trim materials. Fuel injection returned from '84 for V-8s with automatic transmission, like this GT convertible, but internal changes boosted horsepower by 15 to 180. Mustang sales went up for the second year in a row, reaching 156,514.

continued from page 149

properly weighted, braking swift and sure. Performance? Exhilarating, with 0–60 mph in about 7.5 seconds, the quarter-mile in just under 16 seconds at around 90 mph, and top speed near 135 mph. *Road & Track,* long an advocate of Euro-style American cars, was ecstatic. "Given the existing Mustang plat-form, the Ford SVO team could hardly have done a better job of improving [it] to world-class GT standards. Almost all of the things that *R&T* has stressed as important in a well balanced, universally driveable GT coupe have been incorporated [with] few serious compromises…. [The SVO is] suitable for sustained fast driving on any [road] you're likely to find…giving comfort and assurance all the while…. This may be the best all-around car for the enthusiast driver ever produced by the U.S. industry; we hope it's just the start of a new era."

But *R&T* was doomed to disappointment. So was Ford. In the end, the SVO it was just another sophisticated screamer that "buff books" liked and buyers didn't. And at over $16,000 out the door, it looked way too expensive next to the V-8 GT, which deliv-ered similar style and sizzle for a whopping $6000–$7000 less. Ford thus retailed fewer than 4000 SVOs for model-year '84, though it had the capacity to build some four times that number.

Together, the V-8 and SVO killed off the Turbo GT after fewer than 3000 hatchbacks and about 600 convertibles were built for 1983–84. All early-'84 GTs, both V-8 and Turbo, were virtual '83 reruns except for a split rear seatback, also newly standard for most lesser hatchbacks, and substitution of solid front head restraints for the previous open type. December 1983 brought several welcome changes, including Quadra-Shock rear suspen-sion, a revised front spoiler, and closer SVO-style throttle and brake-pedal spacing to assist heel-and-toe artists.

There was little news for other '84 Mustangs. The entry-level L notchback got a hatchback sister, while GL and GLX models were replaced by LX versions with roughly the same features, plus a newly standard V-6 for the convertible. Interiors were spruced up with a new steering wheel and dashboard facing. Dash lighting switched from green to racy red.

There was also a second, tamer 302 V-8 for '84, with throttle-body electronic fuel injection (TBI) and 10 fewer horses than the carbureted H.O. (165 total). This was reserved for non-GTs with automatic, which now came in two forms as well: the familiar three-speeder and Ford's corporate four-speed unit, whose over-drive top gear allowed use of a shorter (numerically higher) final-drive ratio (3.27:1 versus 2.73:1) with no ill effects on mileage. TBI was also applied to the Essex V-6, bringing it up to 120 bhp and 205 lb-ft; here, three-speed SelectShift was now your only transmission choice. In line with a widening industry trend, all manual-shift Mustangs received a starter interlock that prevented accidental lurching should you forget to depress the clutch pedal before cranking the starter.

Eighties Enigma

By this time, gasoline was not only plentiful again but was even becoming *cheaper* in some places. Not surprisingly, many folks just had to have a good old-fashioned V-8. This illustrates a pecu-liar irony of the 1980s: the renewed popularity of relatively large-

Mustang's carbureted V-8 also got more wallop for '85, going to 210 bhp with a more aggressive camshaft, low-friction roller tappets, and freer-flow exhaust system with straight tailpipes (just visible on the GT hatchback below). The 35-bhp gain was impressive considering that emissions limits were still tightening and that Mustangs had to help Ford meet its "fleet average" fuel economy targets.

displacement engines at a time when automakers were discouraged from selling them by government regulations now out of synch with market forces and a worldwide oil glut. It was all too bad, for the Turbo GT and SVO were honest attempts at reconciling performance with economy, a worthy goal. A shame most buyers didn't care.

The 1985 SVO made a midseason debut with 205 bhp, up 30, thanks to a hotter cam, new exhaust system, higher-boost turbo, and other "hot-rodding tricks." SVO's cockpit remained Euro-purposeful, if not functionally ideal. New flush-mount "composite" headlamps were SVO's major '85 style change, though base price fell to a three-year low of $14,521.

Birthday Present

Mustang reached the ripe old age of 20 in 1984. To mark the occasion, Ford dusted off the GT-350 name from Shelby days for a limited-edition model. It amounted to a trim option for the V-8 GT convertible and hatchback consisting of Oxford White paint, Canyon Red rocker-panel stripes, and matching red interior with "articulated" front seats. At least it didn't cost much: $25–$144 depending on body style and other options. Ford ads promised no more than 5000 copies, but one source says the final tally was 5260. No matter. For such a milestone birthday, this special was no big deal—except for Dearborn lawyers. Mr. Shelby claimed that he owned "GT-350" and had been promised that Ford wouldn't use the name without his okay. Carroll, now working again with his old friend Lee Iacocca at Chrysler, may have been thinking of it for one of the hot Dodges he was building at a small-scale facility in California. In any case, he was miffed enough to hit Ford with a copyright infringement suit. Sometimes, it just doesn't pay to be sentimental.

Mustang sales were a pretty good barometer of the mid-Eighties new-car market and national economy. Demand hit

bottom for model-year 1983 at 120,873 units, then strengthened to 141,480, followed by 156,514. By contrast, Camaro/Firebird sales, initially higher, began trending down and by 1987 would trail those of Ford's veteran ponycar.

Production-based Mustangs were always serious contenders in late-1980s road racing. They did especially well in the SCCA Trans-Am but also proved their mettle in the competing IMSA GT series. Each series had its own rules, but both allowed liberal modifications to bodywork, chassis, and powertrain, as on this IMSA contestant.

Staying Competitive

Which was quite remarkable considering that Mustang was an older design with a less sophisticated chassis and somewhat lower handling/roadholding limits. Yet these apparent minuses were actually pluses. Many buyers preferred the Mustang's more traditional road manners and generally superior ride. What's more, earlier amortization of tooling costs allowed Ford to keep prices somewhat lower than GM could, even though the end of a decade-long inflationary spiral was helping both companies in that regard. But Ford also seemed to build its cars better each year—GM didn't—and kept improving them, too.

With all this, Mustang emerged as uncommonly good sporty-car value. The '85 price range ran from just $6885 for the LX notchback to $13,585 for the top-line GT convertible and $14,521 for the slow-selling SVO. Though much costlier in raw dollars, those figures were mighty competitive for the time, especially once a stronger yen began boosting prices of four-cylinder Japanese models that couldn't match the V-8 Mustang for performance or charisma.

Both those qualities were enhanced for '85. Low-friction roller tappets and a new high-performance camshaft lifted the carbureted H.O. V-8 to 210 bhp, an impressive 35-bhp increase. Similar changes brought the injected 302 (still restricted to automatic) to 180 bhp. As before, the H.O. was available only with five-speed manual, which came in for revised intermediate-gear ratios and a more precise linkage. Also improving the GT were beefier P225/60VR15 "Gatorback" tires on seven-inch-wide cast-aluminum

wheels, both lifted from the SVO, plus variable-rate springs, gas-pressurized front shock absorbers, higher-rate rear shocks, and a thicker rear antiroll bar. A three-spoke SVO-style steering wheel freshened the interior (a running change from mid-'84), as did revised dashboard and door-panel trim and comfortable new multi-adjustable bucket seats by Lear Siegler.

Elsewhere, the cheap L models were canceled and remaining Mustangs got an SVO-style nose cap with integral air dam and a simple air slot above the bumper. The SVO itself returned at midyear with flush-mount "composite" headlights, newly allowed by the government, plus 30 more horsepower from a hotter cam and exhaust system, larger fuel injectors, and a revised turbo-charger with higher boost pressure. This basic 205-bhp engine was also used for a short-lived revival of the Turbo GT, which vanished again after miniscule sales. Its vastly more popular V-8 brother kept trading points with Camaro/Firebird in magazine showdown tests. In all, Mustang attracted about 15,000 additional buyers for the model year.

Sales spurted to near 224,500 for 1986, a decade production high achieved with few changes. The main one was adoption of more precise sequential port fuel injection for a single 302 V-8 rated at 200 bhp and offered with either five-speed manual or four-speed automatic. The rear axle was beefed up to handle peak torque that now stood at 285 lb-ft. Both the V-8 and V-6 offered smoother running via viscous (fluid-filled) engine mounts, an SVO upgrade from '85. Buyers this year also enjoyed a longer

THIS PAGE, TOP: Despite few changes for '86, Mustang notched decade-high model-year sales of nearly a quarter-million units. As before, small "5.0" front-fender badges signaled V-8 power, as in this tame-looking LX notchback. LEFT: Mustang went to a single V-8 for '86, a new 200-bhp H.O. with electronic port fuel injection that split the power difference between the previous carbureted and throttle-body-injected versions. ABOVE: GT hoods for 1985–86 wore a simple black patch decal with bold model i.d. cutout. OPPOSITE PAGE: Answering a request from the California Highway Patrol, Ford devised a high-speed Mustang pursuit package in 1983. Within three years, thousands of such cars were catching speeders in 14 other states. This one served in Florida.

anti-corrosion warranty, extra sound-deadening material, and a more convenient single-key locking system.

The '86s got the inevitable yearly price hikes, though they were fairly modest all things considered. The notchback LX went up to $7295, the GT convertible to $14,220. The SVO was still around—and costlier than ever at $15,272—but its days were numbered. With demand still far below even Ford's modest projections, it was just too unprofitable to keep around, and it would not return for '87. Respective model year production for 1984–86 was 4508, 1954, and 3382—just 9844 in all.

Fox Finale?

If nothing else, the SVO highlighted the adaptability and staying power of the "New Breed" Mustang. But by the seventh year of the Fox generation, some observers felt a replacement was past due. To be sure, Ford had done an admirable job of keeping the car interesting and competitive. Indeed, no less a power than president Don Petersen favored "continuous improvement," the strategy that was then helping Japanese automakers make serious inroads into the U.S. car market. But though many journalists were amazed by how good the old Mustang still was, they couldn't help wonder when a new one would appear. Noting how "German" the GT had become for 1985, *Car and Driver*'s Pat Bedard wrote, "You don't expect such refinement this late in the model cycle…. But the Germans keep after their stock, always improving, and the German influence in Ford is being felt. It's a good thing, too, because the Mustang is going to get older still before it's replaced, probably in 1988. But if it keeps aging this gracefully, who cares?"

Bedard was both right and wrong. Though a new Mustang was being groomed for '88, the no-longer-new New Breed still had a long road to travel.

Chapter Nine:
1987-1993

The Fox generation got a new lease on life with a handsome 1987 restyle and further refinements into the early Nineties. More than ever, Mustang sold as the king of "bang for the buck," but Ford worried the car was standing still even as rivals were moving forward. So how to change Mustang without really changing it? Ah, *that* was the question.

Mustang's rapidly improved fortunes in 1982–86 mirrored those of Ford Motor Company itself. After teetering on the financial brink, Ford not only roared back to profitability, it became the most profitable outfit in Detroit. By 1987 it was earning more money each year than giant General Motors—and on only *half* the sales volume. Critics were baffled, stockholders relieved, the automotive press impressed.

There was no secret to this. Like Chrysler under Lee Iaccoca, Ford under Don Petersen (who moved up to chairman in 1985) became more efficient, closing old factories, modernizing others, slashing overhead, and laying off workers (only to rehire some later). Though such steps were most always painful, there was no choice in the face of unprecedented foreign competition. But where Chrysler put all its chips on one basic platform, the adaptable K-car, Ford trotted out a slew of new models with much broader sales appeal.

Part of that appeal stemmed from a new aerodynamic styling signature instigated by Jack Telnack. It proved so popular that he was promoted in mid-1987 to replace Don Kopka as design vice-president for the entire company. Telnack's passion for "aero" had a practical side. As he had shown with the '79 Mustang, reducing air drag improves fuel economy. And as CAFE standards were not going away, that was still vital in the 1980s. But shapes born of the wind tunnel also gave Ford a way to stand apart from the herd at a time when design—good design—was again influencing sales more than EPA mileage numbers. Sure enough, amidst a sea of mostly square-rigged Chrysler products and lookalike GM cars, buyers flocked to smooth, unmistakable new Dearborn offerings like the 1983 Thunderbird and especially the 1986 Ford Taurus and Mercury Sable, affordable midsize sedans that looked like pricey German Audis.

But the key to Mustang's success in these years was performance, not styling. Of course, it helped greatly that an economic recovery took hold in 1982, boosting personal income even as inflation, interest rates, unemployment, and especially gas prices all came down. As we've seen, Ford also helped Mustang's cause with the same sort of relentless refining that Porsche used to keep its Sixties-era 911 sports car so evergreen. This not only involved more power most every year but also new features and options, plus much improved workmanship.

Yet the more things stay the same, the harder they can be to change, to paraphrase an old saw. Even as it got better and better, Mustang increasingly seemed a relic of Ford's past—and ever more dated next to newer sporty cars. But sales were on the upswing, and nostalgia was a big factor, even for younger types who had missed "Mustang Mania" in the Sixties. Still, Ford fretted over what would happen to sales should the market suddenly reverse again or if competitors mounted a strong new challenge. With all this, Ford reasoned, a next-generation Mustang ought to appear by 1989 at the latest.

Hands Across the Sea

As it happened, work toward that car had been underway since early 1982, just as the reborn GT and H.O. V-8 were starting to rekindle the old Mustang excitement. Initiated as project SN8— "sporty car, North America, 8"—this effort envisioned a smaller, lighter pony like the old Mustang II or European Capri, but with aero styling, front-wheel drive to optimize interior space, and high-efficiency four-cylinder engines instead of a thirsty low-tech V-8. Unfortunately, early proposals around this concept did not suit decision-makers. So just a year into the program, Ford turned to longtime Japanese partner Mazda, whose small-car expertise was at least equal to Ford's own.

Dearborn went calling at an opportune time. Mazda was then planning the next version of its front-drive 626 series, which included a coupe, one of Mustang's new-wave rivals. Ford figured to save money and get a better new Mustang by joining in. The result would be two models, each with its own styling identity and sales networks, but sharing basic chassis, running gear, and some inner structure. The idea became even more attractive once Mazda decided to build a plant in Flat Rock, Michigan, near the historic River Rouge factory where Mustangs were made, and to make part of its output available to Ford.

It seemed a match made in heaven. Ford would get a new

Mustang for far less money than by developing it alone. Mazda also liked the economics (the yen was very strong against the dollar) as well as the deal's "politically correct" image. With "Japan Inc." taking ever-larger chunks out of Detroit's sales hide, Congress was threatening protectionist legislation that the Japanese hoped to forestall with "transplant" factories employing U.S. workers.

Message to Dearborn

What Ford hadn't counted on was the near-universal outrage among Mustang fans once word of the plan leaked out. A new Mustang was a good thing, even overdue. But *Japanese* engineering? No way! Mustang was an all-American icon. How dare they put the name on a "badge-engineered" import. And looky here, Ford. Front-wheel drive may be okay for little econoboxes, but *real* performance cars put power to the pavement with the *back* tires.

Dearborn got the message and released the "626 Mustang" (which Mazda sold as the MX-6) as the 1989 Probe (named after Ford's recent series of aerodynamic show cars). The decision wasn't made until the last minute, but it was both wise and correct. Though capable and spirited in turbocharged GT form,

Mustang got a full makover for 1987. Opinions divided over the style merits of deep perimeter "skirts" and busy "cheese-grater" taillights on GTs, but most everyone liked its handsome new wheels. And no one griped about the new-design '87 dashboard or the GT's standard "articulated" front seats.

the Probe was too just "foreign" to pass as a ponycar—an American invention, after all—even if it *was* styled in Dearborn.

Meanwhile, rising demand had convinced Ford to rejuvenate the aging Mustang, something it could well afford amid record profits. The aim was not just bringing the old warrior in line with the new design theme but to make it more competitive in an increasingly tough sporty-car market, especially against the newer Chevrolet Camaro and Pontiac Firebird.

The Same but Different

The result bowed for 1987 as the most thoroughly changed Mustang since the Fox generation's debut. The slow-selling SVO was gone, but LX notchback, hatchback, and convertible returned along with the popular GT hatch and ragtop. Significantly, Ford planners also decided to axe Mercury's Mustang, the Fox-based Capri, after eight years of curiously disappointing sales.

Despite a familiar basic shape, Mustang looked slicker than ever for '87. A smoother nose sandwiched flush-mount head-lamps between triangular inboard parking lights and wraparound turn-signal lamps. Rear side glass on coupes was pulled flush with surrounding sheetmetal, with a wide black band where the vertical slats had been. But though the side windows looked larg-er, the "daylight openings" they covered were unchanged, so over-the-shoulder visibility remained a bit constricted. Restyled taillamps were evident, and most exterior moldings were finished in black. Beside a more contemporary appearance, these changes lowered drag coefficients: now 0.40 for notchbacks, 0.42 for convertibles, and 0.36 for the LX hatchback; the three-door GT tested out at a slightly blockier 0.38. The restyle had little

effect on dimensions inside or out. Wheelbase remained at 100.5 inches, while overall length measured 179 inches, width 68.3, and height about 52 inches. Track widths were 56.6 inches fore, 57 aft. Curb weights did change—for the worse—adding about 100 pounds on average.

LXs remained more visually restrained than GTs. Their grille, for instance, was a simple slot with a horizontal bar bearing a small Ford oval. Below was a body-color bumper with integral spoiler and wide, black rubstrips that wrapped around as body-side protection moldings to a color-keyed rear bumper. GTs wore sculpted rocker-panel skirts that looked like the add-ons they were, plus a dummy scoop ahead of each wheel, a burly spoiler on the hatchback, and busy "cheese-grater" taillamps instead of the LX's simple tri-color clusters. At least the grille-less GT face was aggressively handsome—rather like the SVO's—with a wide "mouth" intake in a forward-jutting airdam with flanking round foglamps. So you shouldn't miss it, large "Mustang GT" lettering was molded into the rocker extensions and rear bumper cover.

RIGHT: Mustang's trusty 302 V-8 was again muscled up for 1987, tack-ing on 25 horsepower for a total of 225. A return to freer-breathing cylinder heads and other induction changes did the trick. Mustang now matched max Chevy Camaro/Pontiac Firebird power but offered man-ual as well as automatic transmission. BELOW: A smoother new nose helped lower the '87 GT hatchback's drag coefficient to a worthy 0.38.

TOP: A growing number of Mustangers in '87 took their V-8 in one of the less-showy LX models like this 5.0 notchback. So did John Law. RIGHT: Mustang's new '87 instrument panel was quite "international" in appearance and function with its useful package shelf, simple rotary climate control, and BMW-style air vents. BELOW: As before, the stealthiest way to go fast in an '87 Mustang was to option an LX with the $1885 V-8 package. This hatchback is so equipped.

A Dash of Distinction

Because instrument panels are among the costliest components for a carmaker to change, the brand-new '87 dashboard implied the foxy Mustang might hang on for more than a few years (as indeed it would). The design could have come from Mazda. The right side was cut away on top to form a useful package shelf and lend a greater sense of interior spaciousness. Drivers faced an upright instrument pod with side-mount rocker switches for lights, hazard flasher, and rear-window defroster. Column stalks again looked after wipers and turn signals, while cruise-control buttons remained conveniently in the steering-wheel spokes. Dropping down from dash center was a broad console housing rotary knobs for temperature, fan speed, and air distribution, all lifted from the new Euro-style Taurus. A quartet of large, square vents marched across the middle of the dash, BMW-fashion. Modernization was also evident in a new-design steering wheel, armrests, door panels, and seat adjusters.

More V-8 Vitamins

The most noteworthy mechanical alterations involved the venerable small-block V-8—no surprise, as it was pulling even with the 2.3-liter four in customer preference. A return to freer-breathing, pre-1986 cylinder heads and other induction changes added 25 horses for a total of 225, thus matching the top Chevy Camaro/Pontiac Firebird option, a 5.7-liter Corvette mill. Torque also improved, swelling to a stout 300 pound-feet. The 302—a.k.a. "5.0-liter" (it was actually closer to 4.9)—remained standard on GTs, which also received larger front-disc brakes (10.9 inches

Flush-mount headlamps, a legacy of the late Mustang SVO, gave all '87s a smoother, more coherent face. LXs like this four-cylinder ragtop had a simple central air slot instead of the GT's solid front fascia, but all models still "breathed" mainly through an under-bumper intake. Multipoint electronic fuel injection was a new '87 upgrade for the 2.3-liter four, but horsepower and torque were only a little higher.

versus 10.1) and recalibrated suspension.

The four-banger wasn't overlooked for '87, exchanging a dull one-barrel carburetor for state-of-the-art multipoint electronic fuel injection. Though the engine was little more potent at 90 bhp and 130 lb-ft, it now teamed with the V-8's five-speed manual and optional four-speed automatic transmissions (vs. the previous four-speed stick and three-speed slushbox), which helped maximize what grunt it had. A big surprise was deletion of the 3.8-liter V-6, leaving a huge power and performance gap between the four and V-8. With that, CONSUMER GUIDE®'s *Auto 1987* predicted "Ford plans on selling mostly V-8-powered Mustangs this year."

Ford did, only a lot of them were LXs with an $1885 V-8 package that also included the GT's uprated chassis and tires. In fact, demand for 5.0-liter LXs proved so strong that Ford ran short of engines during the '87 season. Buyers were told that if they wanted a V-8 Mustang, it would have to be a GT. There were reasons for this. Many people thought the new GT either too ugly, too outlandish, or both, which must have dismayed Jack Telnack. Others simply preferred their V-8 in the quieter-looking LX because it was less likely to be noticed by the law. Besides, it cost less that way.

More Than Skin Deep

Mustang's '87 makeover wasn't all about styling and power. *Motor Trend*'s Rick Titus took note of the "sizeable effort [made] to improve the sound deadening.... Corrugated firewall panels and sound-deadening adhesives give the '87 Mustang a rock-solid feel. It is, in fact, one of the first things you notice when you close the door. Road noise and engine vibration are cut nearly in half, and yet you still get the benefit of race-bred Ford small-block, as the Mustang's exhaust note puts that certain little magic in the air." Titus did take Ford to task over brakes, at least for racing purposes. "Ford's designers chose to enlarge the front vented discs, but continued to use leftover Pinto drums on the rear.... It seems [rear disc brakes] died with the SVO. This is appalling,

Sun-loving Mustangers with $24,700 to spare could get into this new customized 1987 rag-top from Michigan's ASC, a.k.a. Automobile Specialty Company. It was basically a stock V-8 LX convertible with a more steeply sloped windshield, heavy structural reinforcing, unique lower-body skirting, leather interior, and a slick steel tonneau to cover the folded top. The back seat was removed, as were all Mustang badges. Only about 1000 were built.

considering the Ford flies the tall flag of performance over the Mustang, yet doles its best brakes out to whiney little four-bangers and their luxo lines."

But Britisher Mel Nichols, testing a new GT for *Automobile* magazine, thought "the SVO did not come and go in vain…. At the front, caster changes reduce camber loss in the corners, and [there are SVO] plastic ball joints, retuned bushings, and better mounts for the antiroll bar…. The Special Vehicle Operations development of a new crossmember allowed different front suspension pickup points, which in turn permit the fitting of decently large P225/60VR15 Goodyear Gatorbacks running 35 psi for reduced rolling resistance." Nichols also decried the small rear drum brakes but approved a stronger axle, retuned rear suspension bushes, rear antiroll bar, and premium gas-pressurized shock absorbers all around.

Hedonist's Hot Rod

For such a familiar and relatively simple chassis, the '87 GT earned unusual praise for its driver-pleasing road-carving ability. "The Mustang is a hedonist's car," declared *AutoWeek*'s Phil Berg, "one that makes you want to go somewhere—anywhere—alone. Somewhere out in the tules with little road-hogging traffic…. You look forward to cornering with a passionate grip on the steering wheel. You start to believe the only reason for the quick [V-8] is to keep you from wasting valuable time on straights so

Ford spent some $200 million on Mustang's '87 restyle, so no one was surprised when the '88s arrived looking exactly the same. Little else changed too, though LXs did benefit from a higher-capacity battery. Prices continued an upward gallop from '87, rising another $700–$1100. This four-cylinder LX notchback now started at $8726.

you can find more rewarding section of two-lane. It's a very personal thing."

Nichols was more specific, describing GT handling as "predictable and progressive, so effortless and enjoyable…. The car turned into the bends cleanly, with understeer never passing the point of pleasing stability, then nudged through a long period of neutrality into progressive oversteer, talking all the way. A nudge of opposite lock held the tail. A touch more power pushed it out farther, with a little more lock balancing that, too. From the outset, the Mustang felt like a car that could driven fast and safely and satisfyingly. It had all the right sporting attributes, yet there was also something quite nice about its character. It came down to one word: forgiving…. Even on the narrow stretches and where the bends were visibly off-camber, there was nothing intimidating about driving it hard and fast."

The Good Old Days Are Now

Speaking of fast, the fortified small-block delivered straightline performance even more reminiscent of the good old days. Ford claimed 0–60 mph took 6.1 seconds with manual shift, and most magazine tests got close to that. *AutoWeek,* for example, clocked 6.5 seconds, "well into Corvette, Porsche 928S and Lotus Turbo Esprit territory. Two years ago it was about a second slower. Top speed of the new Mustang GT has also risen from the mid 130s to just under 150 mph. Not only is that faster than the high-tech coupes from Toyota, Nissan and Mazda, it beats Ferrari's [V-8] Mondial and closes in on the [six-cylinder BMW] 328. This is the cheapest car in America that will even come close to the revered one-five-oh."

Obviously, new technology was allowing Ford (and others) to deliver the kind of performance that had previously been

achieved only through big displacement. For example, to get around 225 net horses in, say, a '72 Mustang, you had to order an optional 351 V-8 rated at 168–275 net bhp. Yet the '87 small-block was thriftier and smoother-running, needed less upkeep, and was more reliable—pure, unadulterated progress.

Most Bang For The Buck

While progress often exacts a price, Mustang remained an exception. "Though far from perfect—or perfected—the Mustang GT is put together well enough and offers a ton of go for your dough," said CONSUMER GUIDE®'s *Auto Test 1987.* "Despite a full option load—air, premium sound system, cruise control, and power windows, door locks, and mirrors—our [hatchback] came to $14,352, which is an exceptional value when IROC-Z Camaros, Toyota Supras, and Nissan 300ZXs can go for $5000 more."

It's striking how often reviewers mentioned Mustang's high "bang for the buck" value, as indeed they still do. Even General Motors didn't argue with that. As a Chevy engineer told *AutoWeek's* Christopher A. Sawyer in early 1988: "We're stuck now in (the rut) that the Camaro costs more from a production standpoint…. If you want a T-roofed IROC that's pretty close to loaded, you're going to be over twenty grand. An equivalent Mustang is about $3500 cheaper." But that's the beauty of hanging on to a basic design. Once tooling and development are paid off, and assuming no costly changes later, you can usually keep the lid on price and still make good money with every sale.

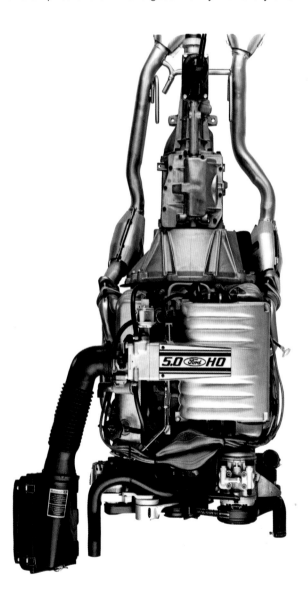

ABOVE: Mustang's T-top option did not return for '88, in part due to continuing strong convertible sales. LEFT: This unusual view of Mustang's V-8 powertrain spotlights the high-volume air cleaner (lower left), handsome head cover with 5.0 H.O. legend, and catalytic converters tucked close to the engine for quicker, more efficient "light off."

New Praise from the Press

So although the Fox was getting on in years, Ford's makeover artists were hiding its gray hairs very well, and Mustang's combination of low price and high performance was more irresistible than ever. "Mustang was born a legend, but it is value for the performance dollar that really draws the customers through the door," said Sawyer. "Grudgingly or not, there is something that folks at both Ford and GM can agree on, the Mustang is the best value for the money in its market segment." Other magazines also recognized this. In 1988 the GT was named one of *Road & Track's* "Ten Best Cars in the World" and made *Car and Driver's* "Ten Best" cars list. The following year, *Motor Trend* named the GT a "Top Ten Performance Car."

But a better car and "best buy" status don't necessarily guarantee better sales. Despite the extensive '87 remodeling, Mustang volume crumbled by over 65,000 units. Still, 159,000 total sales was good going, all things considered. (One problem was tax reform, which took effect on January 1, 1987, and eliminated the time-honored deduction for interest on car loans.) The facelift wasn't cheap at some $200 million, but it included upgrading the Dearborn assembly plant and would be soon paid off.

And sales promptly recovered. Indeed, Mustang widened its lead over GM's ponycars despite only token changes through decade's end. There were just two for '88: a higher-capacity battery for LXs and deletion of the T-bar roof from the options list. The latter really wasn't needed anymore, as convertible sales remained strong. For 1989, Ford acknowledged recent buying

TOP: A 1989 GT ragtop sidles next to a classic '65 in a widely circulated Ford PR photo announcing Mustang's 25th anniversary. Ford's arithmetic puzzled many, as the car's 20th birthday had been observed only four years before. Evidently, Dearborn had decided 1964, not '65, was the ponycar's proper birth year. ABOVE: As before, comfortable "articulated" front seats were standard on '89 GTs and V-8 LXs. They offered multiple adjustments including thigh and lumbar supports.

patterns by making the LX V-8 package into a distinct model trio called LX 5.0L Sport—and throwing in the GT's multi-adjustable sports seats. The only other news of consequence that year was standard power windows for convertibles.

Model-year sales jumped to 211,225 for '88. The '89s did almost as well with 209,769. These totals were all the more impressive in light of prices that were bounding upward—by some $900 for '87, another $700–$1100 for '88, then $300–$400 more. By 1989, only the four-cylinder LX notchback and hatchback still started below the psychologically important $10,000 mark. GTs were up to $13,272 for the hatch and $17,512 for the ragtop, so the new V-8 LX Sports looked like very good buys at $13,000–$17,000.

Great Expectations

Most everyone expected a very special Mustang during 1989. After all, the original ponycar had been around for 25 years, and Ford had issued a 20th anniversary package for '84. Yet no silver-anniversary special appeared right away, which only fueled speculation that Ford was working up something truly spectacular. Rumors circulated through most of '88 about a tricked-out GT with extra-heavy-duty suspension to handle a 351 V-8, borrowed from the Ford truck line and fortified with twin turbochargers for a Ferrari-baiting 400 bhp. At least one prototype was engineered

THIS PAGE: After five years of building V-8 Mustangs with racier looks and trackworthy chassis, Southern California's Steve Saleen offered his first "tuned" Mustang, the SSC. Introduced on April 17, 1989, Mustang's exact 25th birthday, it packed 292 horsepower—67 more than stock—yet was street-legal in all states, quite a feat for a small company. Special bracing in the engine and cargo bays (center and bottom left) made for a solid driving feel and more precise handling. Saleen built only 161 SSCs in '89, all hatchbacks. OPPOSITE PAGE: Few Saleens were built alike, but Steve still offered a stock-power hatchback and convertible for '89. Both had many unique features, including Saleen's own Racecraft suspension. This ragtop priced from $26,450. Saleen Autosport was thriving and now reached a new sales high with 734 total units, of which 165 were ragtops.

and built by longtime Ford contractor Jack Roush, but the project ran afoul of development delays, fuel-economy concerns, and excessive costs for the planned 2000-unit run. There was also talk of a less radical hot one with 260–275 bhp, suspension upgrades, distinct bolt-on body pieces, and possibly four-wheel disc brakes left over from the SVO. Also whispered was a transplant of the supercharged 3.8-liter V-6 from the '89 Thunderbird Super Coupe. But none of this came to pass.

Why No Silver

Shortly before the actual April 1989 celebration, a Ford spokesman told *AutoWeek* why there wasn't a silver-anniversary Mustang for Mustang's silver anniversary. "First, we wanted to do more than a paint and stripe job. If we couldn't do a proper vehicle, we weren't going to do one at all. Second, the company doesn't feel that it would be honest to put its name on someone else's work"—meaning Roush's rip-snorter. "We never really considered that car," the Ford man said, "because we felt that it was overkill." In fact, *AutoWeek* noted that "Ford never considered going outside for [any] help with the anniversary Mustang."

Still, it's fair to ask, was a golden marketing opportunity squandered through poor planning? Was it really better to do nothing if a "proper vehicle" wasn't possible? Mustangers still debate the answers, but they were certainly disappointed at the time. Ford's only gesture at a 25th Anniversary Mustang was small indeed: a passenger-side dashboard emblem with galloping-horse logo affixed to all models built between March 27, 1989, and the end of model-year 1990.

Car Trek

Of course, a milestone Mustang birthday was too important for Ford marketers to ignore, and they didn't. Highlighting the celebration was the American Ponycar Drive, a six-week, 7000-mile coast-to-coast trek involving over 100 European Mustang owners and their cars. Convening at the port of Jacksonville, Florida, participants headed west to Southern California for a big all-Dearborn classic-car show, "Fabulous Fords Forever." This was staged on Sunday, April 16, just a day shy of 25 years from the original New York World's Fair debut. The group then headed back east toward Dearborn for a tour of the Mustang plant and

Mustang styling was again all but untouched for 1990, and there was lit-tle new in equipment or features, either. Sales plunged some 57 per-cent from '89, mainly due to a sharp recession that set in that year. BELOW: Mustang's steadily improved workmanship was especially evi-dent inside. Optional leather, as shown here, returned for 1990 at $489.

other festivities. From there it was on to Baltimore and a boat back home. Along the way, the Ponycar Drive stopped in some 25 cities, where local Mustangers rolled out the red carpet. Some individuals even joined the rally, which had been suggested by a Mustang enthusiast in Switzerland.

Sorry, Lee

That same April Sunday, Ford threw a big birthday bash at the Dearborn plant, which had recently built the six-millionth Mustang. The party generated wide media coverage, including a *Wall Street Journal* piece on the rather touchy matter of inviting the Mustang's "father," now chairman of Chrysler. The story quot-ed a Ford official saying the company came very close to asking Lee Iaccoca, "but we just couldn't bring ourselves to do it." Instead, the *Journal* reported, "Ford relied on surrogate fathers. The main was one Jack Telnack [who said] 'I'd like to stand here and tell you I was the father' of the original Mustang, 'but my biggest contribution was designing the wheel covers.' So, he was asked, who was the father? 'Well, there were several...Joe Oros and Dave Ash, who headed its design. There was a team of six or seven product planners, including Don Petersen.... And then there was Lee Iacocca.'" Petersen himself gave Iacocca a "more generous mention" in Southern California, the *Journal* quoting him as saying, "Fortunately, Lee Iacocca kept our spirits up" early in the program. Typical of the man, Iacocca got in a little dig at his old outfit. As the *Journal* reported: "Ford feared that [he] might have stolen the spotlight and hawked Chrysler products. In fact, that's exactly what he did in a short prepared statement on the anniversary. 'Just like our minivans,' Mr. Iacocca said, 'the Mustang pushed all the right buttons for the customer.'" The story concluded on an amusing note. "One Ford official put the reason for not inviting Mr. Iacocca this way: 'Hell, he might have come.'"

Saleen Solution

Though Ford itself didn't do a 25th-birthday Mustang, Steve Saleen did, introducing his new SSC on April 17, 1989. Saleen, based in Orange County, California, south of L.A., was a veteran of SCCA Trans-Am and Formula Atlantic racing. He also had a business-school degree—and several Shelby-Mustangs in his garage. Encouraged by the H.O. V-8's 1982 revival, he decided to follow in Shelby's footsteps and make stock Mustangs into very personal high-performance cars. For the first five years he focused on everything except the powertrain to avoid the high costs involved with emissions certification for a tuned engine. Saleen developed his own suspension upgrades under the Racecraft brand and also installed special wheels, fatter tires,

Arriving in January 1990, this "Limited Edition" LX 5.0L convertible was not an official 25th anniversary Mustang, though Ford didn't mind if people took it as such. The main attraction was new "deep emerald green" clearcoat metallic paint complemented by a white-leather interior and color-keyed top boot. Base price was a stiff $18,949. Planned production was 3800, but some sources say only 3600 were built.

various aerodynamic add-ons, racy cosmetics, and driver-oriented cockpit features like extra gauges and better seats. He managed only three cars in 1984, all GT hatchbacks, but the next year he worked a deal with Ford to supply him with conversion-ready hatchbacks and convertibles. These cars even got a special factory order code. That's because Dearborn decided to sell Saleen Mustangs through select Ford dealers and to maintain the factory warranty on unmodified components. Steve's company would guarantee its modifications and non-stock components. Saleen Autosport was on its way, turning out 132 cars in calendar '85, 201 the following year, and 280 in 1987.

It was all very like the early Shelby-Mustang days, including frequent running changes to fix unforeseen problems or take advantage of newer, better components as they became available. But Saleens could also be personalized to a much greater extent than Shelbys; Steve offered customers a very wide choice of colors and upholstery, wheels, spoilers, sound systems, and gadgets. This meant few Saleens were built exactly the same way, which made prices highly variable, but "regular" 1985–86 models listed in the $17,000–$20,000 range. Prices were near $25,000 for a "basic" '88 convertible, but sales soared that year to 708 units. Obviously, Steve was on to something.

Street-Legal Sizzler

Up to now, his cars were simply Saleen Mustangs with basically unaltered powertrains, but that changed with the '89 SSC— "Saleen Super Car." Starting with a V-8 LX hatchback or convertible, Steve enlarged the ports and added a larger throttle body, a new intake plenum, different rocker arms, stainless-steel tubular headers, Walker Dynomax mufflers, and heavy-duty cooling system. The result: 292 horsepower. And it was street-legal in all 50 states, remarkable for a "tuner" David against a Goliath EPA. Other SSC features included heavy-duty Borg-Warner five-speed

TOP: Mustang sales fell again for '91, aggravated by a 3-percent price hike that put the basic four-cylinder notchback (shown) over $10,000 for the first time. ABOVE: A reworked top with a lower folded "stack height" tidied up the convertibles appearance.

with Hurst linkage, all-disc brakes from the late SVO, three-way electronically adjustable Monroe Formula GA shock absorbers with cockpit switch, and fat 245/50R16 tires on five-spoke eight-inch-wide DP wheels. Inside were bolstered FloFit leather seats and matching door panels, a *200-mph* speedometer, and a booming CD stereo instead of a back seat. According to Mustang chronicler Brad Bowling, "the asking price for this 'unofficial' 25th anniversary model was $36,500."

Tony Assenza tested an SSC for the May 1989 *Car and Driver*. After noting the suspension "evolved from Steve Saleen's years of racing Showroom Stock Mustangs" in SCCA, Assenza explained how "the chassis is subjected to considerable stiffening by what Saleen calls a 'Chassis Support System.' This includes a triangulated tube arrangement that ties the front strut towers to the firewall, a rear chassis support in the hatch area that looks like half of a roll cage, and a K-member under the front box section…. The chassis and suspension changes make the Saleen SSC a stiff piece that never stops reminding you that it's very much a single-purpose car. That purpose being to carve up twisty roads and terrorize fellow motorists at red lights."

That it could do, with an observed 0–60 of 5.9 seconds and a standing quarter-mile of 14.2 at 98 mph. Sure, the SCC was stiff-riding, noisy, and not much fun in traffic. But as Assenza summed-up: "If you can live with some of this car's less refined qualities and can justify the big asking price, you'll be able to make the biggest noise on your block since Carroll Shelby's GT350 came to town." Few got the chance. Saleen built only 161 of the '89 SSCs, plus 734 "standard" models.

Recession Retreat

With its birthday party over, Mustang carried on for the next three years without major change—except on the sales chart, where the numbers plunged alarmingly. The two were not unrelated, but the real culprit was the onset of a sharp recession.

Model-year 1990 ushered in federally required "passive restraints." Mustang complied with a driver's airbag mounted in the steering wheel, which eliminated the tilt-wheel option, unfortunately. Door map pockets and clearcoat paint were also standard across the board, while options expanded with the addition of leather interior trim. Announced in mid-January was a special "Limited Edition" LX 5.0L convertible, of which 3600–3800 were built. Base-priced at $18,949, this featured "deep emerald green" clearcoat metallic paint, color-keyed bodyside moldings, GT aluminum wheels, white convertible top, and a white leather interior with the GT's "articulated" sport buckets. An available "special value package" added air conditioning, cruise control, premium AM/FM/cassette stereo, and a clock. To its credit, Ford didn't try to pass this off as a belated birthday present, though a company press release did try to make a connection, saying the "entire Mustang lineup, which celebrated its 25th anniversary in 1989, continues a tradition of value leadership in the 1990-model year." Actually, prices were still going up but remained competitive: under $9500 for a four-cylinder LX notchback, less than $19,000 for the top-line GT convertible. Even so, model-year volume plunged nearly 50 percent to 128,189.

Sales dropped again for '91, skidding to 98,737. More detail updates occurred. The anemic four now claimed 105 bhp via a new eight-plug cylinder head, but only rental-car fleet managers cared. Convertibles sported a power top that folded closer to the body for a neater appearance, and automatic-transmission cars met yet another new federal edict by adding an interlock that required pushing the brake pedal before the shifter would move out of Park. V-8 models got pretty new five-spoke alloy wheels of 16-inch diameter, an inch larger than before. LX 5.0s switched from tough-looking but rough-riding Goodyear Eagle GT+4 tires to more compliant 225/55ZR16 all-season Michelins. GTs retained the unidirectional Goodyears in that same size but offered the Michelins as a no-cost alternative. Prices rose a bit more, the base LX notchback going just above $10,000, but V-8 convertibles still started below $20,000.

Mustang seemed stuck in a rut during the early 1990s, with little new to offer from year to year and sales dropping to record lows. But what few changes did occur were generally spot-on. Among the best was a pretty new five-spoke 16-inch alloy wheel as standard for 1991 V-8 models, complete with the traditional "pony tricolor" insignia.

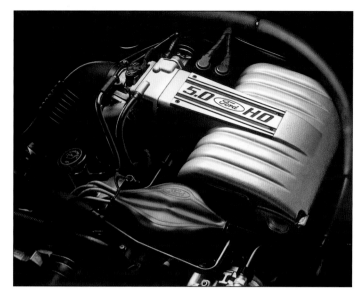

TOP: Like the Mustangs it powered, Ford's 302 V-8 had become a modern classic—and a favorite of hop-up artists who developed all manner of speed equipment for it. ABOVE: As always, the GT convertible offered hot fun in the summer sun—and most everywhere else. Still top of the line, it priced from $19,864 for '91. BELOW: The '91 GT hatchback started at $15,034. V-8 sales had been steadily growing and were now two times that of four-cylinder models, split evenly between GTs and LXs.

Still Little New, Still Lower Sales

Once more, news was sparse for '92. Color-keyed bodyside moldings and bumper rubstrips enhanced LX appearance. And wonder of wonders, those old optional favorites, whitewall tires and wire-wheel covers, vanished from the list. But sales now really tanked, hitting an all-time low of just 79,280 units. The only comfort for Ford was that Camaro and Firebird had been sinking even faster, allowing Mustang to stretch its lead. More telling is the fact that even in a slump, Mustang was consistently outselling the Probe, its one-time replacement.

Though you might think otherwise, Mustang's "vintage" character had actually become a sales asset. Buyers were starting to lose interest in high-tech sporty imports, perhaps because they were all so much alike. But Mustang remained unique—big, bold, and brash, old-fashioned and flawed certainly, but mighty appealing for precisely those reasons. By standing still, as it were, Mustang now stood alone.

This unique character came through clearly in two 1989 "buff book" tests. Running a new five-speed LX 5.0 hatchback, *Motor Trend* praised "its limitless supply of rich, creamy torque at any rpm, and all the wonderful things that it made possible." That comment came in a "Bang for the Buck!" showdown of 16 contestants, including the Plymouth Laser RS Turbo, Nissan 300ZX, Ford's own supercharged Thunderbird, and even an L98 Corvette. In acceleration, braking, and handling, the Mustang finished as high as fourth only in quarter-mile performance, with an ET of 15.38 seconds at 91.5 mph (a 20th Anniversary Pontiac Trans Am turbo was fastest with 14.18 at 98.8 mph). Mustang was mid-pack or lower in the skidpad, slalom, and road-course contests, and dead last in braking, taking 159 feet to stop from 60 mph (the 300ZX was shortest, 120 feet). But with a base price of only $12,765, nothing could match its all-round performance for the money, and *MT* declared it the winner. "Mustang truly

defines the concept of Bang for the Buck. It's probably the most fun for the money in America today."

In a similar vein, the July 1989 *Car and Driver* gathered up eight sporty coupes to answer the question, "What's the most fun you can have for $20,000?" All the cars were Japanese built or designed save a five-speed LX 5.0, which finished fourth in cumulative rankings of performance, ergonomics, styling, utility, and driving fun. Though not the most polished contender, the LX was the most affordable—and the quickest, running 0–60 mph in 6.2 seconds and the quarter-mile in 14.8 at 95 mph. A Mitsubishi Eclipse GS Turbo won this showdown, but it cost $16,000 and was only two mph faster than the LX all-out. "If the Mustang sold for $20,000, we would probably be put off by its age and accompanying disadvantages," *C/D* concluded. "But at $13,671, including a generous load of creature comforts, the LX 5.0 is an incredible performance-car bargain."

Mustang was selling on performance more than ever. Among '91s, for example, V-8s outpolled four-cylinder models by two-to-one, with LXs accounting for almost half. Moreover, fully 49 percent of V-8 buyers chose five-speed manual transmission, a very high rate for an American car. By contrast, manual transmission accounted for just 13 percent of '91 Camaro sales and only 30 percent of Corvette's.

Cobra Strikes Again

The economy started to perk up by model-year 1993, and Mustang sales rebounded to 114,228—to Ford's undoubted relief. In a way, this shouldn't have happened. Mustang was virtually unchanged, yet now faced a swoopy all-new Camaro/Firebird offering a 275-bhp version of the latest 5.7-liter Corvette V-8. Worse, having admitted to literally overrating the Mustang V-8, Ford adjusted outputs down to 205 bhp and 275 lb-ft.

But a hot new Cobra hatchback more than made up for that.

TOP: In what some said was a boon to good taste, optional whitewalls and wire-look wheel covers were dumped for '92. LXs like this 5.0L ragtop sported color-keyed bumper and bodyside rub strips, one of the year's few changes. Model-year sales plunged to an all-time low. ABOVE: A new four-way power driver's seat joined the options list for '92.

Road & Track called it the "best of an aging breed," and by most any measure it was. Developed by Dearborn's new Special Vehicle Team (SVT, the successor to SVO), it packed a new higher-output Cobra 302 producing 235 horsepower via special big-port "GT40" heads, tuned-runner intake manifold, revised cam, and other muscle-building measures. Torque, a stout 285 lb-ft, was channeled through a beefier five-speed manual gearbox—the sole transmission choice—and corralled in corners by sticky 245/45ZR17 Goodyear Eagle performance radials. Also on hand, or rather under foot, were rear disc brakes instead of drums—the first factory Mustang since the SVO to have them. Ford also touted "balanced" suspension tuning that went against conventional hot-car wisdom by using *softer* springs, shocks, and bushings and a smaller front stabilizer bar vs. the GT. Interior furnishings were basically GT stock, while the exterior was almost LX modest. Spotter's points included SVO taillamps, handsome seven-blade alloy wheels—and specific nose with a small running-horse emblem. An hefty rear spoiler was the one arguably jarring note to this speedy, sophisticated package.

Speedy *And* Sophisticated

Did we say speedy? Try 5.9 seconds 0–60 mph, according to *R&T,* whose test Cobra also clocked 14.5 seconds at 98 mph in the standing quarter-mile and less than 16 seconds from 0 to 100 mph. As for sophisticated, *Car and Driver*'s Don Schroeder termed this "a nicer-riding, more supple car [than the GT]. Although it can feel less buttoned down...the Cobra makes better use of its tires and rewards coordinated hands and feet with clearly higher limits and cornering speeds...."

Nevertheless, a few cynics thought this Cobra just a ploy to keep Ford's old ponycar from being completely eclipsed by GM's new ones. *Motor Trend,* in fact, called it a "shake-and-bake bridge to '94." Still, it was eloquent testimony to the Fox plat-

Loyal Mustangers got a heartening 1993 surprise in the new SVT Cobra hatchback with a 235-horse V-8, good for 0–60 mph in under six seconds. The Cobra was conceived by Ford's two-year-old Special Vehicle Team and went on sale in February along with a muscled-up F-150 pickup, the Lightning. Starting right at $20,000, the Cobra boasted 17-inch wheels, sticky Goodyear tires, recalibrated chassis, and unique styling touches. Exactly 4993 were built.

Though the new '93 Cobra looked ready to race, the Cobra R actually could, being optimized for the track and barely street-legal. Upgrades included bigger four-wheel disc brakes, wider wheels, competition chassis tuning, structural bracing in the engine bay and elsewhere, unique high-rise spoiler, and an interior shorn of back seat, air conditioning, and other niceties to save a crucial 60 pounds vs. the road model. With only 107 built for '93, this Cobra R was a fast sellout despite a $25,692 base price.

form's stamina and versatility. And with only some 5000 built, the '93 Cobra will be a prized example of this long-lived breed.

More collectible still is the Cobra R, which saw only 107 copies. Of course, the "R" stood for racing, which meant track use only. Alterations to the street-legal Cobra included much larger front brakes, competition-caliber cooling system and suspension tuning, appropriately wider wheels and tires, and added structural reinforcements. In yet another echo of Carroll Shelby, Ford omitted the back seat, air conditioning, and most power accessories to trim curb weight by some 60 pounds—not much on the road but crucial for the track. Ford sold every R-model for the full $25,692 sticker price vs. about $20,000 for a regular Cobra, itself a bona fide bargain.

At Long Last, Time to Move On

Either way, the '93 Cobra was a happy surprise for a car that had stayed so much the same for so long. But life at Ford had been anything but static. Another historic changing of the guard occurred in 1990 when Donald Petersen took early retirement, ushering in Harold A. "Red" Poling as chairman and Philip E. Benton, Jr. as president. By the end of 1993, however, Alex Trotman had taken over both positions, outlining a bold new vision for Ford's future. Part of that future would soon arrive in the car everyone had been waiting for: the next new Mustang.

The '93s were the last Mustangs with the basic '87 styling. Cobra was the big news, but special white- and yellow-themed appearance packages (above and left) took their inspiration from the previous year's Performance Red Limited Edition 5.0L LX convertible (top). The White Feature package cost $976; the Yellow went for $1488, but included chrome alloy wheels. Both came with white or black leather, and fewer than 1500 of each were made. Overall, Mustang calendar-1993 sales recovered to 98,648, up 12,600 units. One '93 change was slightly embarrassing to Ford: The V-8 was downrated from 225 to 205 horses with adoption of a more accurate rating method. The 5.0 itself was unaltered.

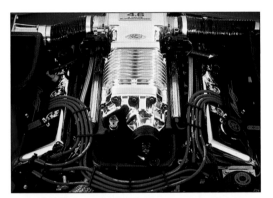

Perhaps to dispel any doubts over Mustang's future, Ford took this racy concept to various 1992 auto shows. Created by the company's new Special Vehicle Team, the Mustang Mach III provided an exaggerated preview of next-generation production styling. Designed with no thought of a top, the two-seat body was paneled in high-tech carbon-fiber above outsize 19-inch chrome wheels. A front-mounted 4.6-liter supercharged V-8 sent 450 horsepower through a six-speed manual gearbox. Ford claimed 0–60 mph in under 4.5 seconds.

Chapter Ten:
1994-1998

Hard to believe, but Ford actually thought of putting Mustang out to pasture—until it learned of General Motors' latest ponycar plans. Dearborn met the challenge by keeping the best and changing the rest to create a stronger, sleeker, more agile new Mustang. Arriving in time for the original ponycar's 30th birthday, it was the best Mustang in years.

A mostly new Mustang rode in for 1994 on a tidal wave of anticipation and nostalgia. Ads pictured it with a classic '65 to declare, "It is what it was." Actually, it almost wasn't.

As related in Chapter Nine, the uproar over the Mazda-based Probe had shown Ford that Mustang fans would never accept a Japanese-style substitute for their car. But with demand for "real" ponycars lagging again by the late 1980s, some in Dearborn began to question the need for another new Mustang. Besides, Ford had more profitable product fish to fry (the Explorer sport-utility for one), and the old Mustangs were still selling pretty well, so why rush? With that, planning floundered for a good two years. Then Ford learned that General Motors was abandoning a planned front-drive Camaro/Firebird for a new rear-drive 1993 concept. Corporate pride demanded a proper reply, so a new Mustang program was underway by early 1989.

Code named SN95, this effort began with a round of consumer clinics per Dearborn tradition—what PR flacks later called "gallop polls." This time, however, unusual weight was given to the views of Mustang owners. Topping the wish lists were modern styling with hints of the original, a cheap and easily serviced V-8, rear-wheel drive, a low base price, and plenty of options—in short, a brand-new good old Mustang.

Because Ford had become a leaner organization, and with the "team concept" now gospel throughout Detroit, SN95 developed quite differently from earlier Mustangs. The big departure was forming a fairly small, independent multi-profession project group. Key figures included overall manager Mike Zevalkink, business manager John Coletti, designer manager Bud Magaldi, interior designer Emeline King, engineering manager Kurt Achenbach, and powertrain manager John Bicanich. All reported to Will Boddie, then director for small and midsize cars.

Considering the legend entrusted to them, the SN95 team worked on a surprisingly modest budget: $700 million in all, with a mere $200 million earmarked for design and engineering. By contrast, Ford spent an industry-record $3 billion on the trend-setting 1986 Taurus. The limited funds ruled out a new platform, even though Mustang was now the sole survivor of the original

Fox family and Ford had newer foundations available. (Rumors briefly swirled about a cut-down version of the '89 MN12 Thunderbird.) The timing was also stingy: just 36 months.

"Schwarzenegger" Wins

Recalling earlier Mustangs, initial SN95 styling concepts did not "clinic" well, being "too smooth, too clean and friendly, too nice," according to design manager Magaldi. After much further work, the choice came down to three proposals presented for executive review in the autumn of 1990. All carried the desired "retro" signatures: a running steed in the grille, simulated side scoops ahead of the rear wheels, triple-element taillamps, and, of course, long-hood/short-deck proportions. But they also shared a new shape: muscular, slightly wedgy, but also "aero" slick in Ford's now-established idiom. The differences were mainly of degree. The tamest was the "Bruce Jenner," described as a "trim, athletic" design that nevertheless scored low as looking too "soft." At the other extreme was "Rambo," an aggressive, exaggerated interpretation that struck most people as looking too mean. This left the in-between "Arnold Schwarzenegger" to win the day. Only minor changes were made before production.

Like the '79 Mustang, SN95 finalists were modeled as notch-back coupes. While a new convertible was never in doubt, engineers and marketers decided to forget the hatchback body style despite its past sales importance. Ford's stated reason was the greater difficulty of achieving acceptable rigidity in a structure with such a large opening at the rear, but the decision more likely reflected the fact that Americans no longer cared much for hatchbacks. Regardless, the coupe ended up with a conventional trunklid and a compromise slantback roof profile faintly reminiscent of the 1965–66 semi-fastback 2+2.

Interior designers also strove for a "classic Mustang" feel while incorporating 30 years of government safety mandates, including new requirements for dual airbags and anti-intrusion door beams. The result was a traditional Mustang cockpit with a heavily sculpted new "twin-cowl" instrument panel flowing smoothly into the doors, a faint homage to early models.

Stronger, Not Heavier

Body engineers worked to increase structural strength without adding weight, and they largely succeeded. Against the previous notchback, the SN95 coupe was some 56 percent stiffer in bending (resistance to flex in the horizontal plane) and 44 percent in torsion (lateral plane). Respective convertible numbers were 76 percent and an amazing 150 percent. Despite these impressive improvements, curb weights ended up only some 200 pounds higher than for equivalent '93 models.

The SN95 team naturally relied heavily on the latest computer modeling tools but also common sense, their own considerable experience, and no small measure of trial and error. This led to numerous under-skin alterations that improved crash performance as well as resistance to squeaks and rattles. For example, coupes replaced open-section roof rails with sturdier closed members, frame rails were beefed up, a hefty inverted-U beam was added to link the B-pillars, and there were reinforcements in a dozen other places. Convertibles added a transverse beam between the rear wheelhouses and a stout underbody X-brace to reduce twist and shake. For the same reason, GTs got diagonal bracing between the firewall and front strut towers.

With all this, the venerable Fox platform was changed so much that Ford renamed it "Fox-4," the number denoting 1994, the targeted model year. "This is not a carryover platform," Boddie declared, noting that of 1850 total parts, 1330 were redesigned or significantly modified. To convince skeptical journalists, Ford built full-size cutaway models with new components painted various colors to contrast with white carryover parts. One of this book's editors remembers it as a riotous rainbow.

Roadworthier

Steering and suspension were left basically as they'd been since 1979, Quadra-Shock rear end included, but the stiffened structure allowed slightly softer springs and shock absorbers for enhanced ride comfort. A repositioned front crossmember and longer lower control arms improved geometry and increased wheelbase by 0.75-inch to 100.3. For better directional stability, front caster was dialed up from 1.5 to 4 degrees, and tracks were widened at each end—by a whopping 3.7 inches in front on base

Design work for the '94 SN95 Mustang was underway by early 1989. Opinion data from consumer clinics showed strong preference for modern lines blended with traditional Mustang signatures. Though this mandate quickly led to a basic theme, early concept sketches, like those shown here, varied from mild (top) to wild (above) to everywhere in between (below). Note, however, the shared "big-wheel" look.

SN95 styling came down to three full-size fiberglass mockups examined in fall 1990 by representatives of Ford sales, marketing, product development, and upper management. The "Bruce Jenner" (top) was rejected as too tame. The aggressive "Rambo" (above) and in-between "Arnold Schwarzenegger" (below) ran about even in consumer clinics, but the Arnold was OKed for production with relatively few changes.

models, 1.9 inches on GTs. To save weight, antiroll bars went from solid to tubular, with larger front/rear diameters for 27/21mm for base models and 30/24mm for GTs.

Other exterior dimensions went up a bit, the SN95s measuring 181.5 inches long, 71.8 inches wide, and 52.9 inches high. Helped by a "faster" 60-degree windshield, the new styling was measurably more "aero," with stated drag coefficients of 0.34 for base models, 0.36 for GTs—small but useful gains.

Larger rolling stock was a growing industry trend, and the new Mustangs got their share. Base models, no longer called LX, came on 6.5 × 15-inch steel rims with 205/65 Eagle GA touring tires and offered three-spoke 7.5-inch-wide alloys at extra cost. GTs were treated to standard 7.5 × 16 five-spoke alloys with high-speed Z-rated P255/55 all-season tires; 8 × 17 five-spoke rims were optional. Brake upgrades were extensive. All-disc brakes were standard (at last) and quite large with diameters of 10.9 inches for the vented front rotors, 10.5 inches for the solid rears. Also new were a larger brake booster, asbestos-free brake pads, and an optional Bosch antilock brake system (ABS).

Powering Up

There was more welcome news under base-model hoods, where the anemic four-cylinder engine gave way to a 3.8-liter V-6. This was basically the same overhead-valve engine last offered in '86 Mustangs but with all the interim improvements made for its use in the Taurus and other newer Dearborn models. Horsepower was 145, up 38 percent from the final four-cylinder figure. Torque swelled no less than 59 percent to 215 pound-feet.

The GT's venerable 302 V-8 got a low-profile intake manifold (to clear the lower new hood), plus aluminum pistons and Ford's latest EEC-V electronic engine controller, all of which upped horsepower by 10 to 215. Torque improved to 285 lb-ft, the same output as the '93 Cobra. Both engines teamed with five-speed manual or optional four-speed automatic, but the latter was Ford's latest "AOD-E" unit with electronic shift control.

New Enough?

Overall, the '94 Mustang represented the kind of thorough modernization that Ford had already lavished on its full-size sedans. Still, some critics huffed that after such a long wait, this "all-new" Mustang wasn't really *all* new. Ford defended the car on two grounds. First, it pointed to all those new and modified parts. Second, as Will Boddie pointed out, a ground-up redesign would have forced Ford to raise prices. "When we talked with Mustang owners... they kept saying, 'What can you do to keep it affordable, to give us value?' We listened to them."

Fair enough, but some buyers must have suffered sticker shock anyway. The entry-level coupe, for example, jumped from $10,810 to $13,365, though the extra money admittedly bought a larger engine, much better brakes, and the dual airbags, plus a tilt steering wheel and four-way power driver's seat that had cost extra before. The GT coupe started at $17,280 vs. $15,850 for its '93 counterpart, but it boasted all the same upgrades, plus bigger wheels and tires and expected standards like front foglights, rear spoiler, sport seats, and leather-rim steering wheel. The base convertible looked like a fine value at a little-changed $20,160; the GT version stickered at a reasonable $21,970.

For the first time since 1973, ragtops were built entirely in-house, right alongside coupes. A power top with glass rear window remained standard, joined by a rear-window defogger. Recalling the 1963 Mustang II show car was an announced Corvette-style liftoff hardtop. Though too bulky for one person, it weighed a manageable 80 pounds and had the same look as the coupe's fixed steel roof. It was a nice idea, but production glitches delayed availability to model-year '95, by which time buyers had apparently lost interest, and the option was canceled after only 499 installations.

Meet The Press

To Ford's undoubted dismay, the '94 Mustang garnered mixed reviews. While road-testers lauded the many changes, there was general head-scratching over the GT's 60-horsepower deficit with the latest 275-bhp Camaro Z28 and Firebird Trans Am. "The carryover power may challenge the loyalty of some [Mustang] fans," mused *Car and Driver*, "[though] with substantial improvements in braking and body structure, the Mustang [GT still] offers tremendous performance for the dollar." Proving the point, *C/D*'s five-speed V-8 coupe ran 0–60 mph in a brisk 6.1 seconds and the standing quarter-mile in 14.9 at 93 mph—not bad for an engine now well past middle age. The automatic version was no slouch either, CONSUMER GUIDE® timing a brisk 7.4 seconds. But as *Road & Track* pointedly noted: "A 60-horsepower shortfall is a lot of horsepower." Ford shot back that Mustang aimed at those who valued overall finesse, not just straight-ahead thrust. Going toe-to-toe with GM power was not the first priority.

So what was? Well, several team members admitted the main mission was to satisfy the 6.1 million folks who'd bought Mustangs since day one. While that implied sizable demand for the new models, it also suggested that sights hadn't been set very high. As *Motor Trend* observed: "Mustang fans have been deprived of a new platform for so long they would've accepted almost anything with a chrome horse on it."

Of course, they *did* accept it, and with enthusiasm. And why not? They had helped to design it. And after *MT*'s editors surveyed the field, what did they choose as "Car of the Year"? Right. "Mustang

TOP: After eight years in the wilderness, a 3.8-liter V-6 returned to the Mustang line as the standard and only engine for 1994 base models, which were no longer called LX. ABOVE: An improved 302 V-8 was the only choice for 1994 GTs. It had 215 horsepower. BELOW: Mustang's long-serving platform changed so much for '94 that Ford renamed it "Fox-4." Four-wheel disc brakes were now standard across the board.

is once again a car to be coveted.... Viewed from both an industry and buyer's perspective, we weighed technological advancement, value and performance to determine the one standout car for '94. The Ford Mustang is that car."

Another Happy Birthday

The *MT* award was a nice kickoff for Mustang's 30th anniversary year. Ford hosted several big parties on Sunday, April 17. One was staged in conjunction with the Mustang Club of America at Charlotte Motor Speedway. Among the throng of people and cars on hand was one William Jefferson Clinton and his rather well-used '67 convertible. The event also welcomed 200 cars driven from as far away as Sacramento, California, in a six-day "Mustangs Across America" rally. Down L.A. way, the "Fabulous Fords Forever" show, then in its ninth year, was the end point for a cross-country "International Mustang Roundup" comprising 16 cars from three European countries.

The celebrating didn't stop there. Recalling 1964, Ford got Mustang selected as Indy 500 pace car. Engine master Jack Roush souped up a trio of new Cobra convertibles for Memorial Day track-wheeling by Ford CEO Alex Trotman and legendary drivers Parnelli Jones and A. J. Foyt. It was the first public outing for the '94 Cobra, though it had started production in February and was always part of SN95 planning.

Snake Charming

Like its '93 predecessor, this new Cobra was the work of Ford's Special Vehicle Team. Exclusives began with a unique front fascia and rear spoiler, 17-inch five-spoke wheels with gumball P245/45ZR Eagle GS-C tires, another discreet chrome snake on each front fender, and a leather-lined interior with trendy white-faced gauges (including a 160-mph speedometer). The chassis remained stock GT but was again made a bit softer for "controlled compliance" handling. ABS was newly standard for much-enlarged disc brakes: 13 inches in front, clamped by new dual-piston calipers, and 10.5 inches in back. For the 302 V-8, SVT

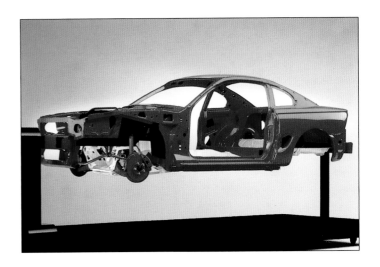

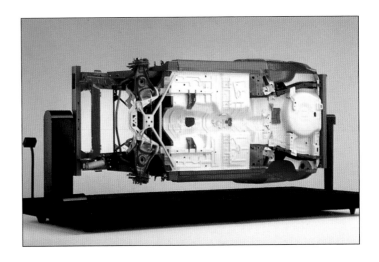

TOP: Another illustration by artist Dave Kimble showcases '94 Mustang packaging on a GT coupe. Cockpit remained a cozy 2+2 affair. CENTER AND ABOVE: Ford built life-size cutaway displays to highlight the Fox-4 platform's extensive changes. Its floorpan (in white) was the major carryover structural component. Front X-brace (in yellow) was one of several measures enhancing overall rigidity.

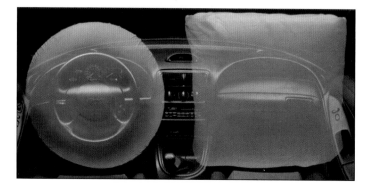

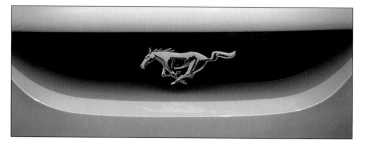

THIS PAGE: Like all '94s, the GT coupe (top) sported a "twin-cowl" dashboard with full gauges and dual airbags, plus engine-bay bracing. V-6 and V-8 models each offered two different wheel treatments (below). OPPOSITE PAGE, TOP: At $13,365, the '94 V-6 coupe started quite a bit higher than the prior four-cylinder LX. BOTTOM: Convertible tops, as on this GT, were power-operated and now folded nearly flat.

applied larger valves, higher-flow exhuast manifolds, extruded-aluminum rocker arms with roller followers, low-drag accessory drive, and lightened flywheel. Yet all this yielded just five more horsepower, 240 in all. Motor-noters heaved more sighs. Even this new Cobra was 35 horses shy of a box-stock Z28.

The Cobra narrowed Mustang's performance gap with GM, but not much. *Car and Driver* clocked a five-speed coupe at 5.9 seconds 0–60 and 14.7 at 96 mph in the standing quarter-mile, both timings a full half-second adrift of a Z28's. The Cobra "is undoubtedly the most muscular Mustang available," *C/D* concluded, "and at $21,240 for the coupe and $24,010 for the convertible, the most expensive. At those prices, this package will appeal to Mustang enthusiasts, but we have a hard time imagining that a new breed of customers will be flocking into SVT showrooms [some 750 participating Ford dealers]."

Still Out Front in Sales

If Mustang remained second-best in a drag race, it was still first in the sales race, with a '94 model-year total of 137,074 units, a whopping 17,245 ahead of Camaro. V-6s predictably outsold GTs but by lesser margins than in recent years. Among Cobras, Ford ended up building about 1000 more coupes than

projected—5009 in all. Convertibles were deliberately limited to 1000, as planned. All were essentially pace-car replicas done in Rio Red with saddle tops and saddle leather interiors, but without the actual pacers' special over-cockpit hoop/light bar. Race-day decals were naturally included.

Sales jumped to 185,986 for model-year '95 despite few changes, though CONSUMER GUIDE® was pleased to note tidier detail workmanship and a more solid overall driving feel. A confusing footnote was an announced GTS model, a GT with base-level trim and a $1200 lighter sticker, which was yanked before '95 sales began. *AutoWeek* later reported the GTS would be a midyear addition priced $2000 below the GT, but it never showed up on factory price lists, nor did a rumored GTS package for '96.

Get the Catalog

But Ford had another way to low-frills high-performance. Remember SVO, Special Vehicle Operations? Well, by 1995 it was the Special Vehicle *Organization* with a new emphasis on developing over-the-counter speed parts. Various kits allowed Mustangers to go as they paid. "If we had to choose just one," *Motor Trend* advised, "it would be the 3.55:1-ratio rear-end gearset. The stock GT comes with 2.73:1 gears for optimum fuel

economy. The Cobra SVT uses a more performance-themed 3.08:1 set. But if you're willing to pay a fuel-economy penalty and $257...the 3.55:1 gears get the most out of the torquey 5.0-liter V-8 engine." SVO also offered this in a $2995 "GT40" engine kit that upped horsepower to 290—50 more than a stock Cobra, 75 more than a stock GT. Featured were big-valve "GT40" aluminum heads (vs. smaller-valve cast-iron units), a new intake manifold with tubular runners, a larger throttle body, tubular exhaust headers, and low-drag accessory drive. So equipped, *Car and Driver's* GT coupe ran 0–60 mph in 5.5 seconds and the quarter-mile in 14.2 at 100 mph. "That puts this garage-built Trojan horse in the speed ballpark with the Z28," said *C/D,* which noted that "you can pay any Ford dealer the 10-hour flat-rate charge (about $500) to do the installation honors." Still not enough? SVO also listed a factory-approved Powerdyne supercharger with a choice of 6- and 9-psi puff, starting at $2600.

ABOVE: Despite much massaging by Ford's SVT division, the '94 Cobra V-8 made only 5 bhp more than the '93 version. BELOW: Compared to GTs, Fox-4 Cobras had larger wheels and tires, different suspension tuning, and a unique hood and fascias. BOTTOM: Cobra added its first ragtop for '94. Only 1000 were built, all Indy Pace Car Replicas like this.

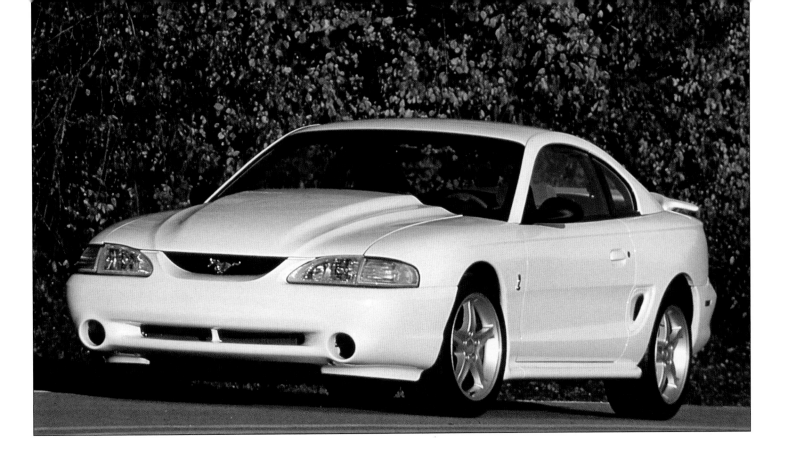

TOP AND ABOVE: SVT issued a new Cobra R for 1995, this time with a 351 V-8 tuned for 300 street-legal horses. Only 250 were built, all white coupes with bulging fiberglass hoods and no weighty back seat or air conditioning. Yet even this "racing" Cobra was no quicker than a street Camaro Z28 and cost some $13,000 more at $35,499 list. BELOW: Ford won the 1994 Manufacturer's Cup in SCCA's Trans-Am series thanks to the speed and stamina of Mustangs prepped by Jack Roush Racing.

ABOVE AND ABOVE RIGHT: Mustang power entered the modern era for 1996 with adoption of Ford's overhead-cam 4.6-liter modular V-8s. GTs ran a single-cam version with the same 215 bhp as the last pushrod 302. Designed for future emissions standards, the new mill required extensive underhood changes to fit but was announced outside only by small front-fender badges. RIGHT AND BELOW: That year's SVT Cobras switched to a twincam "4.6" whose 305 bhp finally brought Mustang up to performance parity with larger-engine GM ponycars. All '96 Mustangs boasted improved transmissions and minor style changes.

Not to be outdone, SVT whipped up a new Cobra R, this time with a *351* V-8 based on its hot-rod F-150 Lightning pickup engine—and completely street-legal. Higher compression (9.2:1), a wilder cam, and larger throttle body yielded 300 bhp and a thumping 365 lb-ft. But despite that, another stripped interior and a fiberglass hood (domed for clearance), *Car and Driver*'s prototype managed only 5.4 seconds 0–60 and a 14-second/99-mph standing-quarter—still only even with an everyday Z28. No matter. With only 250 copies, all coupes, this Cobra R was an instant sellout. Most were modified for road-course and drag racing.

"Mod" Squad

It was a last hurrah anyway. After nearly 40 years, Ford retired its overhead-valve small-block for 1996 Mustangs and bolted in the overhead-cam "modular" V-8 introduced five years before in the big Lincoln Town Car. There were two versions of this 4.6-liter (281-cubic-inch) engine. GTs used a single-cam iron-block iteration with two valves per cylinder in aluminum heads. It didn't look like progress, claiming the same power and torque as the 302. And straightline performance was down a bit, *C/D* netting 6.6 seconds 0–60 mph and a quarter-mile of 15.1 at 92 mph. But the "mod" would rev faster and higher, made similar torque at low rpm, and was smoother and quieter. More pointedly, it was able to meet future emissions standards; the old pushrod V-8 couldn't. The largely hand-assembled Cobra version looked more exciting, sporting twin cams, four valves per cylinder, and a special cast-aluminum block. With 305 bhp at 5800 rpm and 300 lb-ft at 4800, Mustangers no longer needed to fear stoplight encounters with GM ponycars. After testing all three, *C/D* ranked the Cobra behind a top-power '96 Camaro SS but ahead of a similarly optioned Firebird Formula. "It's the best daily-driver muscle car," *C/D* asserted. "Its DOHC 32-valve V-8 is the smallest but highest-

tech of the engines here. It convincingly makes as much horse-power but less torque than the 5.7-liter powerhouses, [yet the Cobra] turned in darn near the same performance, thanks to its lighter weight. True, it was slower than the Camaro and only marginally quicker than the Firebird in several areas, but it [was] the one car we would most want to drive home at the end of a long day." Some things never change.

Other things did. Because the "mod" engines were taller than the pushrod V-8, Ford had to redesign the front chassis cross-member, reposition the steering rack and lower front suspension arms, change engine mounting points, and devise a more compact brake booster. Slightly sprightlier handling was a happy benefit of these changes to accommodate the lighter engines. Underhood clutter was reduced by attaching the alternator, A/C compressor, and power-steering pump directly to the blocks. The "mod" V-8s also introduced modern "coil-on-plug" ignition with no distributor, improving efficiency and reliability.

Elsewhere for '96, Mustang's V-6 received a stiffer block and 10 more horsepower for 150 total, plus the new V-8's platinum-tipped spark plugs, designed to last 100,000 miles. Transmissions were ostensibly the same, but the five-speed manual was exchanged for Borg-Warner's beefier new T45 unit, and the AOD automatic was swapped for Ford's latest 4R70W transmission with more sophisticated electronic controls. Outside, the pony grille emblem got a mesh backdrop, and the horizontal taillamps gave way to three-element vertical clusters, which made the car

Roush Racing Mustangs and driver Tommy Kendall dominated Trans-Am in the late 1990s. Kendall was top driver in '95, '96, and again in '97, when he broke Mark Donohue's string of consecutive series wins and set a new record for total wins. He also won the '95 IMSA 24 Hours of Daytona with copilots Mark Martin and actor Paul Newman.

look narrower to some eyes. A sign of the times was a new "passive anti-theft system" (PATS) for GTs and Cobras. Optional for base models, this used a special ignition switch that required a matching coded key for starting. In the event of a hot-wiring attempt, the ignition system shut down altogether.

Down and Up

Despite the new V-8s, Mustang sales for '96 dropped a steep 27 percent to 135,620, of which 10,006 were SVT Cobras. The tally plunged another 20 percent for '97 to 108,344, though Cobra volume stayed about the same. There were few changes: standard PATS for base models, monotone instead of two-tone interiors (save black dashtops), available new "diamond-cut" 17-inch alloy wheels for GTs, and gray instead of white for the base convertible's optional leather upholstery.

Sales went the other way for '98, jumping 62 percent to 175,522. Again, updates were modest. Retuning took the GT's sohc V-8 to 225 bhp, and a GT Sport Group arrived offering five-spoke 17-inch wheels, engine-oil cooler, and hood and front-fender stripes for $595. A new $345 V-6 Sport Appearance Group bundled 16-inch alloy wheels and rear spoiler with body accent stripes and leather-rim steering wheel. All '98s got safer "depowered" dashboard airbags per federal decree. Prices were still creeping up, now running from $15,970 for the V-6 coupe to $28,135 for the Cobra convertible. Incidentally, Cobra sales this year were exactly the same as for '97, because SVT was at its yearly limit of around 10,000 units.

Muscle, Memories, and Another Milestone

Mustang by now had been America's top-selling sporty car for 12 straight years and was outselling Camaro and Firebird *combined*. The achievement was remarkable, but not surprising. As Peter Bohr noted in a January 2000 *Road & Track* owner survey of 1994–98 models: "'Muscle and memories' is how some describe [the] seemingly eternal Mustang. It was…a favorite from the start. And because the folks at Ford have continued to hone the car over the years, the Mustang has earned a fiercely loyal following equaled by few other automobiles." More than ever, there was still nothing else quite like a Mustang.

But the future always beckons, and another milestone Mustang birthday lay ahead in 1999. Once again, the press and loyal Mustangers expected Ford to do something special for the occasion. They would not be disappointed.

This ad for the '97 GT recalls a late-Sixties Dodge theme with its story of an average guy in a hot car drawing undesired attention. Unlike the old days, though, muscle is implied rather than broadcast with horsepower or test-track numbers. Ford pitched Mustang as a performance car that could handle, stop, rock-out, and keep running for years.

Jack had the monster (aka: Mustang GT) at the world's longest red light.

And he was putting every watt in that MACH 460 sound system to very good use. That's when Jack saw him:

an eager trooper, sitting in his squad car. Waiting. Their eyes met .

The trooper's hand twitched over his holstered radar gun. When the light finally changed,

4.6-LITER SEFI V-8

just so Smokey could take one last, long look. After all, why try to inspire "fear" or "respect"

4-WHEEL DISC BRAKES WITH AVAILABLE ABS

17" WHEELS WITH 245/45ZR17 TIRES*

ROCKIN' 460-WATT SOUND SYSTEM*

*Optional equipment.

Jack eased the monster's V-8 into "slow cruise,"

when "envy" is perfectly legal?

Built Ford to Last Mustang GT

1-800-258-FORD or
www.ford.com

SVT Cobras remained visually stealthy versus the more ubiquitous Mustang GTs. This 1998 coupe shows off the newly standard "star" alloy wheels, very similar to those used for '93. All Fox-4 Cobras boasted larger-than-stock disc brakes with "Cobra" lettering on the calipers, a subtle spotter's point. White-faced gauges were another Cobra exclusive among Fox-4 Mustangs. Ford's Windsor, Ontario, plant built the twincam Cobra "mod" V-8, whose aluminum block was cast in Italy. The crankshaft was forged in Germany. Cobra coupes listed for $25,630, convertibles for $28,430.

Chapter Eleven:

1999-2004

Ford's ageless ponycar was rejuvenated one more time for 1999 with "New Edge" styling, more power, and many key refinements. Though Dearborn soon ran into very stormy weather, Mustang cantered into the new century with its fastest, most roadable models yet. By 2003 it was once again the only ponycar in America, a worthy survivor with a bright new future.

Nineteen ninety-nine was a very good year for Ford Motor Company. Corporate profits hit a record $7.2 billion as the stock market and new-vehicle demand kept going strong in an unprecedented boom economy. Ford Division remained America's number-one-selling nameplate, owning five of the country's top-10 favorites including the full-size F-Series pickup, then in its 19th straight year as the most popular vehicle of any kind. Dearborn also owned Jaguar and Aston Martin (purchased in the 1980s) and would soon add Land Rover, another British icon, plus well-regarded Volvo of Sweden. Ultimately, these four makes would be combined into a new luxury division, Premier Automotive Group (PAG), under Wolfgang Reitzle, the successful former product-development meister at BMW. While looking ahead to its historic June 2003 centennial, Ford made another significant leadership change as Alex Trotman stepped down after five successful years as chairman. Taking over the reins was 42-year-old William Clay Ford, Jr., great-grandson of the company founder, nephew of the late Henry Ford II. Hard-charger Jacques Nasser moved up to president and chief executive officer after two years as head of Ford North American Operations.

But suddenly, it all turned sour. First, the economy started to unravel as overvalued "tech stocks" tanked, taking Wall Street down with them. Then, in 2000, Ford's cash-cow Explorer sport-utility and its original-equipment Firestone tires were implicated in rollover crashes that ultimately claimed almost 300 lives and caused scores of injuries. Nasser played a blame game with Firestone boss John Lampe in the media and before Congressional investigators, then ponied up $3.5 billion to replace some 6.5 million tires. But months of damning publicity battered Ford's claim to industry-leading quality—and its stock price. So did a string of embarassing glitches and recalls involving a redesigned Explorer, Ford's new Escape compact SUV, a revived two-seat Thunderbird, and the small Focus, Ford's latest attempt at a "world car." Other new models like the European-inspired Lincoln LS and its Jaguar S-Type sister did not sell as expected. Mazda, Dearborn's longtime Japanese affiliate, was having sales trouble, too, a further drain on corporate coffers.

And there was worse. After burning through more than $15 bil-

lion since 1999, Ford lost a staggering $5.45 billion in 2001, which only accelerated declines in market share and stock price. Then, in the wake of the horrific September 11 terrorist attacks, Ford was forced to match General Motors' zero-percent financing and other costly market-priming moves, which contributed to a loss of almost a billion bucks in 2002. Equally ominous, the near-term product pipeline looked almost dry, and PAG suffered a setback when Reitzle left in early 2002.

Back to Basics

Many things had clearly gone wrong. Most pundits blamed Jacques Nasser. So did the chairman and his board. Thus did "Jac" get the sack in October 2001 after less than three years as CEO. A reluctant Bill Ford took command.

Basically, Nasser had overreached. Snapping up Volvo and Land Rover was costly enough, but Nasser also bought into Internet retailing and other "e-commerce" ventures, a chain of auto repair shops in Britain, Norwegian-built electric cars, even junkyards. "The plan, theoretically, had promise," opined *Automotive News*. "Mix the old-school nuts-and-bolts strengths of an automaker with the razzle-dazzle of the computer era to create a new-age consumer products company that delivered cradle-to-grave transportation services. [But the] acerbic Nasser left out a couple of ingredients: building reliable vehicles, and keeping the troops happy…. Ford Motor says it is returning to its roots. Once again, a Ford is at the helm [and he has] decided Ford Motor is an auto company. Period."

Many wondered whether Bill Ford was up to the job. But what he may have lacked in managerial experience, he more than made up for in determination. "Look, I am in this for my children and grandchildren," he told *Automotive News* soon after firing Nasser. "I'll be as tough as I have to be, because the viability of this company over the next 100 years is what keeps me going. And I know we are not going to have 100 years if we don't get the next five nailed down."

To answer critics and calm shareholders, the new CEO quickly secured an able chief operating officer in Nicholas Scheele, the mastermind behind recent turnarounds at Jaguar and Ford

Europe. To get a grip on financials, the young scion coaxed former CFO Alan Gilmour out of retirement. The organization chart was again redrawn and an ambitious recovery plan forged. Key goals included slashing unit production costs by $700 or more, trashing a controversial employee-evaluation system instituted under Nasser, closing unneeded plants, and dealing with soaring employee health-care costs and a huge pension-fund shortfall. And, oh, yes: putting the rush on profitable new products built to world-class standards.

We mention all this because it helps in understanding Mustang's path into the new millennium. And for all the corporate turmoil, Mustang fared quite well—starting with the major makeover of the SN95/Fox-4 for 35th-anniversary '99.

New Edge, New Look

The most obvious change was a lower-body reskin exemplifying "New Edge Design." Instigated by Jack Telnack before his 1997 retirement, New Edge was both a follow-on and antidote to his aerodynamic "jelly-bean" styling, which had been so widely imitated that buyers had had enough. Because it was basically a "geometric" approach, with crisp lines and deliberately jarring graphic elements set against rounded forms, New Edge did not translate easily to the SN95. *AutoWeek* likened the restyled coupe as "akin to putting a baseball cap on a shoebox." Still, Mustang designers under Ken Grant managed a fresh look that was also "retro" and fun.

The grille was a narrowed but deeper trapezoid whose running-horse mascot was again corraled in chrome on base and GT

Mustang adopted Ford's "New Edge Design" theme for 1999, with fresh lower-body sheetmetal over the existing SN95/Fox-4 structure. Note the standard foglights and larger wheels on the V-8 GT ragtop versus the V-6 base coupe behind it. BELOW: All '99 Mustangs were considered 35th Anniversary models (dated from 1964, of course), but only base and GT versions wore this celebratory front-fender emblem.

models. A large dummy scoop was set into a more visibly domed hood above wider wraparound headlamp clusters. Bodysides were pulled out, wheel openings newly flared. The signature C-shape side graphic and its simulated rear air scoop were enlarged, but the sheetmetal within was now flat rather than "pre-dented." The rear end was modernized with larger, squared-up vertical taillamps and a trunklid made of light, plasticlike sheet molding compound. Bumpers bulked up as well. Coupes got a revised rear roofline with no quarter-window "kink." Last but not least were front-fender emblems proclaiming Mustang's 35th birthday with a traditional "pony tricolor" circled in chrome.

Smoother, Quieter, Snappier

Improved handling and refinement were the goals of chassis engineers under Paul Giltinan. Side rails were fully boxed, with insulating foam in the rocker-panel areas. Better floorpan sealing also helped lessen road noise. Convertibles gained underbody "rail extenders" designed to reduce structural shudder. For agility, rear track on all models was widened by 1.4 inches (thus equaling the front dimension), and a 1.5-inch higher transmission tunnel allowed a little more upward wheel travel.

Smaller-diameter antiroll bars and retuned shock absorbers were specified to improve ride compliance with no harm to handling despite adoption of firmer springs. GTs switched from variable- to linear-rate coils for the same reasons. Steering was revised with less boost, better on-center feel, and a useful three-foot tighter turning circle. The front disc brakes gained aluminum twin-piston calipers saving 10 pounds apiece in unneeded unsprung weight. New pad material and a larger master cylinder provided more positive braking feel with less pedal effort.

Powertrain engineers under Bill Koche focused on pumping up power. The 3.8-liter pushrod V-6 with "split-port induction" received new cylinder heads, a freer-breathing intake manifold with two runners for each cylinder, high-tech piston coatings that reduced friction, and new aluminum main and thrust bearings. Horsepower jumped by 40 to 190, torque by five pound-feet to 215. A new contra-rotating "balancer" shaft did nothing for performance but did dampen second-order vibrations for smoother running. Improvements were no less extensive for the GT's 4.6-liter single-cam V-8: bigger valves, reshaped combustion chambers, a new higher-lift longer-duration camshaft, straighter manifold runners for better airflow, and improved crankshaft, conrod, and thrust bearings. Horsepower here expanded by 35 to 250, torque by 10 lb-ft to 302. In addition, the former 3.27:1 "performance" axle was now standard for both engines, improving off-the-line snap.

As before, an antilock brake system (ABS) was standard for GTs and optional on base models ($500). An extra $230 bought the additional "active safety" of traction control, Mustang's first. Spearheaded by chief project engineer Janine Bay, this used the ABS wheel-speed sensors to detect wheel slippage. In the

event, system electronics would retard spark and reduce throttle opening until traction was restored (wheel speeds equalized). At higher road speeds (up to 62 mph), the system could also brake either rear wheel as needed, hence the advertising moniker "all-speed traction control." A dashboard "off" switch enabled drivers to let it literally all hang out when conditions—and skill—allowed.

Independence at Last

And what of the SVT Cobras? As in prior years, the '99s bowed a few months after mainstream models and shared most all their improvements, with ABS and traction control standard. SVT treated the twincam 4.6 V-8 to new "tumble-port" cylinder heads and other revisions that extracted an extra 15 bhp for 320 total—the same as a top-option Chevy Camaro/Pontiac Firebird. Also new were big Brembo disc brakes with diameters of 13 inches in front, 11.65 inches in back.

But the most-talked about innovation was the first independent rear suspension (IRS) in Mustang history. It used unequal-length lower control arms, upper toe-control links, high-rate coil springs, and a thicker (26mm) antiroll bar. All were mounted to a welded-up tubular subframe. Along with an aluminum differential housing (from the late Lincoln Mark VIII coupe) that had Cobra-specific halfshafts. In a triumph of inventiveness, SVT designed the IRS as a straight bolt-in replacement for the regular solid-axle suspension; all it took was adding two holes with "weld nuts" to the SN95 structure. That meant the IRS could be installed on the regular Mustang assembly line—and on regular Mustangs post-purchase, though it's doubtful that happened very often. Incidentally, the IRS was supplied as a preassembled module by Bentler, an outside contractor.

Mustang's '99 restyle imparted a crisper, slightly huskier "retro" look, with new iterations of trademark elements like triple taillamps (above left) and simulated bodyside scoops (below center). A "corral" for the running-horse grille mascot returned (above center). Headlamps (above right) were reshaped. A new hood with nonfunctional scoop (below left) was standard for GTs, as were new-design alloy wheels (below right).

LEFT: The 1999 GT convertible started at $24,870. BELOW LEFT: Mustang's V-6 (left) gained a useful 40 horses for '99, while the GT's single-cam 4.6-liter V-8 added 35. BELOW: Though not vastly changed, the '99 interior boasted slightly longer front-seat tracks and less noise, thanks to improved floor-pan sealing and the addition of insulating foam in the rocker-panel areas. BOTTOM: This '99 coupe might look like a $20,870 GT, but it's really the $16,470 base version with the V-6 Sport Appearance Group offering rear spoiler, alloy wheels, and other sporty features for $310.

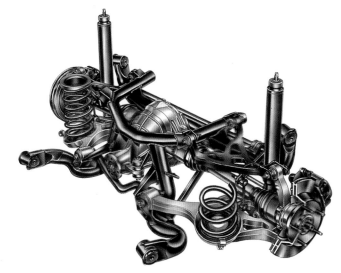

The SVT Cobra again wore small foglamps and an unfenced grille pony for '99. Cobra's twincam V-8 claimed 320 horses for '99, but manufacturing glitches forced a recall to liberate the whole herd. Mustang's first independent rear suspension was a '99 Cobra exclusive and worked wonders for cornering. Like previous SVT Cobras, the '99s featured white-faced gauges and other special cockpit touches. Base price was $27,470 for the coupe, $31,470 for the Cobra convertible.

Thumbs Up

Except for styling, which drew mixed reviews, the press gave a hearty thumbs-up to the '99 Mustangs. *Road & Track* pronounced the fortified V-6 "a respectable performer. It's not as quick or smooth as the GT, but it's no slouch." *AutoWeek*'s Daniel Pund agreed and applauded all models for a more solid driving feel. Though Ford initially claimed slightly improved rigidity, Pund quoted Giltinan as saying this was virtually unchanged. "The perceived solidity is a byproduct of reduced road noise, a more supple ride, and heavier, more direct steering," Pund surmised.

The GT earned its own kudos. *Motor Trend* found its "tidy dimensions, precise steering and torquey [V-8] make it one of the easiest cars to place on line; even at the edge of the tires' limits...." As for straightline go, the magazine's five-speed coupe dashed from 0 to 60 mph in 5.4 seconds and ran the quarter-mile in 14.0 seconds at 100.2 mph—not tops in the modern muscle class, but "as good or better than any stock Mustang we've ever tested, Cobra or not." *AutoWeek* soon got into a GT ragtop, which clocked 5.9 seconds to 60 mph and the quarter-mile in 14.44 at 96.9 mph despite a 150-pound weight penalty. "[This] is one trick pony, but finally, it's not a one-trick pony. It goes, and it stops, and it turns, but it doesn't twitch."

How Many Horses?

All was not right with the Cobra, however. *Motor Trend* noted that despite smaller tires and a solid axle, the GT's slalom and skidpad numbers were surprisingly close "at 66.8 mph and 0.86g, respectively [vs.] 67.8 mph and 0.88g. Viewed in this way, the SVT superpony seems hardly worth the extra $7000"—a starting tab of $27,470 for the coupe, $31,470 for the ragtop. *Car and*

Driver praised the IRS for erasing 125 pounds of unsprung weight, even though it was 80 pounds heavier than the solid-axle assembly. On the other hand, curb weight was down by a worthwhile 110 pounds, and it was split more evenly front to rear. With that, *C/D*'s Barry Winfield judged the '99 Cobra "more supple and thus more readable in corners. The rear end is less susceptible to bump-steer...off-center steering response is better, and [the] handling is more neutral at the limit." But straightline performance was a puzzle. "We expected to hit 60 mph in about five seconds flat," Winfield said, "but 5.5 was the best we could do—0.1-second slower than the previous model. Top speed was also down, from 153 to 149 mph...all of which confirms that our low-mileage prototype test car wasn't making a full head of steam."

Sure enough, a manufacturing glitch had left Cobra intake runners and some exhaust components with internal aluminum residue or "flash" that upset air flow and kept over 30 horses from showing up. After fielding a few dozen owner complaints, mostly from drag racers, Ford recalled all '99s on the ground to replace the manifold or roto-rooter the existing one. Ford also charged nothing to replace mufflers (found to be too restrictive), recalibrate the engine computer, and substitute a more durable accessory-belt tensioner. A decal was affixed in the engine bay to certify the work once it was done. Though Cobra owners didn't seem to mind the recall or its inconvenience, the episode was a black

continued on page 204

John Force and his Mustang funny cars dominated that National Hot Rod Association drag-racing class in the 1990s and into the 2000s. Force won his 10th class championship in 2000 and would go on to claim two more. In 2003, his three-Mustang team won at 13 of 23 NHRA Nationals to finish 1-3-5 in the Funny Car standings.

Stung by the "lost horsepower" glitch in '99 street Cobras, SVT skipped a 2000 model but unleashed the fastest factory Mustang yet. Packing a 385-bhp 5.4 V-8, the newest race-ready Cobra R could do 0–60 in under 5 seconds, 13-second quarter-mile blasts, and a stunning 1.0g on the skidpad. A deep front airdam, high-flying rear spoiler, big Brembo brakes, and Recaro racing seats were all standard. Only 300 were built, all red coupes.

SVT: Passion for Performance

Stay with us. This gets a little tricky. Despite the short-lived Mustang SVO, Ford execs were generally pleased with the work of their Special Vehicle Operations unit (see Chapter Eight). By the early Nineties, however, SVO had become a victim of its own success, with too much work to do and too few people to do it. Accordingly, Ford reorganized and refocused its performance and competition activities. SVO would continue running corporate racing programs and developing over-the-counter speed parts, but the task of coming up with hot limited-edition street cars passed to a new Special Vehicle Team (SVT) headed by John Plant. At about the same time, a Special Vehicle Engineering staff (SVE) was formed to support both SVT and SVO.

As one press release stated it, SVT's mission was "to use the best-available resources from both inside and outside Ford [Motor Company] to explore new ways of creating and marketing high-performance vehicles. The cross-functional team is charged with delivering limited-edition, high-performance derivative cars and trucks designed to delight serious drivers.... SVT's refined, understated 'form follows function' philosophy reflects our passion for multi-dimensional performance." Sales and service would be handled "through a select network of specially trained and certified Ford dealers who are prepared to satisfy discriminating driving enthusiasts before, during and after the sale."

SVT unveiled its first two progeny at the 1992 Chicago Auto Show. Both were early-'93 models: the SVT Mustang Cobra and a hot-rod full-size pickup, the SVT F-150 Lightning. Respective model-year production was 4993 and 5276. Within a year, SVT had added a racing-only Mustang Cobra R, which saw but 107 copies. While the 240-horsepower 5.8-liter V-8 Lightning continued through 1995 and another 6287 units, SVT tuned up its engine to 300 bhp for a new SN95-based Cobra R, of which just 250 were built for '95.

Then, for the next two years, nothing. Several factors were at work. First, Plant retired in March 1995, and though his successor, Tim Boyd, made no big changes to planned projects, the team apparently ran into engineering delays on its next Lightning, a supercharged stormer based on the redesigned '94 F-Series. SVT was also busy with its first sports sedan, a tuned version of the Euro-style Ford Contour, for which top brass had high sales hopes. SVT might have been created to "polish the Ford oval," but it was also expected to make money, or at least break even.

But the main problem was some evident grumbling in the dealer ranks. As *Car and Driver* reported in August 1995, each Ford store paid a $4000 annual fee to be an SVT agent, not to mention investment in special equipment and training. Yet some dealers had bailed, in part because SVT Mustangs couldn't compete on muscle with top-power, *regular-production* General Motors rivals. "If these dealers lose interest, Ford loses interest," *C/D* intoned, "and that could mean all the SVT employees and engineers go back to designing cupholders for the Crown Victoria."

Happily for Ford fans, that wouldn't happen. The SVT Contour, appearing on cue for 1998, was a fair commercial success with 11,445 sales through model-year 2000, after which Ford canceled the Contour itself. The Lightning became even more popular once it got a specially built 5.4-liter supercharged V-8. The 360-bhp 1999–2000 version attracted 8966 buyers; even happier were the 11,107 folks who bought the 380-bhp 2001–02. Meanwhile, as this chapter relates, the SVT Cobra became a permanent and, yes, profitable part of the Mustang line, a bread-and-butter model to rival the Lightning in yearly sales, monetary return, and publicity value. For 2002, the team stepped into the youthful, fast-growing "sport compact" market with the SVT Focus.

By that point, SVT was under the enthusiastic command of John Coletti, who had led the 1994 SN95 Mustang program. Assisting him were chief engineer Mike Zevalkink, who'd been powertrain manager for SN95, and marketing and sales manager Tom Scarpello. By the time SVT marked its 10th birthday as part of Ford's 2003 centennial, it had built over 100,000 vehicles, no mean feat for what remained a small part of a big corporation. "Ten years and we're just picking up speed," Coletti said at the time. "You haven't seen half of what we can do."

Soon after, SVT and Ford Racing (*nee* SVO) were rolled into a new Ford Performance Group, and SVT turned to even more potent and exclusive rides. Pointing the way are the supercharged 2003–04 Cobra, a new 500-bhp Lightning—and the mid-engine Ford GT supercar. With such a passion for performance, SVT's future looks very bright indeed.

Mustang's star attraction for 2001 was the midyear GT-based Bullitt coupe, named for the classic 1968 movie starring Steve McQueen and a hot '68 fastback. Ford PR staged an "air" shot (bottom left) evoking the film's climactic chase on the streets of San Francisco. Another press photo (right) posed the Bullitt with an excellent replica of the movie car (owned by L.A. TV reporter Dave Kunz) against the San Fran skyline. Though little faster than a stock GT, the Bullitt was a great nostalgia trip. Most of the 6500 built were painted the same Dark Highland Park Green as McQueen's car. Features included aluminum interior accents, "retro" wheels, red brake calipers, and a neat-sounding exhaust.

continued from page 200

eye for Ford and SVT—enough that they decided not to do a 2000 Cobra. As the SVT website advised at the time, fixing the '99s had top priority. "Rather than rushing to produce a limited number of 2000 models—and risking production/manufacturing issues by hurrying—we're choosing to focus our efforts on the timely production of the ['01 versions]."

Birthday Special, A Special Stamp

Among happier '99 highlights was the 35th Anniversary trim package applied to about 5000 GTs. Priced at $2695, it included 17-inch five-spoke wheels, applied side scoops, another raised scoop and black striping for the hood, unique rocker moldings, rear spoiler, taillamp appliqués, and a specific black-and-silver interior with leather upholstery, aluminum shift knob, and logo floormats. As expected, mid-April brought more birthday bashes at Charlotte and in Southern California. And in a nice bit of timing, the U.S. Postal Service issued a special stamp late in the year to honor Mustang as one of 15 American icons of the 1960s. Pictured on the stamp was—what else?—a red '65 convertible.

There was little celebrating in the sales office, however, as model-year volume dropped by nearly a fourth to 133,637 units. The "dot-bomb" debacle and other bad economic news didn't help, nor did higher prices for the many '99 upgrades. Base stickers went up $500 on V-6 models, $900 on GTs, lifting the range to $16,500–$25,000. Cobra sales were also down but not mortally wounded by the AWOL-horsepower flap, and convertibles outsold coupes for the first time (4055 vs. 4040 units).

Price hikes were quite modest for 2000—just $50 to $150. Despite a worsening economy and little new among mainstream models, sales actually turned up on a *calendar-year* basis, gaining 4.1 percent to 173,676 units.

The Cobra Strikes Back

Mustang's main event of 2000 was the new Cobra R that roared in about eight months after a birthday-party preview at Charlotte. Like the last R-model of '95, this one was street-legal but obviously track-oriented—"a turn-key racing machine," as *Road & Track* called it. Speed freaks salivated over a 5.4-liter 32-valve twincam V-8 like that in the big Lincoln Navigator SUV, thoroughly massaged by SVT and Ford's Special Vehicle Engineering group headed by John Coletti. As usual, the focus was on better breathing. A new intake manifold sported large, curved "air trumpets," exhaust ports were enlarged, and there were tubular headers connected to X-pipes ahead of Borla mufflers and twin side-exit exhausts. Because of its extra height, the 5.4 nestled beneath a very bulged hood with functional vents on a rear-facing scoop. A high-riding spoiler helped keep the tail down at speed, as did an aerodynamic front-fascia "air splitter." Suspension was beefed up with ultra-stiff Eibach springs, hard bushings, and premium Bilstein shock absorbers that slammed ride height by 1.5 inches at the front, an inch at the rear. Heavy-duty halfshafts were specified, along with jumbo Brembo disc brakes clamped by four-piston calipers. Tires were purpose-designed 265/40ZR Goodrich "g-Force KD" on 9.5 × 18 forged-aluminum wheels. Completing the package was a short-throw six-speed manual transmission by Tremec—Mustang's first six-cog gearbox—working through a stock Cobra clutch to a special Gerodisc hydro-mechanial differential with 3.55:1 gearing.

SVT again omitted the back seat, air conditioning, sound system—and a lot of sound insulation. Curb weight was variously quoted at 3580–3610 pounds, far from feathery but light enough for the new R-model's 385 bhp and 385 lb-ft of torque. The result was the fastest factory Mustang yet. *Car and Driver* timed 0–60 mph at just 4.7 seconds and a standing quarter-mile of 13.2 at 110 mph. *Road & Track* got 4.8 and 13.2/109.1 mph, but these and other published numbers slightly *bettered* Ford claims. More importantly, they bettered top Camaro/Firebird performance and at least equaled that of the Chevy Corvette. Skidpad grip was worthy of the standard Recaro racing front buckets. *R&T* measured 0.99g, *C/D* an astounding 1.01. "Handling is dead-solid predictable up to the considerable limits, [when] gentle understeer suggests you back off a bit," *C/D* said, "but there is not a hint of tail-happiness. The brakes…are superb, with stunningly little fade even over extended periods of hard use." *R&T* noted surprising civility: "Out on the street, the Cobra R…doesn't inflict the same kind of body punches you'd expect from a race car. Despite the heft of the suspension and the absolute lack of body roll, there is enough fore-and-aft compliance to make the ride bearable."

At last, Mustang could claim a place at the very top of the performance hill. The only downers were a fairly formidable price—$54,995, *plus* luxury and gas-guzzler taxes—and just 300 copies available, all red coupes and all quickly sold. *R&T* was sympathetic: "The Cobra R is a nice start—now let's see some real numbers, as in volume, out on the street."

Street Cobra Transformed

Ford partly answered that challenge for 2001 by reinstating the regular Cobra with all 320 horses accounted for. *Car and Driver* put two cars on a dynamometer just to be sure, then reeled off 0–60 in 4.8 seconds and a stunning quarter-mile of 13.5 seconds at 105 mph. But that was "only part of the story," said tester Larry Webster, "as the Cobra has left its crude ponycar roots and joined the ranks of competent sports coupes.... Now you can point the Cobra exactly where you want and assume it will go there." Webster declared the 2001 was "nothing short of a Cobra transformation…a superb all-arounder."

OPPOSITE PAGE: The GT coupe and other Mustangs were little changed for 2002, a likely reason sales were down for the second straight year. THIS PAGE, ABOVE: Mustang celebrated Ford's 100th birthday in 2003 with a mild Centennial trim package, shown here on a GT ragtop. BELOW: New for 2003 V-6 models was a Pony Appearance Package that delivered Bullitt-style wheels and most GT styling features for $595.

The same could be said for other 2001 Mustangs notwithstanding their less impressive performance. Unlike the Cobra, the base and GT models added several styling features of the 35th Anniversary package, including a raised (but still nonfunctioning) hood scoop, special side scoops, and a reshaped trunklid spoiler, plus black headlamp surrounds. Changes were otherwise few— a new console, standard 17-inch wheels for GTs, a few options shuffles—until midseason, when Ford fired a Bullitt.

The Spirit of '68

Previewed as a 2000 concept, this specially equipped GT coupe was brokered by styling chief J Mays (Jack Telnack's successor) in a nostalgic nod to the iconic 1968 Steve McQueen film (see pg. 59). Mays, who'd help create the ultra-clean Audi TT, had issues with Mustang's '99 styling and did his best to correct them on the Bullitt, omitting the rear spoiler and adding a unique hood scoop, rear-roof-pillar trim and rocker moldings, plus a brushed-aluminum fuel-filler door. The cockpit was dressed with special seats and leather upholstery, an aluminum shift knob and pedal trim, Sixties-style gauge graphics, and chrome door-sill

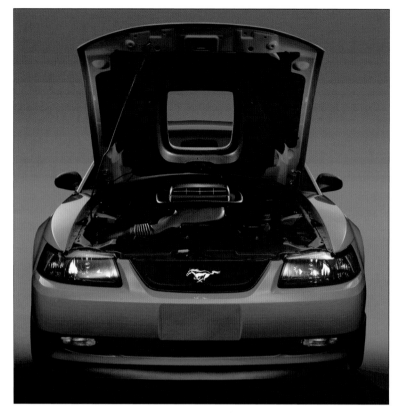

plates with "Bullitt" in Art Deco type. Ride height lowered by 0.75-inch also helped appearance, as did red-painted brake calipers peeking through five-spoke 17-inch American Racing "Torq Thrust" wheels mimicking those of McQueen's movie ride. Ford also retuned the GT's Tokico shock/strut units, installed specific antiroll bars, and added "frame-rail connectors" to calm body shake. Finally, the GT V-8 got a larger throttle body, cast-aluminum intake manifold, smaller accessory-drive pulleys, and a freer-flow exhaust system. The result was a mere five extra horses and three lb-ft of torque, so the Bullitt was not usefully faster than a stock GT coupe

Mustang again played the nostalgia card for 2003, adding a GT-based Mach 1 coupe that not only revived a famous name but the "shaker" hood scoop associated with it. The scoop fed air to a 300-horse version of the 4.6 twincam V-8 from earlier SVT Cobras. Priced from $28,370, the new Mach 1 also featured a firm suspension with slightly lower ride height, retro gauge graphics, unique trim, and leather upholstery.

despite costing $3500 more—$26,230 and up. Still, Ford had no trouble moving the planned 6500 units. Most were painted Dark Highland Park Green, another echo of Steve's car, though black and dark blue were available, too.

Sales Keep Swinging

Motor Trend reported that the Bullitt was "the first in a series of short-term specials designed to bring extra excitement and collectibility into the current [Mustang line]." Excitement was surely needed, judging by sales, which eased 2.6 percent for calendar '01 to 169,198. The '02 tally was 138,356, a worrisome 18.2-percent drop in a year when zero-percent financing had stoked the general market to red hot. Then again, mainstream Mustangs once more showed little significant change. Indeed, Ford's big move for '02 was to turn popular option groups into prosaically named models: Base Standard, Deluxe, and Premium, (all upgraded to standard 16-inch wheels), and to create Deluxe and Premium GT models.

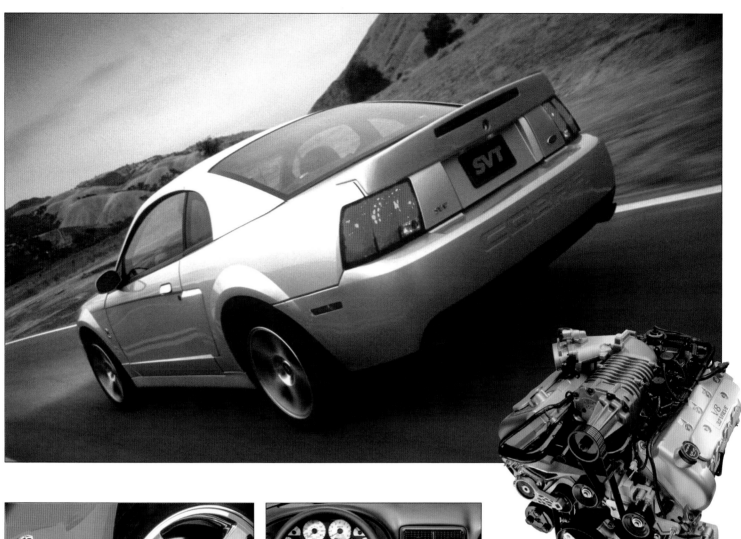

SVT went all out for 2003 by supercharging the Cobra's twincam V-8 to create the most potent street Mustangs ever. With 390 horses and 390 lb-ft of torque, both the coupe (top) and convertible (left) could run 0–60 mph in well under 5 seconds. Larger brakes and rolling stock helped control the formidable thrust. The shifter connected to a mandatory six-speed manual gearbox. A bulging twin-scoop hood was also new. The coupe started at $33,460, the convertible at $37,835.

An exclusive "Mystichrome" paint option was one of the few changes in the '04 supercharged Cobras. It was a new high-tech finish that seemed to change hue depending on ambient light and one's vantage point. The $3650 price included chrome alloy wheels, as shown here, plus some special interior trim. The SVT Cobra remained a terrific performance buy, with the coupe starting at $34,575, the ragtop at $38,950.

SVT Really Blows It

The SVT Cobra was MIA for '02, but only until spring, when the 2003 versions made an early debut packing a huge new wallop: 390 bhp and 390 lb-ft of torque. Taking a page from the hot-rodder's handbook, SVT bolted an Eaton M112 Roots-type centrifugal supercharger to the Cobra's twincam V-8 and made numerous changes to accommodate it. These included using an iron block for durability under pressure, plus a water-to-air intercooler, new cylinder heads, and revised pistons with suitably lower 8.5:1 compression. The only transmission was the Tremec six-speed familiar from the '00 Cobra R. Suspension was naturally recali-

brated, with individual damping rates for the coupe and convertible. Rolling stock comprised inch-wider five-spoke cast-alloy rims wearing 275/40ZR Goodyear Eagle F1 tires. SVT also added a vented hood (necessary with the added engine-bay heat from the blower), revised front fascia and rocker-panel skirts, a rear air diffuser, and a new low-profile decklid spoiler.

With all this, SVT's latest Mustang delivered near 2000 Cobra R thrust at a much friendlier starting price of $33,460. The stats told the tale: 0–60 mph in 4.5–4.9 seconds, quarter-mile ETs around 13 seconds, 0.90g skidpad grip. All this in a car you could drive to work day in and day out. You might not call it refined, as *Road & Track*'s Doug Kott observed, "Yet it's refined enough for those who elevate performance and affordability...above ultimate sophistication.... [T]he SVT crew should be applauded for... breathing new life into Ford's workhorse."

Return of the Mach 1

Even more affordable—and little less spectacular—was a 2003 follow-up to the boomermobile Bullitt. Reviving the Mach 1 name after 25 years, this new variation on the GT coupe carried an unblown twincam Cobra V-8 tuned for 300 bhp and topped by a functional "shaker" hood scoop straight from the Sixties. Base price was $28,370, a stout $3715 above the GT Premium coupe, but that also included a slightly lowered suspension, primo Brembo brakes, a black hood stripe and other unique cosmetics, and "comfort-weave styled" leather upholstery.

Car and Driver pitted the reborn Mach 1 against three new high-tech foreigners for a December 2002 test and ranked it second behind Nissan's formidable, newly reborn Z-car. "The Mach 1 earns its silver medal because it is brute fun. Drop the hammer, and with no especially refined technique, 60 mph is yours in a scalding 5.2 seconds...the fastest time in this test by a full half-second." As ever, there were gripes about solid-axle handling and

RIGHT: Mustang marked its 40th birthday in 2004 with a modest $895 Anniversary Package for base and GT premium models. BELOW: Though '04 would be the last gasp for Mustang's long-serving Fox platform, the trusty steed made one final historic splash when a 2004 GT convertible rolled out of the Dearborn Assembly Plant on November 20, 2003, as the 300-millionth Ford Motor Company vehicle. Chairman and CEO William C. Ford, Jr., came by to help celebrate the milestone.

dated ergonomics. But *C/D* admitted the Mach 1 "generates more grins than grimaces…. [It] is an ode to the past. Perhaps Henry Ford was wrong: History isn't bunk, it's a hoot."

All by themselves, the Mach 1 and the sizzling supercharged street Cobra made 2003 a vintage Mustang year. The only other change of note was a $595 Pony appearance package for V-6 models. Sales improved fractionally, adding a bit over 2000 units for the calendar year. But the trusty old steed was clearly marking time. As everyone knew, a frisky new filly was on the way for 2005, previewed with a pair of concepts at the January 2003 Los Angeles and Detroit Auto Shows.

The Big Four-Oh

That implied few changes for '04, Mustang's 40th anniversary year. Sure enough, there was little news that season: an extra 10 horses for Mach 1, three more for V-6 models. But of course, Ford did deliver the obligatory birthday package, this time an $895 kit for Premium V-6 and GT coupes and convertibles. This bundled an Interior Upgrade Package (normally a $295 stand-alone item) with unique wheels, special badging and trim, and fold-in mirrors; curiously, it deleted the stock rear spoiler. It wasn't much of a present for such a milestone birthday, but it didn't have to be. The real celebration was yet to come.

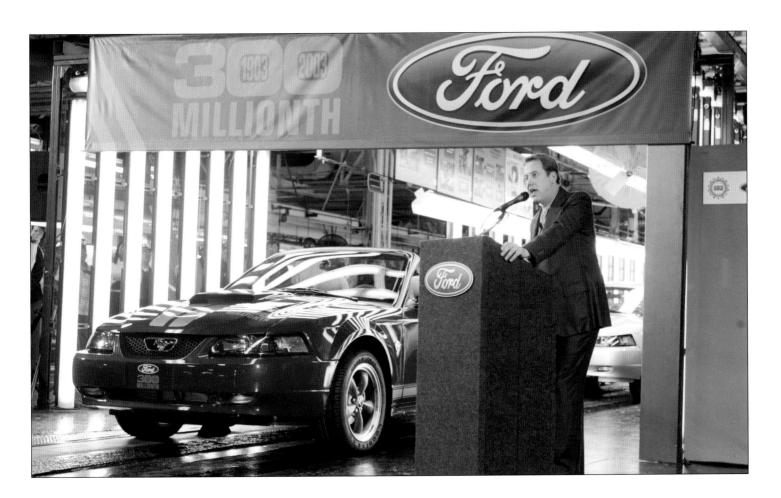

Chapter Twelve:
2005

Its shape was ordained by a superstar
stylist with a European pedigree.
Its engineering was directed by a man
who as a child in wartorn Vietnam
idolized it as a symbol of freedom.
Its personality was inspired
by the most charismatic Mustangs ever.
The original was reborn for 2005,
newer than ever, familiar as always.

No new Mustang was ever newer than the 2005 model. The '65 borrowed the Falcon's frame. The '74 poached Pinto's platform. From 1979 through 2004 it was, by degree, a member of the Fairmont-Fox family.

The '05 was the first Mustang that didn't share its underskin architecture with an existing Ford product. It enjoyed, in the words of its chief engineer, "a purpose-built, muscle-car chassis new from the ground up." It could scarcely have met its cost and performance requirements otherwise.

The new platform ushered in a sweeping change to Mustang's assembly process, a change essential to the car's economic feasibility. The new platform made possible a redesigned suspension tailored precisely to Mustang's cost and performance requirements. And it freed packaging engineers to finally give the car up-to-date ergonomics.

Yet for all that was new, the 2005 Mustang's most-defining trait was its bow to yesteryear. Here was the '65's C-scoop, the '69's fastback, the '67's dashboard, the '70's nose, and—surprise!—the '66 GT350's rear quarter windows.

Cherry-picking the choicest cues from Mustang's back catalog was cooly calculated. Ford wanted to rekindle the warmest feelings about a 40-year love affair, to link the latest version to Mustangs that mattered.

All this—the styling, the innovations in assembly, and platform engineering—everything about the 2005 Mustang had a single focus: to sustain the secret of Mustang's success.

It was simple, really. Mustang had always been able to cut across demographic lines, to attract both the style-seeking budget buyer and the speed-shifting hotshot. That helped it outlast the Chevrolet Camaro, Pontiac Firebird, and every other imitator. And it was the attribute that was being counted on to ensure its survival.

The Choicest Cuts

"Our objective was to bring back everything that was right about the best Mustangs," said the man behind the '05's styling, J Mays, Ford's celebrated chief of design. "If you look back over the 40-year history, there have been some fantastic Mustangs,

some lesser Mustangs, but never has the brand wavered in terms of its popularity for the mass market.

"We've gone from selling 400,000 units a year in '64, '65 to around 170,000 units a year," Mays said in January 2004, as the '05 was being unveiled to the press. "By today's standards, that's an amazing number of two-seat [sic] coupes. This is by far the most popular two-seat coupe in the world. And it also happens to be probably the most successful youth vehicle of all time.

"So when we looked at the greatest Mustangs of all time, we eventually narrowed it down to two kinds of vehicles. There were the ponycars in '64½, '65, and '66. And there were the all-out muscle cars, from '67 through '70.

"Based on the culture we're in today, where everything's a little bit more overt, everything's a little more urban, we thought that if we were going to pick up on any of the design cues of any of the Mustangs over the last 40 years, the '67 through '70 was the way to go," Mays said.

"And we tried to blend cues of those vehicles with modern cues—better stance, more overt flares, and a much larger shoulder than you would have found on a previous generation Mustang—in order to overtly and visually underline the idea of muscle and power."

Walk the Walk

Of course, the engineers had to deliver what the stylists promised. Working with the time-honored rear-wheel-drive, long-hood/short-deck, 2+2 formula, they fashioned a new body structure stouter and safer than any previous Mustang's.

They redesigned the front suspension, revamped the traditional solid rear axle, and engineered for easy integration of independent rear suspension for the highest-performance versions.

They fitted a new-to-Mustang 202-horsepower 4.0-liter V-6, the car's strongest base engine ever. To the familiar 4.6-liter V-8 they added advanced cylinder heads and other new-to-Mustang technology that gave the GT an honest 300 bhp, a summit previously reserved for special editions and '60s legends. They upgraded the front suspension, steering, and brakes and gave the automatic

Among the earliest explorations of what the 21st century's first new Mustang might look like came from the pen of Ford designer Sean Tant. FROM TOP: A cab-forward muscle machine (sketched in 1996); envisioning the return of a forward-canted nose and concave tail (1997); a fastback form that revived the spirit of the roof vents from the 1965–68 Mustangs (1997); a smooth, sexy expansion on the 1994–98 car (1998). RIGHT: Tant drew this view as an inspirational exercise.

transmission a contemporary five speeds.

"It looks fast, and we wanted to back that up," explained Mark Rushbrook, the car's driving dynamics manager. "From the moment you get in, It has to fit right—the seat, the steering wheel and pedals, the gear shift—right where you want them.

"And as you fire it up and hear that throaty exhaust sound, you have to say, 'This is going to be fun to drive.' And when you engage it in gear and drive away, the throttle response has to be what you expect in a car that looks like that. It has to accelerate very quickly, and be fun to steer down a twisty road. And when you stop, the brakes have to be as responsive as what you would expect.

"So [our objective] was to tie all that together as one image that supports the styling—from the time you get in it to the time you park it and look back and say, 'Yeah, that was fun to drive.'"

The Cold Truth

Originally, Mustang's next revamp was to have come for 2001 or early 2002. Ford was mapping it out even as the heavily freshened 1999 model was being launched. But SN95 sold well, and planners got some breathing room to reconsider Mustang's next move. They concluded it was a viable nameplate, and vital to Ford, but they recognized some painful realities.

"We went through it system by system," said Phil Martens, Ford vice president of product creation. "We looked at the suspension, the body structure, the engine, the transmission. We concluded it was better to re-engineer Mustang than to take elements from the 20-year-old Fox platform and bring them into current standards. This way, we could correct some of the deficiencies that had been long-standing issues."

Foremost among these were occupant packaging and mechanical refinement. Strategies were laid out to address both, and by early 2002, Martens was ready to approach Ford's board of directors with the proposed next chapter in Mustang history. Mustang holds a unique place in the hearts of those in the very highest ranks at Ford Motor Company. But even a car so rich with meaning needed an ironclad business case to win over the unsentimental board of directors.

"It wasn't a slam dunk," said Hau Thai-Tang, the '05 Mustang's chief engineer. "We all love the Mustang. We know what it means to the company. It's arguably the second-most significant car in the history of the Ford Motor Company, behind the Model T. But at the same time, we're not going to do it just for the sake of having a Mustang. We have to make money."

Flex Time

One way to appease the profit-minded board was to build the car cost-efficiently. Ford scanned its portfolio of production sites and came up with AutoAlliance International in Flat Rock, Michigan. A Ford-Mazda joint-venture, this modern, flexible-assembly plant could accommodate diverse production. In the 1990s, it made the Mazda 626 sedan, MX-6 coupe, and, in a touch of irony, the presumptive Mustang, the Ford Probe. By late 2003, the facility was churning out Mazda's new compact car, the 6.

Relocating Mustang assembly from the ancient Dearborn Assembly Plant on the Rouge River to AutoAlliance was a tall order. It meant integrating the manufacture of two very different products. Mustang was a domestic rear-drive coupe (and convertible) with longitudinal V-6 and V-8 engines. The 6 was an import-traditional front-drive compact produced in four-door sedan, wagon, and hatchback body styles with transverse-mounted 4- and 6-cylinder engines.

Many modern auto factories are capable of so-called flexible assembly, but few build both front- and rear-drive vehicles or handle such a span of body styles.

At AutoAlliance, body shells of the Ford and Mazda cars, naked except for paint, converged from separate tracks to que up, one after another, on a single assembly line at 60 cars per hour. There, each was fitted with its appropriate suspension system, its powertrain, seats, and instrument panel, its front and rear fascias and built-up doors. It was a daunting undertaking and affected key decisions about the '05 Mustang.

The car had to be planned from the start to draw hundreds of fasteners, nuts, and bolts from the same parts bins as the 6. Its front substructure had to be designed so the two cars' engines could install in similar motions. Workers had to be trained to build both Mustangs and 6s, and their tools had to operate efficiently in both processes. Done properly, the cost-savings in parts, labor, and tooling would be substantial. So would the impact on Ford.

In 2004, Ford projected that by the end of 2010, 75 percent of its plants would employ flexible assembly. Savings from that 15-percent annual boost in efficiency would be redeployed to product development. As Ford Motor Company Chairman and Chief Executive Officer William C. Ford Jr. said in January 2005: "Mustang is a symbol of the Ford brand, and it's also a symbol of where the company is going."

Bandwidth

The other significant influence on design and engineering was Mustang's particular clientele. No sporty-car buyers were more faithful. Mustang owners repurchased a Mustang 33 percent of the time. Among the competitive set, the Mazda Miata and Toyota Celica were second, at 22 percent. The class average was just 17 percent.

Mustang had earned this loyalty by stretching to appeal to a impressively broad audience. Base prices for model-year 2004, for example, ranged from $17,800 to nearly $40,000. And while V-8 editions got the glory, V-6 versions accounted for 70 percent of Mustang sales.

"That poses a real dilemma," explained Thai-Tang. "The challenge was to design a platform that's very affordable, very efficient for the low end, but still capable enough to deliver bang for the buck for the performance enthusiasts."

Ford calls this "bandwidth," and its influence was clear as 2001

Under heritage-conscious styling chief J Mays, the design direction shifted to a modern reworking of vintage-Mustang forms. This full-size clay from early 1999 was a two-sided model. Its left half showed an evolution of the 1999–04 car. The shape and dimensions of its right side would be honed over the next few years into the 2005 Mustang. Note the scale models on the table in the background of the top photo.

drew to a close.

"In early 2002, as the program prepared to go for approval, we made a couple of key decisions," Martens said. "At all costs, we were going to maintain the styling, which turned out to be brilliant. And in a lot of regards, how we could execute and deliver that [styling] became critical.

"The second thing was recognition of the range of Mustang offerings," he said. "From the V-6 with a solid rear axle...all the way up to a V-8 convertible Cobra R with an independent rear suspension—there's no other vehicle in the industry that spans that bandwidth of price—high teens to almost $60,000—and that bandwidth of powertrain and suspension, all in one product architecture.

"We decided in April of 2002, that we had to protect for that bandwidth. We made the decision to proceed...with a dual path on the suspension, with the base being a significantly improved solid rear axle, and the high end being a state-of-the-art fully independent rear suspension.... With all of that being put into play, we knew we had the capability to go for program approval."

Ford's board considered the business plan, scrutinized the cost of building the car, and weighed these factors and others against projected revenues. In June 2002, it gave its blessing to production of what would become the 2005 Mustang.

The car was slated for introduction in fall 2004. It would follow

Mustang's new platform would bear the S197 code, and designers used its dimensions to underpin this full-size clay from September 1999. The study had many features that survived in some form to the production car. These included a bodyside scoop (here both sculpted-in and taped on), pronounced wheel arches, and grille-mounted fog lights. Triple-element taillamps and a big decklid badge would also endure the design gauntlet. But this proposal also held some dead ends: rear side windows, marker lights integrated with the headlamps, and a distinct curvature in the tail. Finally, its relatively low, flat hood would prove untenable as the design process advanced.

Even as clay models were being sculpted, designers were encouraged to continue generating ideas, as these sketches from 2000 demonstrate. TOP ROW: Tant looked at updating the 1969 Mustang's nose and conjured a pony with a sinister visage. ABOVE AND RIGHT: Designer Addam Ebel investigated various hood, fascia, and grille treatments.

by six model years the SN95, which, in Ford code, stood for Sporty, North American market. Ford used a slightly revised code for the new Mustang. It became S197. "S" was for the "sporty" segment, 197 was simply the car's number in the company's product cycle.

No Mystery

"I tell folks," said chief engineer Thai-Tang, "the best thing about working on the Mustang is everybody knows what a Mustang should be. And the worst part about working on the Mustang is everybody knows what a Mustang should be."

Certainly that was true among those creating the car. Mustang attracts engineers, designers, product planners, and stylists whose automotive enthusiasm abounds. Indeed, members of some S197 teams had more Mustangs among them than they had children. That degree of devotion has its downside.

"I knew going into this job that by the time I was done, I was going to upset everybody at least once," Rushbrook said. "We all get pulled in different directions. The studio will want something. The marketing guys want something else. The manufacturing folks want something. The finance team will push for something. It's a constant balance. At the end of the day you just step back and say, what's the right thing for our customer?"

Determining that can require market research. As early as 1998, Dearborn was surveying audiences about what would become the 2005 Mustang. But it was far narrower in scope than

research done for earlier Mustangs. Test groups were shown some styling studies but only well along into the project. It served mostly to validate the direction the car was already taking.

"We did one [styling prototype]," Mays recalled. "We knew what we wanted. I said, 'If we don't know how to design a Mustang, then we should go home.' And I'm confident this is the right one. Everyone who worked on this car is a Mustang fanatic. And when they're all standing in the studio looking at the clay model and smiling, that's all the clinic we need."

Tough Crowd

Outside Ford's walls, one valuable opportunity to "clinic" the car was at Mustang club events. It was a worldwide following, with clubs in 16 countries on five continents—some in places Mustang wasn't even sold. There were more than 250 Mustang clubs in the U.S. alone. They drew the most passionate owners, many of whom gathered to show and race Mustangs of every vintage. "They're a tough crowd," said Bob Johnston, Mustang vehicle engineering manager. "You can't just walk in and pretend you're an enthusiast. You have to earn their respect."

Again, research confirmed what Ford already concluded. Mustang must remain affordable and stylish. It must have appropriate power in V-6 trim, command respect in base V-8 form, and be a solid foundation for performance modifications. A significant number of owners spend thousands on speed accessories from the aftermarket and from Ford's own Racing Performance Parts

Over the course of S197 development, supervision of the styling team passed to several chief designers who were under Mays' direction. Douglas Gaffka supervised creation of this April 2000 study. It had different left- and right-side window treatments, lacked bodyside scoops, and a greenhouse set back to create a pronounced long-hood profile.

arm. Helping them create 500-bhp, 11-second street machines was fundamental to Mustang's credibility and to Ford's bottom line. That's why early planning included input from renowned Mustang tuners such as Roush Performance, Saleen Inc., and Kenny Brown Performance. Ford wanted bolt-in upgrades ready when the car was launched.

Plug and Play

Also consulted early was Ford's Special Vehicle Team, the factory arm behind the independent-rear-suspension Mustang Cobra.

"We worked very closely with them to understand what their design brief looks like as far as performance targets," explained Thai-Tang. "We protected for those things—making sure we can package a larger engine at some point, making sure the rear suspension could handle the added torque." Cost and production efficiencies demanded a platform that integrated SVT's independent rear suspension more simply and with less expense than did the SN95 chassis.

"We decided we shouldn't shoehorn this in," Martens said. "We should design it as a module and design it to plug and play. But it had to perform equal to the best in the world."

Research also included hundreds of miles in competitive machines, gauging acceleration, ride, steering, handling, and the encompassing NVH: noise, vibration, and harshness.

The S197 team evaluated the Chevy Camaro Z28 and C5 Corvette for powertrain performance and the Mazda RX-8 for balance. They liked the Nissan 350Z's manual-shift precision but not its ride quality. They drove two generations of BMW M3 and came away impressed with the German cars' steering precision and feel. In fact, the target for interior packaging was the 3-Series coupe. The team even looked briefly at front-drive sports coupes.

Another Dimension

Putting all this research into practice was done with the help of design tools and processes unavailable to earlier Mustangs. S197 engineers essentially modeled the entire car in 3D computerization. Savings in time and money was enormous. Designers could, for example, conjure a virtual suspension, run it through its range of motion, measure clearances, and create the surrounding sheetmetal without having to build a single physical model. Just 12 months after the first click of the mouse, designers held in their hands tooled parts of significant systems.

"I think this is the first program at Ford in which we didn't build what we call mechanical-package bucks, which is a prototype of every part, and then put them together to make sure the car actually goes together," said packaging supervisor Keith Knudsen, who was responsible for the car's overall mechanical design integration. "We did it all digitally. And the first time we saw it all go together was when we built essentially Job One representative cars."

Those "attribute prototypes" demonstrated certain dynamics and powertrain characteristics. Ford built relatively few of them, and testing revealed only minor changes would be required.

Interestingly, revisions mostly involved what couldn't be modeled with 3D computerization, things that required human interaction. For example, a mock-up of the steering wheel uncovered a problem with the location of a cruse-control button. "If you look

J Mays: In his own words

Rare is the automotive stylist who breaks out of the studio and into the mainstream, but when you're the driving force behind such high-profile designs as the Volkswagen New Beetle, Audi TT, and the Ford GT and Thunderbird, notoriety finds you. It generates articles in Time *and* USA Today *and scores of other publications, awards from such auspicious heights as the Harvard Design School, even a retrospective at the Los Angeles Museum of Contemporary Art. Such is the star power of Ford design chief J Mays. Born in Oklahoma in 1954, he graduated from California's Art Center College of Design and climbed the career ladder in the studios of VW, Audi, and BMW. Mays joined Ford Motor Company in 1997, and in 2003 was named the corporation's Group Vice President, Design, responsible for shaping the design direction of its entire portfolio of brands. He directed the styling of the 2005 Mustang.*

Well, you never want to have anyone say that you've loused up an icon. I've done quite a few icons now in the last 10 years, for this company and other ones. And my biggest nightmare, the thing that made me wake up at night in a cold sweat, was you don't want to be known as the guy that screwed up the Mustang. You'd like to be known as the guy who resurrected everything that was great about it and the fantastic things that we remember about it.

I'm sleeping pretty well...

This is a bit of a cultural game we play. If you look at how this country operates, it operates on a bandwidth that runs from rural to suburban to what we're seeing as an emerging trend— not just with hip-hop artists, but with the entire culture— and that is urban.

Under urban, there are offshoots: urbane and metropolitan. We have, on the rural side, our F-150 trucks. Very successful. And that's how they're positioned culturally and in the mind of our customers. On the suburban end of the spectrum, we have clean, contemporary, modern designs like the Five Hundred and Freestyle that we think fit into the suburban lifestyle. And there's nothing wrong with that. That's the way the majority of us live. And these are contemporary, modern-designed vehicles that happen to fit into that.

But then there's the urban aspect of our culture we wanted address as well. And I think Mustang, just as it did when it was so successful in the late '60s, fits into that bad-boy image pretty successfully.

What we consider to be on the periphery of our culture, urban, is actually not on the periphery. It's increasingly mainstream. I think over the next five years you'll see it integrated more into mainstream culture and be accepted by all ethnicities and all different cultures. And as that happens, yes, our cars will become more edgy.

Hip-hop and, I think, urban culture, has always thrown back to the rest of our culture what they see happening out there. There's a lot of danger and there are a lot of people very unsure of themselves because of the threatening environ-ment in the world today. And I think hip-hop's just a reaction to that. It's holding up a mirror and saying, "This is what we see the world looking like right now." It's overt and it's in your face and it's a little scary and a little dangerous and it can be at times even a little vulgar. But I think that's sort of the world we live in, for better or worse, right now.

And so we know how we want to position this car in the marketplace. This is a "Give-me-a-balls-out muscle car." That's really the only way to say it. And that's what our customer base expects us to deliver. This is not only the most popular muscle car in America, this happens to be the most popular nameplate in America.

I keep saying this car is not a car at all. It's a cultural icon up there with the Marlboro man, the Beach Boys. Things that, if you ask a European, you'll very often get a very clear answer on what's American. Well, Mustang fits into that category. I think the thing's transcended being an automobile and now is such a part of the American cultural fabric that it has a lot to do with patriotism and everything that's right with this country.

...[W]e had the design within the first week. Then we spent about a year refining it. That car is lovingly surfaced, and I'm extremely proud of the team that did it because it's surfaced like a premium German automobile, yet has all these American design cues on it. When I arrived here, we had an inverted process. We would spend about seven-eighths of our time designing and being creative. And then someone would say, "Oh shit, we're out of time." So we'd rush to get the thing into production. And I literally just turned the entire thing on its head. I said, "Look, I'm interested in contemporary, distinctive design. But I'm far more interested in getting the quality right and the execution right." With this car, we've done that.

By this pivotal November 2000 clay, the car's proportions were in place and the window graphics were nailed down with a single pane of side glass and a rear-quarter-panel cutout. The horizontal taillamp treatment would be scuttled along with the "horseshoe" shape at the base of the rear glass. Still being worked out was the route of the upper bodyside crease; here, it travels above the rear wheelarch.

at that digitally it might seem OK," packaging supervisor Knudsen said, "but when you actually try to use it in the car, you found it was too far to reach easily."

And though the computer-modeled rear seat-belt position met regulations for child-safety seats, it allowed test seats too much wiggle to pass muster with designers who were parents.

Test This

The team was pleased with how the car felt, right from start.

"From the first prototypes we built," Rushbrook said, "you could tell the fundamentals were there, that we had done a lot of the right design improvements, like stretching the wheelbase, improving the weight distribution to help steering and handling, upsizing the brakes. But it took a good year of tuning on these individual cars to get everything right and then bring it all back together."

Much of that year was spent traversing the globe in camou-

flaged prototypes. All-weather braking and traction control was measured in northern Sweden to take advantage of its early cold season. Durability was taxed at Ford proving grounds in Michigan, Florida, and Arizona. Prototypes ripped around Mosport racetrack in Ontario, Canada. They were driven for 24 hours straight at Ohio's Nelson Ledges road course.

Of the 6000 different vehicle tests conducted on S197, Ford itself admitted none may have been as important to Mustang fans as the tire spinning full-throttle launch. "We never had a shortage of volunteers to help us with burnouts," Rushbrook acknowledged. "But it's actually a very meticulous process, not just fun and games."

The Appetizers

As all that secret analysis was underway, the public got its first taste of the new Mustang at the 2003 North American

With the car's form settled, stylists labored over other matters. In these March 2001 models, they explored concave and convex rear effects. In front, placing the signal lamp below the headlamp, where it was visible from the side, resolved vexing design and manufacturing issues. The hood showed the curvature it would wear in production, and the upper bodyside crease now ran through the rear wheelarch. Clays didn't yet differentiate between V-6 and GT versions, but drawings on the studio walls did. These studies are shown without the Di-Noc modeling film applied to clay to give it paint-like color.

International Auto Show in Detroit. Presented as concept cars were a fastback coupe and a convertible built by Ford Design CA in Valencia, California.

Officially called the Mustang GT concepts, the silver fastback and gleaming red convertible were a highlight of the show. Their independent rear suspension and 400-bhp supercharged 4.6-liter dohc V-8s were drawn from the SVT Cobra.

Broad and low-slung, with styling drawn from the '69 and '70 Mustangs, it was no secret the GTs were the shape of things to come. But there were notable differences between the show cars and the production Mustang under development. For one thing, the concepts were two-seaters. And some details were pure show-biz, such as the instrument bezels that rotated on precision geared tracks to display rpm and speed.

More significantly, the concept cars were based on a modified DEW98 platform. Engineered jointly by Ford and Jaguar in the 1990s, DEW98 was developed for the Lincoln LS and Jaguar X-Type luxury sedans. In shortened from, it was used by the Thunderbird. The Concept GTs fueled published reports that the production Mustang would be based on a DEW platform.

But Ford was being cagey about the source of the production chassis. And while some press materials claimed the GT concepts "spawned" the production Mustang, the reverse was true: The show cars were basically customized 2005 Mustangs.

"We actually took the data from the production car and shipped it to California," said Larry Erickson, chief stylist on the production '05 Mustang. "They started cuttin' and hacking and doing the usual show car things. The concept is like sectioned an inch through here and an inch through there. And when we

first looked at it, I thought there's some stuff that's nicer [than the production car]. There's like zero ground clearance and 20-inch tires, the usual show-car stuff.

"But then I started looking at it and thinking there's some things that are better about the production car. All my friends who knew we were working on this said, 'Well, I'll bet the production car will never come up to it.' I think in ways the production car is better."

Don't DEW It

Inside Ford, they called it "due ninety-eight" and it was the first new rear-drive car platform developed by the company in years. It schooled Ford in 21st Century design—the importance of locating the wheels as far forward as possible to help weight balance for improved ride and handling, for example.

But the most important lesson of DEW98 was that it wasn't right for the new Mustang. Engineers didn't come to that conclusion immediately. But it didn't take long.

"The LS was a natural starting point," said chief engineer Thai-Tang, who was also vehicle engineering manager for the LS. "We spent about a month studying it. But we quickly realized it wasn't going to work for our purposes. It just didn't make good business sense."

With "business sense" a guiding principle, engineers whittled away at DEW98's suitability. Its front-end architecture was a good example of why it wasn't Mustang-worthy.

Mustang's single-overhead-cam 4.6-liter V-8 was wider than the smaller-displacement V-8s used in the DEW cars. The problem intensified with the wider-still twin-cam 4.6, not to mention

In Spring 2001, the S197 work-in-progress was brought together with two of its primary historical influences. LEFT: Melvin Betancourt, exterior design manager (from left), Doyle Letson, then chief designer, and designer Garen Nicoghosian do some hands-on detailing. BELOW: The 1969–70 Mustang, here represented by a '70 Boss 302, inspired the angle of the S197's nose. BOTTOM: The side-window shape paid allegiance to that of the '67–'68 fastback, as this '67 GT makes clear.

By May 2001, the design of the 2005 Mustang was all but locked in, though some features would still need to be modified for production. For example, stylists liked this hood for the way it recalled the dual-cove '67–'68 design. But it was determined the shape was incompatible with the production panel's aluminum construction. And the contour of the rear fascia would need to be changed to meet bumper-impact standards.

even-larger V-8s planned for Mustang's future.

This was important because cost-efficient AutoAlliance production demanded Mustang move seamlessly along an assembly line that loaded engines from below—a requirement DEW's unequal-length control-arm front suspension was too narrow to accommodate and too expensive to modify.

Engineers also concluded the sound and vibration generated by Mustang's large, powerful V-8s couldn't be addressed by simply applying deadeners to the DEW structure. Mustang would need a purpose-built architecture to manage powertrain NVH.

DEW was designed with an independent rear suspension tuned for touring-car road manners. Mustang had to accommodate both a solid rear axle and—without costly modification—an independent rear that delivered high-performance handling. Re-engineering DEW for such versatility was untenable.

Finally, DEW was developed as a four-door sedan and would not be compatible with a Mustang convertible. DEW was usable for Thunderbird because T-Bird was a two-seat convertible; the space behind its seats could be devoted to a bulkhead that restored structural rigidity. Mustang's convertible needed that

space for a rear seat, so it demanded a platform designed from the ground-up with drop-top rigidity in mind.

"When you factor those physical realities together," Thai-Tang said, "you quickly realize the LS platform's going to have to be modified quite a bit."

That's not to say S197 had nothing in common with DEW98. The design of its central floorpan, fuel tanks, and front chassis rails were patterned after those in the LS, S-Type, and Thunderbird. And parts of the front chassis crossmembers were interchangeable. As a whole, the 2005 Mustang actually shared about 35 percent of its parts with other Ford products—starting with the V-6 from the Explorer, extending to such items as door hinges, bolts and other fasteners, and including hoses, wires, and emissions electronics.

But Thai-Tang, along with other S197 team leaders, insisted componentry shared with DEW98 was too negligible to measure. "It's funny," he said, "we never came out and said we were going to use the LS [platform]. That was conjecture in the media. I read all these things about a 'lightweight LS platform,' and I said, 'Geez, I wonder who's working on that because it's not us.'"

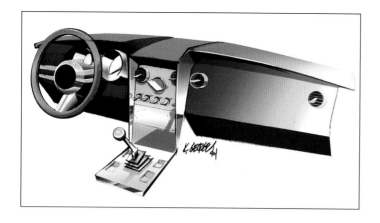

Redistributing weight improved steering and traction, advantages engineers enhanced by relocating the battery from under-hood to the trunk. That also paid dividends in the front crush zone. Including structural advances designed to absorb and re-direct crash forces, Ford called this the safest Mustang ever.

Overall, the car was 4.4 inches longer than the 2004 model, 1.4 inches taller, and 0.8 inch wider. Front and rear track expanded 2.4 inches. The biggest gain in the four-place cabin was in shoulder room: an additional 1.8 inches for the front seats and 1.2 for the rear. Head room increased a half-inch in front, but a sleeker roofline decreased it by as much in the rear. Leg room grew 1.1 inches in the rear but was unchanged in front. Coupe trunk volume expanded 1.4 cubic feet, to 12.3.

If there was a downside to dumping the Fox-derived platform it was that expertise engineers gained over the decades was suddenly of no use. "They had that knowledge base, knowing that platform inside and out, so we lost that," Rushbrook said. "But we used that as an advantage, to say, 'OK...as we design the new platform, let's make sure we don't design in those same short-comings.'"

Still, no one was sorry to see it go. "We've gotten our invest-ment out of the Fox platform," Thai-Tang said. "It's been out there 25 years. It's time to move on."

Out of the Past

Larry Erickson rolled in his chair from the drafting table to rum-mage unruly stacks of books cluttering his office. He excavated one to illustrate a point about the 1967 Mustang. "You'll notice," he said, flipping its pages, "it's not dog-eared and open to any of the Mustang II pictures."

Distinguishing the successful Mustang styling themes from the unsuccessful played a profound role in shaping the 2005 model. Yet, as with most automotive designs, the end result was basical-ly a truce between emotion, function, and cost. If Mustang stylists did their job, emotion would appear to win.

Erickson gained attention as the California-bred designer behind ZZ Top's "Cadzzilla" customized Cadillac, though he also worked at General Motors design and taught at Art Center

Moving On

A new body shell of high-strength steel was conceived to meet Mustang's dynamics, packaging, and NVH criteria. Ford claimed a dramatic leap in body stiffness over SN95: a 31-percent increase for the coupe, a 100-percent improvement for the con-vertible. The structure was especially robust in places like the longitudinal sections below the doors, where stiffness would be taxed most during aggressive driving.

So the coupe wouldn't have to carry unnecessary weight, the platform was designed to accept underbody bracing exclusive to the convertible. Pounds were saved with an aluminum hood and with computer-calculated structural stampings that concentrated mass where needed without being thicker than absolutely neces-sary.

Against the 1999–2004 Mustangs, the 2005 was a larger, roomier car, but not much heavier. The GT gained about 100 pounds over its outgoing counterpart, tipping the scales at 3450 pounds with manual transmission, 3500 with automatic. The V-6 model gained less than 15 pounds, going to 3300 with manual, 3345 with automatic.

Significantly, the weight was distributed over a longer wheel-base: 107.1 inches, up from 101.3. That enhanced ride quality and passenger space. Most of the 5.8-inch increase came by moving the front wheels five inches forward, which stylists liked for the resulting tiny front overhang, and engineers loved because it reapportioned weight rearward. The GT coupe put 53 percent of its load on the front wheels, versus 57 percent for the previous model.

College of Design. He joined Ford in 1999 and was named chief stylist on the S197 project in January 2002. By that time, the car's basic look had been established by J Mays, and Erickson's predecessor, Doyle Letson, along with exterior design manager Melvin Betancourt, were translating it into three-dimensional form.

Ford's stylists and sculptors, their studio walls lined with inspirational photos of American icons and past Mustangs, progressed from drawings and scale models, through full-size clays, to fiberglass shells, with side trips into some digitized prototypes.

Major design issues were still unsettled in early 2002. These included the greenhouse shape and the body's surface development—its creases, bulges, and cutlines. Also unresolved were the car's graphics—the angle at the corner of a window, the placement of a turn-signal lamp. The overarching aim was to create something familiar but fresh. It was a tender balance.

"By the time I came on the program, there was this constant desire to make it as modern as possible," Erickson said. "But I don't believe there was any consideration of [not] tapping the historic context of Mustang. The idea was that we continue the legacy of Mustang."

Lifting the Brush

One risk was that the car would be a pale reflection of past glory, with nothing new to communicate. Its designers, not surprisingly, were quick to defend its 21st century credentials.

"When you take just [the center] portion of the car, without the front and the rear, don't think there's a lot of trade-off as far as 'modern' versus 'Mustang,'" Erickson said. "I think this middle of the car is very modern."

As the cabin progressed into mock-up form, designers had to make it compatible with price and production realities. Toggles gave way to parts-bin Ford switchgear. The classy analog watchface envisioned between the center dash vents got tangled in debates over instrument-panel packaging, and when bean counters realized it duplicated the radio's clock, it was killed. The "spaceball" gear lever shown here was from Ford's Volvo branch, but its linkage didn't mate with Mustang's. Even the see-through steering-wheel spokes would be filled in to accept cruise-control buttons. Tricks of the trade: The clay dashboard got brightwork from restaurant-grade aluminum foil and textured color surfaces from latex house paint.

Mays cited the presence of "a lot of very cool geometric surfaces. When you look at the wheel arches in particular," he said, "this car takes on a modern appearance that separates it from those cars in the past. The wheel arches, both front and rear, are visually almost perfectly round. Certainly the headlamps, and these three vertical taillamps on each side with just a slight amount of trapezoid, are quite a nod to modern design. As is the entire rear of the car, which looks as though it's just been milled off to leave what is essentially a rectangular racetrack around the lamps. I suppose the small window behind the B-pillar is another example of taking and modifying a triangle…. We've tried to take the graphics that were so popular in the '60s and modernize them through giving them slightly more geometry."

As vital as getting Mustang's form, graphics, and details cor-

rect, it was important to recognize when enough was enough. Designers call it "lifting the brush."

"We've got a design philosophy that says, 'Look, just forget the filigree,'" Mays said. "You've got about two or three statements at the most that you can make on a vehicle, and any extra noise is just taking away from what you're trying to say. On the Mustang, there's a lot of filigree we could have added and still made it a Mustang. But this is the contemporary way to express it."

So what did the styling say about this Mustang?

"The proportion is probably the largest statement," Mays said, looking at an '05 GT glowing burgundy under auto-show spotlights. "You've got an endlessly long hood, with the front wheels, like a fist, hooked out just as far as it'll go. That signifies there's a Godawful-big V-8 under there in most cases. That front-wheel-to-

LEFT: Larry Erickson followed Doyle Letson as Mustang chief designer, coming on the project in early 2002, and seeing it to completion. As with all automotive designers, a large part of his job was to reconcile styling, cost, buildability, and taste. Here, from various points in S197 development, are examples. TOP: This clay's bifurcated headlamp treatment was too complex to fit without costly design modification. Stylists salted it away for possible future use on a higher-priced S197 derivative that could absorb the cost. ABOVE: Extra vents in the lower fascia looked cool, but stylists thought they created a fussy nose.

the-front-door cutline is very important in establishing that the proportion of the car is correct. And it's also important in establishing that the vehicle's actually rear drive.

"So you have a very long hood. You have a close-coupled greenhouse with a very short deck. And this close-coupled greenhouse, which has a teardrop effect, then has to anchor itself on the rear wheel. The entire weight of that vehicle has to fall onto the rear wheel, to look as though when you push the accelerator down, all the power's going to be transferred to that. That's a lot for a car to have to visually communicate, but I think that one does it."

Forces in Opposition: The Nose

A balance of forces was evident in most every aspect of the 2005 Mustang's styling. On one side were ideals of nostalgia and authenticity. On the other were realities of how much it would cost to transform thought into sheetmetal, if this combination of shapes could actually be assembled, whether that contour was compatible with a functional requirement.

It started, naturally, at the front of the car.

"I love the front end," Mays said, gazing at the burgundy GT. "It's just a beast. And I love the grille, with those enormous fog lamps that are only about five times as large as they need to be. That is one aggressive front end...you see that coming in your rearview mirror, you're going to pull over."

Each element that contributed to that aggressive character—the missile-cruiser-cant of the grille, the big lights, the "brow" of the hood—was an example of the style/function equilibrium.

For example, the 2005 Mustang's nose was not very aerodynamic.

"I could have made a more aerodynamic car [without] a forward-falling front end, but in my mind, I wouldn't have had a Mustang," Mays said. "So we balanced the need for aerodynamics with the No. 1 hierarchy of importance, which led the entire development of the vehicle: This car has to look right."

Aero-assisting clear plastic panels covered the headlamps, which on the GT were nearly equaled in size by grille-mounted fog lights. This recalled various '60s Mustangs and was obviously a key styling element. But on the '05 GT, the grille-mounted lights also improved airflow to the engine by creating high-pressure zones that funneled air through the radiator with surprising efficiency. In fact, the V-6 model's grille, which didn't get the fog lamps, was fitted with hidden panels designed to produce the same high-pressure effect.

The larger openings in the GT's lower fascia had no effect on engine breathing but were there to emphasize its muscular nature. Interestingly, some designers found the cleaner look of the V-6 fascia more appealing.

The Scoop on the Hood

The two models shared the same aluminum hood, though not necessarily by plan. Stylists explored giving the GT its own hood, but it was too costly and complex to stamp shapes into the big alloy panel. They settled on a common hood, then found they had to make it taller than originally planned to clear the engine—but not the V-8. The V-6 was actually taller. They settled on a hood with a slight barrel curve longitudinally and a subtle downturn at its leading edge and were relieved to find it resulted in a front-end profile that strengthened the character of both the base and GT models.

Of course, the GT could have been differentiated simply by grafting a scoop onto the hood. Decorative hood scoops and vents were part of Mustang heritage. But on the '05, they would have served no function.

Stylists can be compelled to edit out certain features in favor of the bigger picture. Some S197 studies included a ducktail upsweep that gave the car a sportier-looking rear end. It's seen on the car at right and is visible on the clay at the top of page 224. But committing the upsweep to sheetmetal made designers think the V-6 version looked a little too aggressive. They still had to add a performance emphasis to the GT and found that affixing a wing or spoiler to the ducktail looked garish. So the production car emerged without the ducktail, a styling decision that served the needs of both Mustang models.

With development of the 2005 Mustang well along in secret, two 2003 concept cars provided a hint of what was coming. Built on the chassis of the Lincoln LS and Thunderbird, the concept coupe and convertible fueled speculation this so-called DEW98 platform would also underpin the new Mustang. Created by Ford's California design speciality shop, the show cars actually were customized versions of the virtually completed S197 body. The low hoodline wasn't feasible, but 20-inch wheels and aggressive side scoops held some promise.

"There were are a lot of people within our camp that felt we need a scoop," Thai-Tang said. "It's part of Mustang. We could get revenue for it. It differentiates the GT from the base car. But—and I was a very tough proponent of this—I said, 'I want this car to be authentic. I don't want to have any add-on appendages and hood scoops.' If it's not functional, we shouldn't have it. I'm not saying you won't see a hood scoop on a Mustang at some point in time. But it won't happen while I'm running it. Now a 'shaker' hood is functional. I don't have an issue with that."

Balancing Act: The Body

A bodyside scallop. A classic fastback roofline. Sentimental rear quarter windows. Each defined the profile of the 2005 Mustang, and each was a lesson in the handshake between design and engineering.

In a theme that would become familiar, the depth, size, and placement of the C-shaped bodyside scallop was determined with an eye on a future goal in mind, that of preserving a basic shape that could be built on.

"You've probably noticed that we've made less of a feature of

the C shape than subtly alluded to it," Mays said. "Very often in the past we've designed Mustangs—and now I'm going back to the '60s, so it wasn't 'we,' but my predecessors—designed Mustangs so that [the side scoop] became such an element that it was very hard to 'wish it away' once it was in sheetmetal. We've gone the other way. We've said if we wanted to come back with a special version that had a scoop behind the door, then we can add that rather than try to figure out how to take it away."

A more immediate goal influenced the shape of the rear roofline. Engineering insisted it be high enough to meet steadfast margins for rear-seat head clearance. Styling favored a slope that would have been more confining. In the end, both seemed satisfied.

"If we let the [styling] studio have their way, their line would probably result in a decrease in rear head room versus today's car," engineer Thai-Tang said. "The car is physically larger, and when a customer sees a larger car, they expect more interior space. That was something where we went back and forth with the studio. And we're talking millimeters of what that line looked like to achieve a win-win: The fast roofline they wanted, but at the same time, improving the occupant head space, which we wanted."

"We spent a considerable amount of time dealing with the rear head points where the occupant sits in the back seat," stylist Erickson concurred. "But the thing is, a lot of cars, when you look at them, have surfaces that look like a set of compromises. Like, 'Well it had to be that high, and it had to be that wide.' This looks like, 'That's the line I wanted.'"

By most accounts, rear head room was one of the rare points of contention generated by the car's retro-flavored look. That's not to say stylists captured as much of Mustang's past as they may have wanted. For example, Mays was fond of the gentle shoreline of sheetmetal where the first-generation 2+2's rear glass met the trunk. Manufacturing considerations meant it wouldn't be duplicated for 2005.

"Probably the only thing I didn't get that I would really have liked to have, would have been what we call that 'horseshoe' rear window, " Mays said. "That's where it looks as though you've taken the rear-window graphic and stretched it back over the car. Now the original '64 [sic] had that, and I was very intent on getting it into production here.

"But we had to walk away from that because at one point in the program we were considering a hatchback. We ultimately went to a full, enclosed trunk. And as we looked at the trunk, that changed the manufacturing procedure at the base of the C-pillar.

So we lost that horseshoe. I don't think it's decreased the appeal of the car. In fact, in some ways, it's made it more modern. But it's just a very distinctive Mustang cue that I would have liked to get into the vehicle."

By contrast, the 2005's rear-quarter glass was a retro cue that also satisfied a modern functional necessity. Every Mustang since 1969 had a rear side window aft of the door glass. The '05's stylists became disciples of the single-side-window graphic of the 1967–68 fastback. They loved how it focused attention on the driver. But that created a long, solid sail panel that shut out light to the rear seat and blocked driver vision. The solution was triangular windows that recalled those on the '66 Shelby GT-350.

Of course, just as decisions about the '05's body scallop left open the possibility of future side scoops, so the rear quarter windows set the stage for future vents or air intakes. Such intakes were a feature of past Shelby models. In fact, Shelby's crew had removed vents from the production 2+2 to create the original rear-quarter windows. That left glass framed in thin, almost elegant metalwork.

S197 stylists worked closely with manufacturing to achieve their difficult-to-stamp window shape, and elegance was not the affect they were after.

"That's part of this urban design DNA that's worked its way into

From its inception, the S197 program included an open body style, though the production convertible would not be unveiled until some months after the coupe's fall-2004 debut. That didn't stop the concept-car folks, who put together this red ragtop companion to their silver coupe. It also used a 400-bhp supercharged Cobra V-8 and independent rear suspension. Both cars picked up some features already discarded for production, such as the dashboard's analog clock and toggle switches. But they added some beguiling techie touches, like gauge markers that moved on precision geared bezels. The show convertible's cross-body hoop was another flight of fancy.

this vehicle." Mays said. "This vehicle is chunkier [than the first-generation 2+2]. There's a smaller window graphic and a heavier bodyside with a bigger shoulder. Delicacy wasn't what I was trying to avoid, but I was trying to create a tough automobile.

"I think 'tough' fits right into this whole urban mindset," he said. "A Mustang, not unlike an F-150, is a tough vehicle. They're both tough for different reasons, but when we talk about this car with our customers, the word 'beautiful' doesn't ever come up. They talk about how tough and sexy the car is."

Circles and Ovals

However fond he was of the urban-DNA approach, Mays was wise enough to "lift the brush" when he found it threatened to overpower the V-6 car. Some iterations of his initial styling theme "were even more overtly tough than this," Mays said. "But you have to be able to balance that across different wheel and tire sizes. The great thing about this car is it looks absolutely right on 16-inch wheels...and it looks great with 17s and 18s. That's a very important thing, to be able to balance the various models. If I'd made it any tougher or any heavier, the V-6 would have looked overbodied."

Wheel design was itself an element of style, and both the V-6 and GT were introduced with two variations each. All were alloy. The V-6 got 16s in a 10-spoke design. The V-8 got 17s in two five-spoke styles. The uplevel V-6 wheels had a center spinner

like the imitation "knock-off" hubs on some first-generation Mustang wheel covers. The standard GT wheel basically repeated the 1960s aftermarket "torque-thrust" design brought back for the 2001 Bullitt and used on the last SN95 GTs. The GT's optional 17s were patterned after those on the concept GT show cars.

Also borrowed, this time from Ford's midengine GT supercar, was the GT's bodyside badge. The V-6 Mustang wore no unique ID. In fact, the Ford blue oval appeared on either model only on the wheel caps. Curbing the blue ovals was debated within the company. But marketing pointed to customer research in which an '05 Mustang shorn of all badges was recognized as a Ford product by 90 percent of clinic participants.

Dialing Back: The Tail

Just as stylists understated the side scoops to protect for design diversity, they held something back from Mustang's rear end. They had explored a ducktail upsweep, which lent an assertive, sporty finish. But this so-called kicker made the V-6 look too aggressive. To dial up the GT would have required yet an additional spoiler or wing. That would have created an overly busy stern. So they killed the ducktail and created a more-modest shape shared by both models.

The GT got an add-on wing to differentiate it from the V-6. Thai-Tang said the wing helped decrease rear lift above 60 mph, with minimum impact on drag. But mostly it was a bow to market-

ing, and virtually every stylist preferred the cleaner look of the tail without it.

"The spoiler on the GT is a delete option," Mays noted, "and if it were up me I'd take it off. But at the same time, people love it. So there's very little arguing with our customers."

Hold On, It's Coming

From the first drawings and scale models, those who shaped the look of the S197 Mustang were confident the basic theme was the right one—not just for 2005, but for years to come.

"One thing I'm adamant about is the design is correct," Mays said in January 2004. "I see no need to facelift it. But what I do see a need for are special versions. And if you were a betting man...gee, it might someday be nice to have a Bullitt version of this, or a Boss version. I'm not suggesting that we're going to, but if you go through the history of this vehicle, as most fans of Mustang do, there's a lot of anticipation of what kinds of special vehicles will we bring on top of this. You will probably see versions in the future with louvers. And you'll see versions with scoops. It allows us to create a very flexible and modular palette to roll out interesting Mustangs for the next seven years."

It was a plan that turned on the ability to lift the brush.

"We had so many things we wanted to accomplish, the challenge became, how do we edit it down?" Mays said. "How do we pull back and get the first car out on the road, and then save all these goodies for the subsequent models that will come in the next few years?"

That's not to say designers considered the 2005 car in some way unfinished.

"There is not a single line on this car that hasn't had a serious amount of thought into it," insisted Erickson. "Some cars, if you went back in their design sequence, you'd find out that, oh yeah, at the last minute we pulled that front end together. Everything was crafted. Everything had the intent and the time put into it."

Clean-Sheet Cabin

As with the exterior, it was ordained the interior would pay respects to the car's heritage. That evidently did not phase the cabin's designers. In fact, they seemed liberated by the prospect of placing their cockpit in a new structure, a computer-aided 21st-century composition that owed nothing to a sedan or economy car.

"This is a clean-sheet platform," packaging supervisor Knudsen noted. "It was designed from the beginning to be a Mustang, so we had complete flexibility on where we were going to put the control positions relative to having to live with a carryover architecture."

The team spent weeks with wooden interior bucks, rearranging movable components. They sought to erase faults built into the previous generation Mustang and to optimize ergonomics for the sporting driver. "We've put a lot of effort into getting the fundamental relation between the steering wheel, the shifter, and the pedals all correct on this car," Knudsen said.

Addressing a leading complaint, the power seat control was relocated from the seat's front to the side. Helping fine-tune the driving position was a tilt steering wheel; it didn't telescope because Ford said that wasn't a high value priority to Mustang buyers. The three-spoke wheel itself is a throwback design, though its spokes lacked the lightening holes that gave '65 and '66 Mustangs a European-sports-car flavor. "I tried to get them," Mays said. "Couldn't do it. The safety folks and litigation lawyers came back and said, 'No one's gonna get their fingers caught in that spoke.'"

Mays also lost a skirmish over interior materials. The 2005's were clearly a step up in quality, with more padded surfaces, better-grained plastics, and, available on every '05 Mustang, an optional dashboard appliqué of genuine aluminum. "But I would have liked to have even more high-grade materials on the interior," Mays said. "I'm a realist, though, and I realize this car has to sell on a spectrum of over $20,000, from the base to the top-end model that will eventually come out. So I'm pretty happy with it."

Color Me Gone

Interior design development was managed by Kevin George, who had once designed action figures for toymaker Hasbro Inc. This was the first Ford project for the team he headed, and the cabin they worked out was a modern interpretation of Mustang's 1967–68 design.

The dashtop conjured square-arched eyebrows. Its double-barrel speedometer/tachometer layout used classic-'60s typeface and was deepset in bright plastic bezels. The headline act was a color-configurable gauge cluster. Inspired by customized instrumentation seen at Mustang-club events, this was the first such factory setup on any production car.

The configurable cluster was part of the option group that also included the aluminum appliqué, upgraded door panels, a bright-finished gearshift, and a three-button message center. The message center displayed simple trip and fuel-consumption readouts on a screen within the speedometer. One of its buttons accessed a selectable-backlighting menu that enabled the driver to deviate from the standard green instrument illumination and scroll through 125 other hues.

While the outside world looked to the 2003 concept cars for clues about the next Mustang, prototypes of the real thing were undergoing extensive testing around the globe. Camouflaged development cars were subjected to cold-weather work in Sweden, 24-hour endurance runs on race tracks, and countless trials at Ford's proving grounds. OPPOSITE, TOP: This test car wears the GT's standard 17-inch "torque-thrust" wheels. FAR LEFT: Some prototypes that risked public exposure masked their roof and tail with vinyl shrouds. LEFT: The laptop can confirm what the engineer suspects. RIGHT: Of the 6000 different tests to which S197 was subjected, perhaps none was more significant to certain Mustang lovers than the good-old smoky burnout.

The 2005 Mustang hit showrooms in late 2004 as a modern interpretation of the original that won America's heart some 40 years earlier. It was by no means a mere exercise in nostalgia, however. It was in fact the first Mustang constructed on its own purpose-designed chassis. And it used cutting-edge technology to meet the challenge of satisfying a vast range of driving tastes and pocketbooks. The GT version accounted for about 30 percent of Mustang sales but carried the car's bang-for-the-buck banner. Its styling was distinguished by grille-mounted fog lamps, dual exhaust tips, and a "delete option" decklid spoiler. The triple-element taillamps were an honored Mustang styling cue, the trunklid badge recalled the fuel-filler cap on '60s and early-'70 models, and the GT badge was inspired by Ford's midengine 2005 supercar. The car pictured mounts the GT's optional 17-inch alloy wheels.

It worked from a foundation of red, green, and blue light-emitting diodes. Each push of the button would blend and adjust the LEDs through a spectrum of purples, whites, oranges, and grays. The color was dispersed across the backs of the gauges, leaving the etched-on numbers and markings readable in a contrasting shade. Ford press materials said the system would enable owners to "mix and match lighting...to suit their personality, mood, outfit, or whim." If it was a gimmick, it was a popular one.

"When you're looking at the total car, when you're looking at the platform and all this other stuff, these things sometimes seem kind of small," Knudsen said. "But you get with the customers—we've done some focus groups and things like that—and it's amazing how into these things people get."

In the Fold

Interior designers could also become excited about things that on the surface seemed unimportant. For example, they ranked Mustang's rear seat among their most satisfying achievements. It was roomier than before, with a two-pocket cushion far more accommodating than the previous flat seat.

Most importantly, it folded to create cargo-carrying flexibility. That restored, after many years, an important feature to the large number of owners for whom Mustang was their only car. It also was an unlikely battleground among marketing, design, engineering, and finance. It involved arguments over where to locate the fuel tank, how to preserve torsional stiffness, where to absorb incremental costs, even what the rear-seat sew pattern looked like.

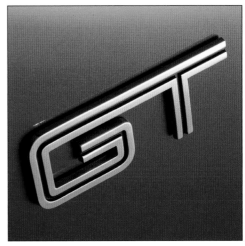

In the end, the pro-folding faction won the day and the feature was made standard on all models. They didn't get their desired flat-floor passage to the trunk; it wasn't possible because of the need to package the solid rear axle. But trunk volume itself grew 13 percent, the lid raised on nicely crafted struts that didn't eat into luggage space, and the audio crew somehow fit an 11-liter subwoofer (part of the newly available 1000-watt Shaker Audiophile System) with room to spare.

The electrical team under Dean Nowicki was especially pleased with the new optional antitheft system, which was designed to lower the cost of performance-car insurance. It employed a separate alarm sounder because thieves' first move was often to disable a horn-linked alarm. The system could also detect a change in vehicle inclination and trigger the alarm to guard against tow-away thefts or wheel removal.

Power to the People

In 2004, 300 horsepower didn't seem so impressive for a "muscle car," not when Pontiac's reborn GTO boasted 350, memories of 330-bhp Firebirds were fresh, and even Subaru furnished 300 turbocharged ponies in a compact sedan. But given the 2005 Mustang GT's middle-$20,000 pricing, and the numbers in which it would be built, no other car could make 300 horses so accessible. This was a baritone exhaust note, rubber in second *and* third, 0–60 mph in about 5.5 seconds—all for regular folks. Mustang!

The '05 GT made its 300 bhp at 6000 rpm and generated 315

pound-feet of torque at 4500. That compared with the previous GT's 260 at 5350 and 302 at 4000. The outgoing $29,000 '04 Mach 1 got 310 bhp and 335 lb-ft from its twin-cam, 32-valve 4.6. Tops for '04 was the supercharged 4.6 SVT Cobra at 390 bhp and 390 lb-ft, but it started at $35,000.

Machs, Bosses, and Shelbys had been there, but this was the first mainstream Mustang GT to scale the 300-bhp summit. It did it on 87-octane fuel and owed much to modern technology, namely a new all-aluminum V-8 with three valves per cylinder and variable cam timing. The base-level Mustang V-6 wasn't so trick but did make a good accounting at 202 bhp, up from 193 bhp.

Drive-by-wire throttle control was first-time technology for both engines. And faster, stronger electronic processors improved fuel economy while cutting exhaust gases enough to earn both models Ultra Low-Emission Vehicle II (ULEV II) status.

For all its technical proficiency, the slide-rule crew had an emo-

tional side, too. An important part of the Mustang experience, they concluded, was the sound of the car. So they conducted listening studies with current and potential owners to identify what engine sounds were "powerful." They fabricated and evaluated more than 100 mufflers before choosing those that best expressed the spirit of the car.

"Everyone has their belief of what a Mustang should sound like," Rushbrook said. "And it's more than exhaust, it's a total sound experience that you get from the engine, the transmission, from the induction of the air into the engine, and from the exhaust out. That's got to support the whole fun-to-drive image."

V-8: The Block

Mustang's V-8 again displaced 4.6 liters but borrowed technology from Ford's modular engine family, which included the F-150's 5.4-liter Triton V-8. The block was similar in design to

Mustang owed much of its survival to the popularity of the V-6 model, which put a sporty, affordable, and reasonably practical ponycar within reach of millions. The '05 model carried on that tradition with a look some of the car's own stylists preferred for its economy of line. Compared to the GT, the V-6 had a grille devoid of foglamps, contrasting-color rocker panels, a spoiler-free tail, and a single exhaust tip. The hood itself was common to both cars, and it was the height of the V-6 engine that determined its shape and crown. A chrome Mustang galloped on every grille, but only the V-6 model showed the emblem on the combination trunk-lock/badge. Rear-quarter windows evoked bygone styling while giving light to the rear seat and aiding driver vision. Overall, the new Mustang was 4.4 inches longer than the '04 version, on a wheelbase stretched by 5.8 inches. Weight increased only modestly.

Mustang's cast-iron predecessor but was a new deep-skirt, aluminum piece. It was stronger, stiffer, and saved 75 pounds, thanks to computer-aided engineering.

The "mod" 4.6 had the same cylinder-bore diameter as the Triton 5.4 but a much shorter stroke—3.54 inches versus 4.17 inches. That gave it the free-revving characteristics a performance car deserved. Mustang's lightweight aluminum pistons had short skirts with an antifriction coating. High-tension piston rings promised long-term durability and low oil consumption. The connecting rods used a cracked-powdered-metal manufacturing technique for precise fit. Five main bearings with cross-bolted main-bearing caps were part of the strength-and-stiffness agenda. A tray attached to the main bearing caps baffled oil flow in the pan, reducing aeration and assuring proper oil feed to the crankshaft during sustained hard lateral maneuvers.

The 4.6 employed liquid-filled engine mounts tuned to quell

specific unwanted vibration. So did the V-6, but the V-8 also used a computer designed triangular cast-aluminum engine-mount bracket.

V-8: The Heads

Displacing 281 cubic inches, the '05 GT was comfortably ahead of the one-horsepower-per-cubic-inch benchmark for naturally aspirated engines. That was due in large measure to a cylinder-head design new to Mustang. Instead of two valves per cylinder, it had three—two intake and one exhaust. Air equals engine power, and two intake valves moved more air into the engine than one. These heads also offered a more direct, ported-style path to the valves for better breathing at peak engine speeds. Exhaust flow was optimized with a new tuned exhaust manifold.

The new heads gave an 9.8:1 compression ratio, higher than Ford could previously deliver on regular-grade gasoline. A center-

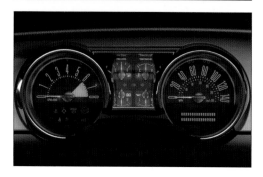

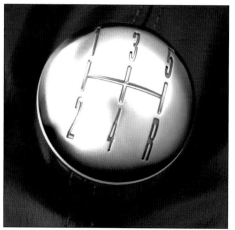

Working with a longer wheelbase and a modern structure, Mustang's interior designers brought the cabin up to date ergonomically while evoking the look and spirit of the classic '67–'68 cockpit. It was comfortably wider than the outgoing Mustang's, with better seats and a standard fold-down rear seatback that enhanced versatility. Pictured is the upgraded trim package that included real aluminum on the instrument panel and shift knob and a color-configurable gauge cluster. A dashboard button allowed the driver to scroll from basic green lighting to 125 other hues. This interior also shows the optional leather upholstery.

mounted sparkplug ensured a symmetrical flame and was longer and narrower than earlier designs. It descended to the center of the cylinder head, leaving lots of room for the valves. The compact coil-on-plug ignition system allowed more precise spark control and saved space under the hood.

The three-valve heads were smaller than the previous two-valve heads, reducing weight. Magnesium cam covers suppressed valvetrain noise and cut still more weight. Taking mass from the top of the engine helped lower the car's center of gravity, a boon to handling.

Finally, Ford gained some manufacturing efficiency because the "mod" architecture allowed Mustang to share its heads and camshaft with the 5.4-liter Triton. They even had the same parts numbers.

V-8: Variable Camshaft Timing

Like Mustang's former 4.6, the "mod" V-8 used a single overhead cam per cylinder head. But it employed variable camshaft timing, previously the province of the SVT Cobra engines.

Variable cam timing operated the valves at optimum points in the combustion cycle, tailored to the engine's speed and load at that instant. The Mustang system shifted timing of both the intake and exhaust valves together. That made it lighter and less complex than variable-cam systems that actuated intake and exhaust valves separately.

The cams operated both sets of valves using low-profile roller-finger followers, helping reduce friction and keeping overall engine height low. Cam position was controlled by an electronic solenoid that modulated oil pressure to advance or retard the cam timing based on engine-computer input.

The 4.0-liter V-6

To those whose budget or driving style didn't fit the V-8 profile, Mustang offered what was arguably its best-ever alternative. As with the "mod" V-8, the '05 drew on Ford's non-car stable for its V-6, a single overhead-cam 4.0-liter also found in the Explorer

SUV and Ranger pickup.

Compared to the outgoing 3.8-liter pushrod 60-degree V-6, this 90-degree six was more powerful, smoother, and quieter. It had an iron block and aluminum heads and made 202 bhp at 5350 rpm and 235 lb-ft at 3500 rpm, up from 193 and 225.

The cams were driven by a slave shaft mounted in the "V" of the engine, for a lower overall engine height than a conventional overhead-cam setup. For duty in the Mustang, the V-6 was treated to a unique camshaft grind, new tuned-length exhaust manifolds, and a new flywheel and oil pan. Noise-reducing features included a girdled crankcase for increased strength and rigidity, a dual-mode crankshaft damper, and isolated composite cam covers.

Breathe In, Breathe Out

Atop both engines was a new intake manifold tuned to meet Mustang's twin aspirations of great sound and maximum airflow. The V-8's manifold incorporated a low-profile, dual-bore throttle body that drew cold air from outside the engine compartment to feed tuned intake runners. At the end of each intake runner was a new-to-Mustang feature Ford called a charge motion control valve. At low engine speeds and light loads, these specially shaped control flaps closed to speed the intake charge and induce a tumble effect in the combustion chamber. That caused the fuel to mix more thoroughly and burn more quickly and efficiently. At higher engine speeds, the charge motion control valves opened fully for maximum flow into the combustion chambers.

Throttle control for both engines was via a new electronic system that inferred the driver's intent from the position of the accelerator pedal. It matched this information against other data—such as engine speed and load—and electrically operated the throttle-body accordingly. Meanwhile, the powertrain computer optimized the variable cam timing, fuel flow, and automatic-transmission shift points to match.

Ford called it torque-based electronic throttle control and claimed better acceleration and more consistent response over a range of operating conditions than with electronic systems that

New front buckets for '05 had relocated seatback releases and held Mustang's first side airbags, which were designed to cover both torso and head in a side collision. Shown is the shift lever for the new five-speed automatic transmission.

simply mimicked the action of a mechanical throttle linkage. And eliminating the stiff metal cable between a traditional accelerator pedal and the engine erased a traditional pathway into the cabin for noise and vibration.

The final piece in the engine-breathing matrix was a new exhaust system for each engine. The V-8's was a true dual system, with 2.5-inch mandrel-bent stainless steel exhaust pipes.

A Shift In Power

Historically, about half of Mustang's V-8 buyers choose a manual transmission, one of the highest take-rates in the industry. By contrast, about 65 percent of Mustang V-6 owners opt for automatic.

Five-speed manual continued as standard with both engines. The Tremec 3650 gearbox returned for the GT, the Tremec T-5 for the V-6. Both were tweaked, getting a flange driveshaft coupling instead of a splined drive for smoothness, and gaining new linkages for quicker engagement with less "notchiness."

Both manuals reduced pedal effort with a boosted hydraulic clutch. The V-6 clutch got new plate materials for durability, the V-8's was enlarged in response to the engine's added power.

The optional transmission for both engines was Mustang's first five speed automatic. Also found in the LS and Thunderbird, this Ford-built 5R55S featured a direct-drive fourth gear and an overdrive fifth. Shift duration and timing were governed by a powertrain computer that communicated with the transmission 10 times faster than before. Mustang engineers now could match transmission controls to variable cam timing and the electronic throttle in their quest to have an entire powertrain work together to deliver smooth performance.

To send power rearward, GTs got a new two-piece driveshaft

THIS PAGE: The GT retained a single-overhead-cam V-8 of 4.6 liters, but its block was aluminum, not iron, for a savings of 75 pounds. Its new cylinder heads incorporated a more-efficient three-valve design—two intake, one exhaust (above). And variable camshaft timing provided ultra-precise valve operation. At 300 horsepower and 315 pound-feet of torque, gains of 40 and 13, respectively, over the '04 GT, it created the most-powerful mainstream Mustang since the days of Machs and Bosses. This modular V-8 burned 87-octane gas and benefited from a true dual-exhaust system (opposite, top). For 2005, V-6 buyers were newly served by an ohc 4.0 liter drawn from the Explorer and tweaked for Mustang duty (opposite, middle). It had 202 bhp and 235 lb-ft, versus 193 and 225 from the outgoing 3.8-liter pushrod V-6.

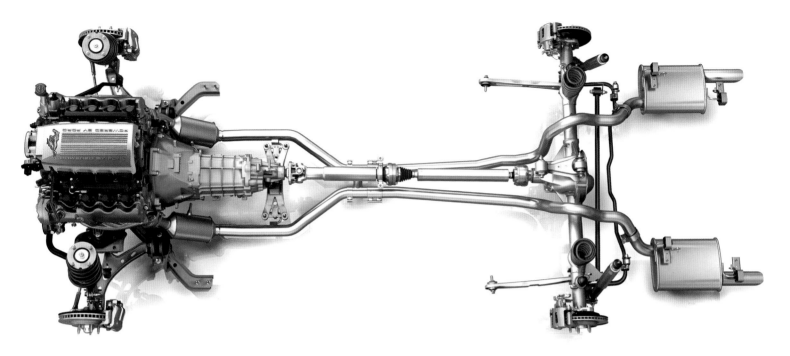

that could withstand higher engine speeds and torque. V-6 models used a slip-in tube driveshaft.

GTs with manual transmission traded a 3.27:1 final-drive ratio for the 3.55:1 gear used by the 2004 Mach 1. All other '05 Mustangs got a 3.31:1 final-drive ratio; previously, automatic-transmission cars came with a 2.29:1 or 2.49:1. Standard on the GT was a traction-lock 8.8-inch rear axle. V-6s had 7.5-inch ring and pinion gears.

No Slipups

Traction control had been a Mustang option for several years, but S197's new all-speed system was the most sophisticated and sensitive ever. It analyzed information from the engine controller and ABS to detect whether the vehicle was on dry pavement or negotiating a slippery surface and modulated the electronic throttle and brakes in concert to reduce wheel spin.

Standard on GT and bundled as an option with ABS on V-6 models, the system was tuned to work with an aggressive driver. Accelerating on dry pavement, it allowed more rear wheel slip to enhance the performance feel, even in turns. If it detected slippery conditions, it acted more aggressively to help maintain stability.

When traction control wasn't desired—smoky burnout, anyone?—a dashboard button deactivated the system. Another push turned the system back on; otherwise, it activated automatically the next time the vehicle was started. No antiskid system was available.

On the Beam

The logical way to examine Mustang's 2005 styling or powertrain was to start from the front. But suspension discussions began at the rear. That's where the car defiantly retained a solid

axle—upon which much engineering attention was lavished, granted—but not the independent setup so many critics expected.

Ford's official line was that the S197 engineering team was free to select any type of rear setup it wanted, including an independent suspension.

So why did it perpetuate a design that dated from the dawn of the motoring age? Why hang the wheels at the ends of a lateral beam—where bumps and cornering forces on one side affected the other—and integrate the whole barbell-like contraption with the differential, so powertrain vibration could migrate back to the body structure?

Thunderbird had an independent rear suspension. Heck, even the Explorer SUV had one. S197 engineers had some explaining to do.

"It's obviously something we struggled with," Thai-Tang said. "We did a lot of research. I hate to generalize, but the majority of our customers don't know and don't care what kind of rear suspension is in the car. They care about the driving dynamics, obviously. And the folks who do care and do know, a large percentage of them wanted a solid rear axle. These are a lot of our core enthusiasts. Then there's a percentage that wanted IRS. For those folks, we will offer something."

It was decided a solid rear axle played to Mustang's strengths as an affordable performance car, one that appealed to the majority of its sporting drivers for straight-line acceleration.

Given that, a solid rear axle was robust enough to survive the torque loads of repeated full-throttle launches. It maintained constant track, toe-in, and camber relative to the road surface. That kept the tires planted during the weight-transferring, tail-slewing,

Hau Thai-Tang: In his own words

As chief engineer for the 2005 Mustang, Hau Thai-Tang was at the epicenter of the project from its beginning. He managed the technical team that designed, developed, and tested the car's every mechanical aspect. And he was responsible for reconciling its engineering with the diverse demands of styling, assembly, and cost. Born in Saigon, Vietnam, Thai-Tang grew up in New York City and joined Ford as a Ford College Graduate trainee in 1988. He spent time on Ford's CART racing crew, was engineering manager for the Lincoln LS, chief engineer for the Thunderbird, and led development and launch of the 2001 Mustang GT, V-6, Cobra, and Bullitt models. He holds engineering degrees form Carnegie-Mellon University and the University of Michigan.

It's a great privilege for me to work on this fifth-generation Mustang. For me, as a kid growing up in Vietnam, my aspirations were to some day *own* a car.

I have one brother, and my parents are both college educated. My mother worked for Chase Manhattan Bank in Saigon. My father was a school teacher. At the end of the war, when we recognized that the Communists were going to win and the U.S. had pulled out all its troops, the people from Chase Manhattan Bank told us, "We're going to help emigrate some of our employees to America."

They went through a selection process and I think what helped us was both my parents were college educated, and they spoke the language—actually they were more fluent in French because we were a French colony—but we had a small family and I think Chase determined that we could probably assimilate over here pretty well. I was nine. We were told, "You're going to America. Listen to this radio and when you hear "White Christmas" by Bing Crosby, you'll have an hour to get to the airlift destination."

We were allowed one carry-on bag each. So we had four bags lined up by the door. One day in April 1975, we heard "White Christmas" and my parents got us into a car, sped over to my grandparents' house, said goodbye, drove to this meeting place. They took us by bus to the airport. We got put on an American military plane. We flew to Guam. The next day Saigon fell to the Communists.

In Vietnam, to have a car was a pretty good thing and we had one, a Citröen *Deux Chevaux*. My grandfather also had a French car, and he had an old Jeep. He was pretty well off. He rented some rooms to American military officers. As kids, we were always hanging around with them. They gave us ice cream. One of the things they left laying around were car magazines. You'd look at them and see all these American cars. And part of the morale-building at the time was they would bring over Mustang race cars as part of the USO tours. That was when I saw my first Mustang. It was a race car. And it was fast. So my connection with America and with cars was forged on those images.

My parents stressed education. Vietnamese culture, you know. They wanted us to be a doctor or a dentist. I decided to be an engineer because I was good in math. Couldn't stand the sight of blood. I graduated from school and came to the auto industry. What attracted me was my love for cars and the fact that [the field] is so dynamic, constantly changing, so competitive.

The best thing is, it's tangible. You know, you can work for NASA, but they're not going to let you try the space shuttle. Here, you can bring it home, you can show it to your friends, you can show it to your spouse, you can show it to your parents, and you can say "I helped do some element of this." That was the attraction.

For me, Mustang has such universal appeal. It stands for, in my mind, everything that's good about America. It's big, powerful, bold. It's accessible. It embodies freedom. I mean, that's the joy of driving a Mustang. That's the American success story. So my perspective may be different from, say, the Midwestern farm boy who grew up playing with his dad's tractor when he was eight. His context with the Mustang is different than mine. But we both have the same love for the car, and for the same reasons.

It has been a remarkable journey. I was born in '66, and under the Chinese zodiac, which in Vietnam we used, that was the year of the horse. So my mother is convinced that this is all fate and destiny. "You were born in the year of the horse. Now you're working on the Horse Car." She thinks it's all intertwined. But I tell her, "Hey, tomorrow I could be working on the Freestar."

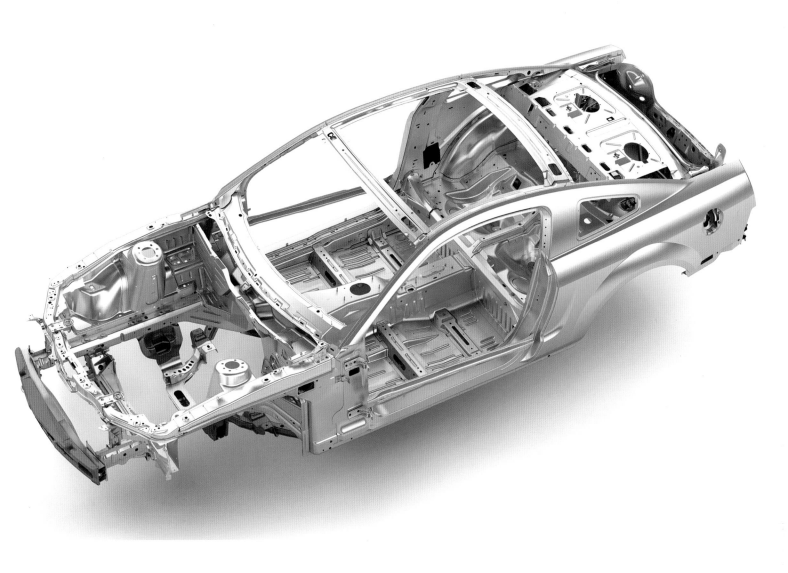

Powertrain testers mated an early 2005 Mustang nose to the structure of a Lincoln LS (below). But using that car's DEW98 platform for the new Mustang proved unsuitable for many reasons: It was too costly to rework for Mustang's solid rear axle, was not designed from the start for a four-seat convertible, and was too narrow to load big V-8s from below, as required on Mustang's assembly line (seen at right in pilot-production mode). ABOVE: The solution, in the words of chief engineer Hau Thai-Tang, was a "muscle-car chassis new from the ground up." Shading on this S197 shell denoted build sequence, not shared parts.

tire-tramping havoc of a 5000-rpm drop-clutch take off.

A solid rear axle was far less expensive to design, build, and service than an independent rear. It made it easier and less costly for drag racers to change rear axle ratios. And finally, chassis engineers were convinced they could give Mustang enough handling and roadholding to satisfy an audience that did not expect razor-sharp moves. For those that did, a Cobra version awaited.

To Each Its Own

The plan was to divide and conquer. The chassis team adopted a strategy in which each rear suspension component addressed its ride and handling assignments as independently as possible.

They wanted to avoid the compromises of Mustang's previous rear suspension. Its main components shared too many duties, doing none particularly well. SN95/Fox-4 attached its axle to the chassis with four control arms that regulated fore, aft, and lateral motions and even moored the springs. At the mounting points of all those arms were rubber bushings that, like the arms, had too many responsibilities. Thus, the bushings were too firm for best ride comfort, too soft for optimal handling and steering precision (yes, a car's rear suspension can affect steering).

The new suspension used separate links to regulate longitudinal and lateral forces. Each was designed for a specific job.

The main lateral link was a tubular Panhard rod. It ran parallel to the axle, attached at one end to the body, at the other to the axle. It stabilized the axle side-to-side as the wheels were jolted and jostled from road imperfections. This lightweight rod also helped limit unwanted axle motion during hard cornering. (The GT had a separate rear stabilizer bar to reduce body lean further.)

The Panhard rod's bushings were very firm, to limit motions that degrade handling and steering. The bushings could be very firm because they did not have to do double duty as connection points for links relied upon to provide a soft ride.

Those links consisted of three control arms mounted longitudinally, or in line with the body. Two—the trailing arms—were at the outboard edges of the axle. The third, called a central torque control arm, was atop the differential housing.

These longitudinal links regulated the axle's fore/aft motions as it hit bumps and ruts. The central torque control arm also provid-

ed leverage against axle wind-up in hard launches. All their bushings were created specifically to promote ride comfort and composure and thus were relatively soft. Given these more-focused roles, the arms themselves were lighter in weight and more elegant in design than their SN95 counterparts.

The springs were also lighter and were mounted directly to the axle for improved ride control. The shock absorbers were outside the rear structural rails, reducing the lever effect of the axle and allowing more exact, slightly softer shock-valve tuning.

In carefully building a case that the rear axle was precisely controlled throughout its range of motion, even over mid-corner bumps, engineers recited bushing rates, degrees of toe, and other suspension arcana.

Ford's PR office simply proclaimed: "The strong, light and function axle works even better than some independent setups in corners and gives Mustang a better dragstrip launch than virtually any production car."

A Call to Arms

Conventional wisdom said a double-wishbone front suspension was performance-car state of the art. But inspired by the BMW M3, S197 engineers instead chose a coil-over MacPherson strut setup.

MacPherson struts were originally developed in the 1940s by Earl S. MacPherson, a Ford engineer. The Mustang team relied on them to deliver comfort and control with no excess weight.

Locating the suspension at its lower outboard points were L-shaped control arms. Engineers asserted these arms gave a

Mustang's front and rear suspension was new for 2005 and was designed so components could concentrate specifically on ride or handling, not try to satisfy both, as in the SN95/Fox-4 generation. THIS PAGE: In front, MacPherson struts teamed with new, L-shaped lower links for a lighter, smarter approach. OPPOSITE TOP: The S197 crew concluded a solid rear axle best met cost, durability, and packaging needs. Their redesigned setup used a Panhard rod to limit side-to-side motions for better handling. Relocated springs and new lateral links— two lower, one atop the differential—focused on ride control. To meet the more-demanding requirements of the planned Cobra model, S197 was also designed to easily accept an independent rear suspension.

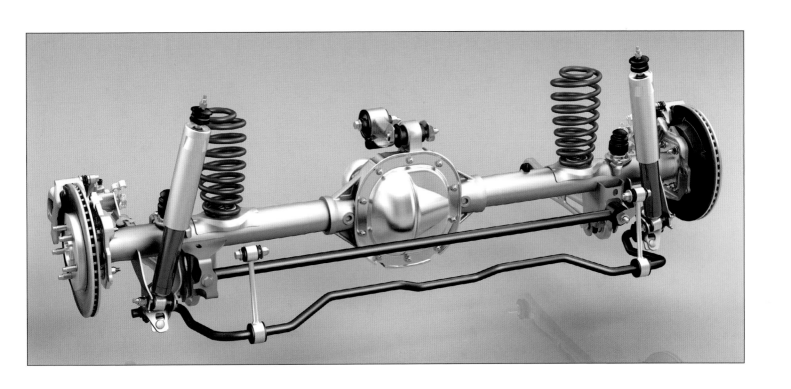

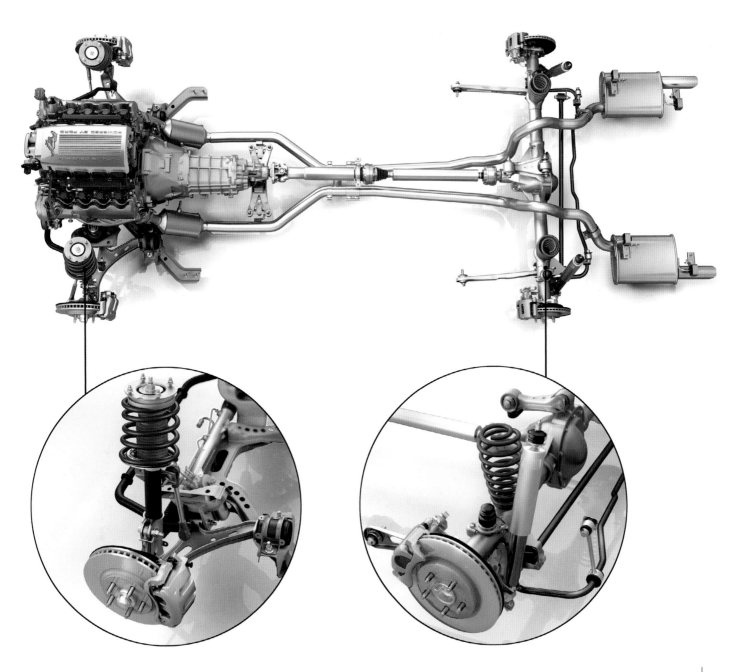

better ride/handling balance than A-arm or wishbone-shaped components. Again, bushing compliance played a key role.

To control side-to-side motion and quicken steering response, a firm bushing mated the forward leg of the L-arm with the chassis. To damp road shocks, fore/aft movements were directed through a softer, compliant bushing at the rear leg of the L-arm.

This separation of duty was owed not only to the particular "reverse-L" shape of the control arms, but to their design. Chassis engineers were effusive about the manufacturing technology behind them, calling it groundbreaking and claiming the relatively inexpensive steel control arms weighed less than comparable cast-aluminum designs. This exceptional strength-to-weight ratio helped minimize unsprung weight, so the suspension could respond better to abrupt road-surface changes.

The front springs were mounted concentrically on the MacPherson struts in a coil-over-shock configuration. That enabled the shocks to damp forces in harmony with the springs, allowing a 44-percent lighter spring than in SN95, and enabling more precise shock-valve tuning. Helping limit body roll was a stabilizer bar—34mm on the GT, 28.6mm for V-6 models.

Along with the new front suspension came a fresh steering system. It again was rack-and-pinion, but new linkage was fitted to provide crisper turn-in, and the turning circle was reduced by nearly 3 feet compared to the '04 Mustang.

Stop That

Like its immediate predecessor, the '05 Mustang had four-wheel disc brakes as standard. But it boasted the biggest rotors and stiffest calipers ever fitted to a mainstream Mustang. The goal was shorter stopping distances, better pedal feel, and longer brake life.

In front, the GT used dual piston aluminum floating calipers to clamp 12.4-inch discs. That was an increase of more than 15 percent in rotor size. These brakes had 14 percent more swept area than those of the previous GT. The rotors were 30mm thick and ventilated to provide consistent stopping power in repeated hard braking.

The V-6 got 11.5-inch ventilated front rotors that also were 30mm thick. That was a 6 percent increase in rotor size over previous V-6 brakes.

Rear brake rotors on both the GT and V-6 were 11.8 inches in diameter—more than 12 percent larger than before—and 19mm thick. And they were vented. Single-piston calipers swept 18 percent more area than the previous rear brakes.

New, four-channel ABS was standard on GT, optional on V-6. It added electronic brake force distribution, which apportioned braking power to the wheels that could use it most effectively.

From Roof to Road

The balance among styling, engineering, and cost that influenced so many aspects of the S197 project was evident right down to its wheels and tires.

For example, taking advantage of how the new rear suspension located the wheels, designers tightened the tire-to-fender gap by 35mm compared to the previous Mustang. And when chassis engineers chose to balance Mustang's ride and handling by specifying tires with a taller sidewall than on many other performance cars, stylists found it enhanced the car's muscle look.

Upon its late-2004 introduction, Mustang GT offered two styles of 17-inch wheels, both 8 inches wide and equipped with Pirelli P235/55ZR17 W-Speed-rated all-season performance tires.

These were narrower than the 2004 GT's 245/45ZR17s and had a sidewall about a half-inch taller. The '04 Cobra had run on wider-still, lower-profile 275/40ZR17s.

BELOW LEFT: V-6 models came with 10-spoke, 16-inch alloys. The uplevel version added this decorative center spinner that recalled the faux knock-off wings on some '60s Mustang hubcaps. Tires were 215/65R16s. BELOW: GTs wore all-season 235/55ZR17s on 8-inch-wide alloys. Standard was a five-spoke design similar to the 2004 GT's. This extra-cost GT wheel was inspired by the split-spoke affair on the '03 concept Mustangs. The only place Ford's blue-oval logo appeared on any '05 Mustang was in the wheel centers. All '05s had four-wheel disc brakes with the biggest rotors and stiffest calipers ever fitted to main-line Mustangs. ABS was standard on GTs, optional on V-6 models.

V-6 models also got two styles of wheel, both 16s, both 7 inches wide. Their tires were S-rated all-season BF Goodrich P215/65R16s and were specified to provide long wear. In concert with the ABS and traction control systems, all these tires were intended to make Mustang more practical in rain, ice, or snow.

Generating friction inside Ford as the car approached introduction were the 18-inch wheels displayed on auto-show Mustang GTs in early 2004. These 9-inch rims wore 255/45WR18 performance tires. This wheel-tire combination hadn't been approved for the '05 model year, and there was debate about whether it would see production at all.

Reflecting upon the engineering and design marathon that was the development of the 2005 Mustang, the give and take, the battles won and lost, chief engineer Hau Thai-Tang said his main regret was that the car wasn't launched with larger available wheels and tires. He would have liked to offer those 18s right off the bat. Hell, he would have loved to have seen 20-inch alloys. No technical reason they weren't available, he rued, just cost and timing. Balance is like that.

Besides being a profit-generator in its own right, the '05 Mustang was counted on to stir showroom interest in all Fords. It bowed as the company struggled with slipping sales and a market share of 19.5 percent, its lowest since 1928. ABOVE: A custom-painted Mustang GT took its place with the midengine GT and 2004 Shelby Cobra concept in a triumvirate designed to pump up the brand's performance image. On stage here are J Mays, Carroll Shelby, and William C. Ford Jr. BELOW: Dearborn envisioned the heritage styling as a bridge to ponies past.

The GT's grille lights were billed as fog lamps and had internal bezels designed to reproduce the lighting pattern of traditional, low-mounted fog lamps. Engineers said their location helped improve airflow through the grille, but the nose as a whole favored style over aero-efficiency. In its defense, designer J Mays explained: "I keep saying to everyone, 'Well, this has certain aerodynamic attributes: That front end actually scares the hell out of the air molecules—it pushes them around the car.'" Mays said the '05's styling was intended to express a tough, urban sensibility.

TOP: Mustang launched without a hood scoop. Designers couldn't justify a functional reason for one. Although the GT's rear wing was a nod to marketing, engineers claimed it did reduce aero lift at speed. Stylists said elements such as the bodyside C-shape were intentionally understated. And designer J Mays promised the basic look of the '05 would be unchanged through the life of the car. ABOVE: The 18-inch wheels that were the subject of debate within Ford. OPPOSITE: Engineers auditioned scores of mufflers to capture just the right Mustang rumble.

Specifications:

1965-2005

Mustang magic has much to do with things facts and figures can't capture. But a lot about the car is quantifiable. This look at Mustang by the numbers opens with graphs comparing it to its historic archrival, the Chevrolet Camaro, in terms of sales and engine power. Charts of key specifications, prices, and production totals follow, grouped by major design periods over the car's first 40 years.

OPPOSITE PAGE: The top graph tracks January-December calendar-year sales, as distinct from model-year production. Camaro was introduced for 1967, discontinued after 2002. The bottom graph shows factory horsepower ratings for regular-production models. It includes SVT Mustangs and SS Camaros, but not special-order models like the Mustang Cobra R or COPO Camaros. The decline in 1971–72 reflects the industry's move from gross to net horsepower ratings.

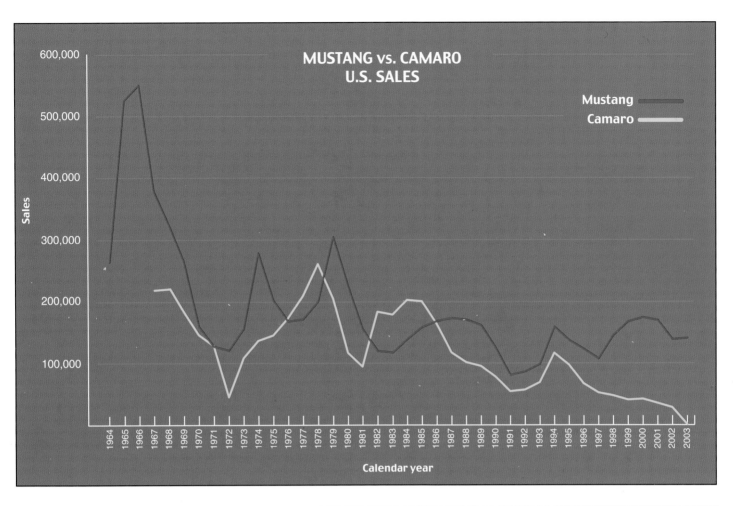

MUSTANG vs. CAMARO
U.S. SALES

Sales

Mustang ———
Camaro ———

Calendar year

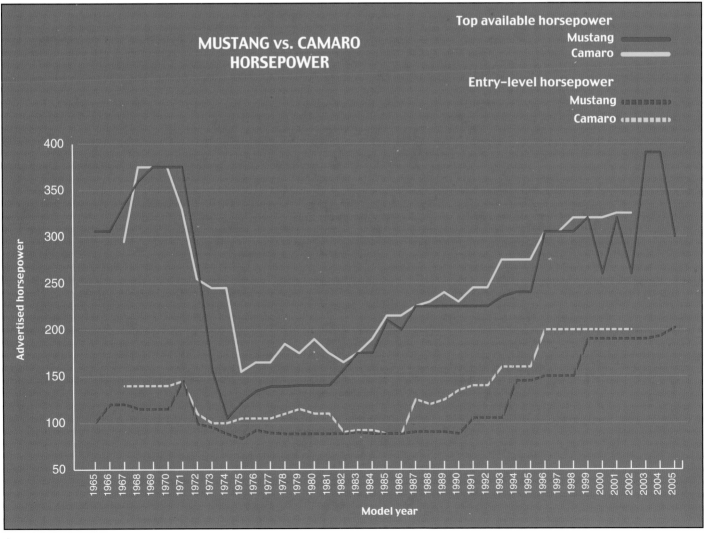

MUSTANG vs. CAMARO
HORSEPOWER

Top available horsepower
Mustang ———
Camaro ———

Entry–level horsepower
Mustang ▪▪▪▪▪▪▪▪
Camaro ▪▪▪▪▪▪▪▪

Advertised horsepower

Model year

1965-1966 Coupe, Convertible, Fastback

Specifications:

Wheelbase, inches:	108.0
Length, inches:	181.6
Curb-weight range, pounds:	1965: 2445–2800
	1966: 2488–2800
Width, inches:	68.2

Engines:

Type	Cubic inches	Horsepower
I-6	170	101
I-6	200	120
V-8	260	164
V-8	289	200–306

Model-year production:

1965: 681,551
1966: 609,946

Transmissions:

Automatic: 3-speed
Manual: 3-speed
4-speed

- Model-year 1965 was April 1964 to August 1965.
- Production totals include GT-350: 562 for 1965, 2378 for 1966.

Base price:

Model	1965	1966
Coupe, I-6	$2372	$2416
Coupe, V-8	2480	—
Convertible, I-6	2614	2653
Convertible, V-8	2722	—
Fastback, I-6	2589	2607
Fastback, V-8	2697	—
GT-350 fastback	4547	4428

1967-1968 Coupe, Convertible, Fastback

Specifications:

Wheelbase, inches:	108.0
Length, inches:	183.6
Curb-weight range, pounds:	1967: 2568–3000
	1968: 2635–3300
Width, inches:	70.9

Engines:

Type	Cubic inches	Horsepower
I-6	200	115–120
V-8	289	195–290
V-8	302	230–250
V-8	390	320–335
V-8	427	390
V-8	428	335–360

Model-year production:

1967: 475,346
1968: 321,854

Transmissions:

Automatic: 3-speed
Manual: 3-speed
4-speed

- Model-year production includes GT-350, GT-500, and GT-500KR: 3225 in 1967 and 4450 in 1968.

Base price:

Model	1967	1968
Coupe, I-6	$2461	$2602
Convertible, I-6	2698	2814
Fastback, I-6	2592	2712
GT-350 fastback	3995	4117
GT-350 convertible	—	4238
GT-500 fastback	4195	4317
GT-500 convertible	—	4439
GT-500KR fastback	—	4473
GT-500KR convertible	—	4594

1969-1970 Coupe, Convertible, Fastback

Specifications:

Wheelbase, inches:	108.0
Length, inches:	187.4
Curb-weight range, pounds:	1969: 2690–3210
	1970: 2721–3240
Width, inches:	71.3–71.7

Engines:

Type	Cubic inches	Horsepower
I-6	200	115
I-6	250	155
V-8	302	220–290
V-8	351	250–300
V-8	390	320
V-8	428	335
V-8	429	375

Base price:

Model	1969	1970
Coupe, I-6	$2635	$2721
Fastback, I-6	2635	2771
Convertible, I-6	2849	3025
Grande coupe, I-6	2866	2926
Coupe, V-8	2740	2822
Fastback, V-8	2740	2872
Boss 302 fastback	3588	3720
Convertible, V-8	2954	3126
Grande coupe, V-8	2971	3028
Mach 1 fastback	3139	3271
GT-350 fastback	4434	4500
GT-350 convertible	4753	4800
GT-500 fastback	4709	4800
GT-500 convertible	5027	5100

Model-year production:

1969: 302,971
1970: 191,363

Transmissions:

Automatic: 3-speed
Manual: 3-speed
4-speed

- Model-year production includes GT-350 and GT-500: 3150 in 1969 and 636 in 1970.

Specifications:

Wheelbase, inches:	109.0
Length, inches:	187.5–190.0
Curb-weight range, pounds:	1971: 2907–3261
	1973: 2995–3216
Width, inches:	75.0

Engines:

Type	Cubic inches	Horsepower
I-6	250	145
V-8	302	210
V-8	351	240–330
V-8	351	168–275 (net)
V-8	429	375

- Starting with model-year 1972, engine output was measured with all accessories attached and stock intake and exhaust systems in place, resulting in a "net" horespower rating.

Model-year production:

1971: 149,678
1972: 125,093
1973: 134,867

Transmissions:

Automatic: 3-speed
Manual: 3-speed
 4-speed

Base price:

Model	1971	1972	1973
Coupe, I-6	$2911	$2729	$2760
Fastback, I-6	2973	2786	2820
Convertible, I-6	3227	3015	3102
Grande coupe, I-6	3117	2915	2946
Coupe, V-8	3006	2816	2897
Fastback, V-8	3068	2873	2907
Boss 351 fastback	4124	—	—
Convertible, V-8	3320	3101	3189
Grande coupe, V-8	3212	3002	3088
Mach 1 fastback	3268	3053	3088

Specifications:

Wheelbase, inches:	96.2
Length, inches:	175.0
Curb-weight range, pounds:	1974: 2620–2886
	1978: 2646–2751
Width, inches:	70.2

Engines:

Type	Cubic inches	Horsepower
I-4	140	83–92
V-6	171	90–105
V-8	302	122–139

Model-year production:

1974: 385,993
1975: 188,575
1976: 187,567
1977: 153,173
1978: 192,410

Transmissions:

Automatic: 3-speed
Manual: 4-speed

Base price:

Model	1974	1975	1976	1977	1978
Coupe, I-4	$3134	$3529	$3525	$3702	$3731
Fastback I-4	3328	3818	3781	3901	3975
Ghia coupe, I-4	3480	3938	3859	4119	4149
Coupe, V-8	3363	3801	3791	3984	3944
Fastback, V-8	3557	4090	4047	4183	4188
Ghia coupe, V-6	3709	4210	4125	4401	4362
Mach 1 fastback	3674	4188	4209	4332	4430

Specifications:

Wheelbase, inches:	100.4
Length, inches:	179.1
Curb-weight range, pounds:	1979: 2530–2672
	1981: 2601–2692
Width, inches:	69.1

Engines:

Type	Cubic inches	Horsepower
ohc I-4	140	88
ohc I-4 Turbo	140	131
ohv V-6	171	109
ohv I-6	200	85
ohv V-8	255	117
ohv V-8	302	140

Model-year production:

1979: 369,936
1980: 271,322
1981: 182,552

Transmissions:

Automatic: 3-speed
Manual: 4-speed
 5-speed

Base price:

Model	1979	1980	1981
Coupe	$4494	$4884	$5980
Fastback	4828	5194	6216
Ghia coupe	5064	5369	6424
Ghia fastback	5216	5512	6538

1982-1986 — Coupe, Convertible, Fastback

Specifications:

Wheelbase, inches:	100.4
Length, inches:	179.1–179.3
Curb-weight range, pounds:	1982: 2568–2636
	1986: 2795–2853
Width, inches:	67.4–69.1

Engines:

Type	Liters	Horsepower
ohc I-4	2.3	88
ohc I-4 Turbo	2.3	145–205
ohv I-6	3.3	88
ohv V-6	3.8	105–120
ohv V-8	4.2	111
ohv V-8	5.0	157–210

Transmissions:

Automatic:	3-speed
	4-speed
Manual:	4-speed
	5-speed

Model-year production:

1982: 130,418
1983: 120,873
1984: 141,480
1985: 156,514
1986: 224,410

- 2.3 liters = 140 cid
  3.3 liters = 200 cid
  3.8 liters = 232 cid
  4.2 liters = 255 cid
  5.0 liters = 302 cid

Base price:

Model	1982	1983	1984	1985	1986
Coupe, L	$6345	$6727	$7088	—	—
Coupe, GL	6844	7264	—	—	—
Coupe, LX	—	—	7290	$6885	$7189
Coupe, GLX	6980	7398	—	—	—
Fastback, L	—	—	7269	—	—
Fastback, GL	6979	7439	—	—	—
Fastback, LX	—	—	7496	7345	7744
Fastback, GLX	7101	7557	—	—	—
Fastback, GT	8308	9328	9578	9885	10,691
Turbo fastback, GT	—	9714	9762	—	—
Convertible, LX	—	—	11,849	11,985	12,821
Convertible, GLX	—	12,467	—	—	—
Convertible, GT	—	13,479	13,051	13,585	14,523
Turbo convertible, GT	—	—	13,245	—	—
SVO fastback	—	—	15,596	14,521	15,272

1987-1993 — Coupe, Convertible, Fastback

Specifications:

Wheelbase, inches:	100.5
Length, inches:	179.6
Curb-weight range, pounds:	2754–3350
Width, inches:	68.3

Engines:

Type	Liters	Horsepower
ohc I-4	2.3	88–105
ohv V-8	5.0	225–235

Model-year production:

1987: 159,145
1988: 211,225
1989: 209,769
1990: 128,189
1991: 98,737
1992: 79,280
1993: 114,228

Transmissions:

Automatic:	4-speed
Manual:	5-speed

Base price:

Model	1987	1988	1989	1990	1991	1992	1993
Coupe, LX	$8043	$8726	$9050	$9456	$10,157	$10,215	$10,719
Fastback, LX	8474	9221	9556	9962	10,663	10,721	11,224
Convertible, LX	12,840	13,702	14,140	15,141	16,222	16,899	17,548
Coupe, LX 5.0 sport	—	—	11,410	12,164	13,270	13,422	13,296
Fastback, LX 5.0 sport	—	—	12,265	13,007	14,055	14,207	14,710
Convt., LX 5.0 sport	—	—	17,001	16,183	19,242	19,644	20,293
Fastback, GT	11,835	12,745	13,272	13,986	15,034	15,243	15,747
Convertible, GT	15,724	16,610	17,512	18,805	19,864	20,199	20,848
Cobra fastback	—	—	—	—	—	—	20,000
Cobra R fastback	—	—	—	—	—	—	25,692

Specifications:
Wheelbase, inches:	101.3
Length, inches:	181.5
Curb-weight range, pounds:	3055–3565
Width, inches:	71.8

Engines:
Type	Liters	Horsepower
ohv V-6	3.8	145
ohc V-6	3.8	150
ohc V-8	5.0	215
ohv V-8	5.0	240
ohv V-8	5.8	300
ohc V-8	4.6	215–225
dohc V-8	4.6	305

Model-year production:
1994: 137,074
1995: 185,986
1996: 135,620
1997: 108,103
1998: 175,763

Transmissions:
Automatic: 4-speed
Manual: 5-speed

- 1998 model-year production extended by 3 months, to November 1999.
- 5.8 liters = 351 cid

Base price:
Model	1994	1995	1996	1997	1998
Coupe	$13,365	$14,330	$15,180	$15,355	$16,070
Coupe, GT	17,280	17,905	17,610	18,000	20,070
Convertible	20,160	20,795	21,060	20,755	20,570
Convertible, GT	21,970	22,595	23,495	23,985	24,070
Cobra coupe	22,425	21,300	24,810	25,335	25,630
Cobra convertible	23,535	25,605	27,580	28,135	28,430
Cobra R coupe	—	—	—	—	34,995

Specifications:
Wheelbase, inches:	101.3
Length, inches:	183.2
Curb-weight range, pounds:	1999: 3069–3386
	2004: 3290–3469
Width, inches:	73.1

Engines:
Type	Liters	Horsepower
ohv V-6	3.8	190
ohc V-8	4.6	260
dohc V-8	4.6	305–320
dohc V-8, supercharged	4.6	390

Calendar-year sales:
1999: 166,915
2000: 173,676
2001: 169,198
2002: 138,356
2003: 140,350
2004: NA

Transmissions:
Automatic: 4-speed
Manual: 5-speed
                  6-speed

- 5.4 liters = 330 cid

Base price:
Model	1999	2000	2001	2002	2003	2004
Coupe	$16,470	$16,520	$16,805	$17,220	$17,475	$17,720
Convertible	21,070	21,370	22,220	—	—	—
Deluxe coupe	—	—	—	17,825	18,205	18,450
Deluxe convertible	—	—	—	22,540	23,145	23,455
Premium coupe	—	—	—	18,940	19,320	19,105
Premium convertible	—	—	—	25,125	25,730	25,580
GT coupe	20,870	21,015	22,440	—	—	—
GT convertible	24,870	25,270	26,695	—	—	—
GT Deluxe coupe	—	—	—	22,760	23,345	23,245
GT Deluxe convertible	—	—	—	27,015	27,620	27,585
GT Premium coupe	—	—	—	23,930	24,515	24,415
GT Premium convertible	—	—	—	28,185	28,770	28,755
Bullitt coupe	—	—	26,230	—	—	—
Mach 1 coupe	—	—	—	—	28,705	28,820
Cobra coupe	27,470	—	28,605	33,125	33,460	34,575
Cobra convertible	31,470	—	32,605	37,370	37,835	38,950
Cobra R coupe	—	54,995	—	—	—	—

Specifications:
Wheelbase, inches:	107.1
Length, inches:	183.2
Curb-weight range, pounds:	3300–3500
Width, inches:	73.9

Engines:
Type	Liters	Horsepower
ohc V-6	4.0	202
ohc V-8	4.6	300

- 4.0 liters = 245 cid
- Specifications are for coupe only.

Base price: NA

Calendar-year sales: NA

Transmissions: Automatic: 5-speed
Manual: 5-speed

Index